T0318350

In this book, Professor Spulber traces the role of the state in both the West and the East for more than two centuries. His discussion proceeds along parallel lines – notably from the creation of the welfare state in the West and the all-encompassing party-state in the East, to reform of the Western welfare state by means of privatization and entitlement changes, to transmutations in the East through large-scale privatizations and the creation of the "nomenklatura (former communist officialdom) capitalism." The book establishes an original and unusual connection between the dismantling of state enterprises and the limitation of government functions at all levels in the West, and the collapse and then restructuring of the state on new foundations in the East. No other current work of scholarship explores this topic in comparable scope, impartiality, or historical breadth. The author's approach is both theoretical and empirical, and the nonideological analysis has topicality and immediate relevance to policy making.

Redefining the State

Redefining the State

Privatization and Welfare Reform
in Industrial and Transitional Economies

Nicolas Spulber
Indiana University

CAMBRIDGE
UNIVERSITY PRESS

CAMBRIDGE UNIVERSITY PRESS
Cambridge, New York, Melbourne, Madrid, Cape Town, Singapore, São Paulo

Cambridge University Press
The Edinburgh Building, Cambridge CB2 2RU, UK

Published in the United States of America by Cambridge University Press, New York

www.cambridge.org
Information on this title: www.cambridge.org/9780521594257

First published 1997
This digitally printed first paperback version 2006

A catalogue record for this publication is available from the British Library

Library of Congress Cataloguing in Publication data
Spulber, Nicolas.
Redefining the state : privatization and welfare reform in
industrial and transitional economies / Nicolas Spulber.
p. cm.
Includes index.
ISBN 0-521-59425-1 (hb)
1. State, The. 2. Comparative government. 3. Comparative
economics. 4. Post-communism. 5. Privatization. I. Title.
JC11.S69   1997
320.1 – dc21   97-6654
                                            CIP

ISBN-13 978-0-521-59425-7 hardback
ISBN-10 0-521-59425-1 hardback

ISBN-13 978-0-521-02418-1 paperback
ISBN-10 0-521-02418-8 paperback

For Pauline, with love

Contents

Figures and Tables

Preface

This book examines, in historical perspective, changes in the role of the state with regard to public ownership and the scope of welfare in the main industrial and transitional economies. These changes have stimulated illuminating debates on the state's size, range, and functions. They have also involved important transformations – the shifting of boundaries between the public and private sectors, the carrying out of large privatization programs, and the reevaluation of the nature and content of public welfare. These debates and transformations are of singular importance for understanding the actual and potential scope of the state in any economy.

The term *industrial economies* refers herein first and foremost to the main Western European countries – namely, the United Kingdom, France, and Germany – and to the United States. Whenever appropriate, the framework is expanded to include the entire so-called Group of Seven (G7) industrialized countries. The term *transitional economies* refers first of all to Russia and, whenever necessary, to its former Central and Southern European satellites. I believe that the developments in these Western and Eastern countries since World War I concerning public ownership and welfare present compelling correspondences, notwithstanding great differences in scope, timing, and type of system. These correspondences deserve to be brought to light and examined on a comparative basis. (The focus on West and East as defined does not mean, of course, that detailed examinations of germane reforms in other countries are of less importance or interest.) The choice made here was further guided by the desire to delineate as clearly as possible the basic correlations between the historic evolutions of these areas over more than two centuries and to avoid allowing the discussion to branch out into secondary directions.

What exactly is meant by the term *the state* depends, of course, on which society one refers to and at what point in time. In Western Europe, for instance, the state is generally viewed as consisting of two distinct elements: a transient one, the government, subject to change through elections or, in the intervals between elections, through the formation of government coalitions; and a stable centralized administration, comprising distinct, hierarchical structures independent of the legislative system – the civil service, the judiciary, the army, and also the police. The official head of state may be a president (elected or forcibly imposed under a dictatorship), a king, or an emperor, who may or may not have any real power in appointing or in changing the government and shaping its policies. In the United States, on the other hand, the separation between the transient federal government and what is called in Europe the state's "administration" is less sharp. The structure, tasks, and performance of the federal civil service are viewed as closely dependent on the policies of the government in power and on the political party that it represents. A traditional conservative tendency in U.S. politics perceives the entire federal civil service as a sprawling, cumbersome, and wasteful conglomerate that it derisively calls "the Washington bureaucracy," some of whose main functions could, according to the critics, be eliminated, while its services could be taken over by the civil administrations of the fifty states and the municipalities. The issue of downsizing the federal civil service, that is, downsizing the centralized civil administration structure of the entire United States, particularly concerning public ownership, welfare, and regulation, is at the heart of many conflicts between Republicans and Democrats. To add to the possible confusion of the noninitiated, the terms *Republican* and *Democratic administration* refer to the government they lead, as well as to the ways in which they structure and redefine civil services and appoint their chiefs, along with the new justices and the army's high command.

In the East, the state as it functioned under the Communist Party's command-and-control system evidently differed in many respects from the structure and goals of the states that finally emerged after the collapse of the USSR. The traditional communist state system was modeled in many respects after Germany's World War I *Kriegswirtschaft* (war economy), while the newly emerging state systems are modeling themselves on those based on market-directed relations. And, of course, their approaches differ greatly with regard to both public ownership and welfare, with which we are here concerned.

A state's approaches to the issues of public ownership and welfare define in a significant way its nature, functions, and goals. Which factors have led historically to the expansion of public ownership – up to and including total state ownership – and which factors have led to the growth of state welfare systems? Which factors have contributed to the reversal of these tendencies, that is, to the methodical transfer of public property to the private sector through privatizations, as well as to the methodical shrinkage of state income transfers for welfare purposes? To what extent do these tendencies portend an even broader policy of downsizing the scope, size, and economic functions of the state? Or, on the other hand, are there various other factors at work that may favor, not further downsizing, but rather a renewed expansion of the state's economic activities? These are the questions that this book attempts to address.

The work consists of four parts. Part I in its first chapter broadly sketches the conditions that led to the systematic expansion of public ownership (with regard to certain industries and public transportation) and of the role of the state in the main European economies (and subsequently also in the United States). The survey starts with the era of so-called merchant capitalism, which began with the formation of modern states through the eighteenth century, goes through the growth of "industrial capitalism" during the nineteenth century and into the twentieth – up to and including World War I – and continues finally through the Great Depression and the post–World War II years. The analysis brings into relief the interrelation of all these changes with a succession of connected economic theories, starting with mercantilism and continuing (notwithstanding its forceful critique by the classical school) in the form of various liberal–mercantilist approaches through the nineteenth century and then with renewed strength through the Great Depression and after World War II.

Chapter 2 examines the functions of the state both before and after the transformation of Russia into the first Soviet-type state. The chapter begins with a brief survey of the expansion of the state and of public property in imperial Russia up to 1917. It then sketches the ways in which, under the aegis of the Bolsheviks and their Marxian-Leninist ideas, the state established its complete ownership over land, industry, transportation, banking, insurance services, and trade, as well as how the new leaders attempted to command and control this allegedly "unified enterprise" as a kind of engineering servomechanism. It then shows how this system experienced increasing failures, discusses its unsuccessful attempts to reform itself, and finally analyzes its collapse, leading to the disaggregation of the great multiethnic Soviet composite. This collapse forced the emerging states – including, first of all, Russia itself – to recast their state structures and try to remodel them on those of market-directed economies.

Parts II and III focus on attempts to negate various consequences of state expansion. Such attempts, starting from the late 1970s, aimed in the West to downsize the role of the state, in particular with respect to public ownership and to welfare. In the East, beginning in the late 1980s, the goals were the overturning of the old state construct and the building of new state structures.

Both the Western and the Eastern reforms have involved redefinitions of the state's functions, and both have resorted in practice to the use of similar instruments, namely privatization and welfare change. But in the West, the main concern was setting limits to some of the state's intrusions on the economy, while in the East the main concern bore on the essence of the state and on ways of recasting its important structures on new bases. I pay close attention to both the debates involved and the actual transformations carried out, in the West and in the East. To begin with, Chapter 3 focuses specifically on the discussions that took place – notably during the Thatcher (UK) and Reagan (U.S.) administrations – concerning the nature and scope of state enterprises and their role in the economy, as well as on the extent and eventual consequences of income transfers for welfare purposes. The views exchanged in these debates illuminate the rationale for the creation of multiple forms of state-owned companies, their possible use to circumvent certain budget constraints, their role as channels of governmental subsidies and credits in chosen directions, their importance in securing certain ailing industries, and their use as instruments of technological modernization and control in various "strategic" sectors. The measures actually carried out then and since, involving the massive privatization of public enterprises in Western Europe and the potential and actual changes in the scope of welfare programs, notably in the United States, convey a clear view of the multiple possible ways of downsizing the state.

Chapter 4 examines the factors shaping the amplitude, diversity, and contradictoriness of the remodeling of the Russian Federation's structures, which emerged from the collapsing structures of the disintegrating USSR. Crucial efforts were devoted to carrying forward (1) policies of price liberalization and massive privatization of state holdings, (2) attempts at consolidating an effective central state power while subduing the powers of the economic "fiefdoms" led by the old officials (the nomenklatura), and (3) overcoming widespread tendencies toward crime and corruption. All these efforts turned out in many ways to be disappointing and/or totally ineffective. The chapter indicates how and why the processes of transformation have assumed at times a chaotic and uncontrollable character and have led to massive declines in income, output, and employment, along with high inflation, general poverty, and a torn safety net.

Part III places the Western and Eastern changes in larger, comparative frameworks. The Western changes are examined in the broader industrial framework of the G7 economies; the Eastern ones, in the broader transitional economic framework including, along with Russia, its former European satellites. Many of the Western ways of defining the role of the state are deeply rooted in certain theoretical approaches concerning output, employment, and growth. Chapter 5 sketches the basic conflict existing in this respect between the classical economic school and its Keynesian critique, and then extends the discussion to the differences from today's offshoots of both the classical school and Keynesianism. Against this background, the chapter examines the scope of the state within classical and modern frameworks with reference to the United States, compares the centralized civil administration of the latter with those of the other G7 countries, and points out that the U.S. administration, contrary to the assertions of its critics, is in many respects smaller than that of the other members of the G7. The chapter focuses then on the specific problems posed by variations in the ways in which the disposal of public property may take place – variations that necessarily involve specific conceptions of the role of the state and its relations to the market. The chapter next details both the preparatory procedures and the most common methods of privatization, and finally evaluates the results of these activities in relation to their usual stated goals, namely the achievement of greater competition and efficiency.

Chapter 6 examines the changes in both Russia and Eastern Europe concerning first the legal frameworks of these countries, and then the patterns of large-scale privatization and their consequences, namely the conditions whereby privatized firms adapted to changes in ownership, new coordinating mechanisms, and new contractual relationships. The focus is on what I call the "first critical phase of the transition" (from 1989/1991 to 1995) and on the results achieved concerning overall transformations; the paths of change in incomes, output, investment, and employment; the readjustments of the systems of social protection; and the prospects of full economic recovery.

Part IV examines, from the perspective of the twenty-first century, the prospects concerning the scope of the state, both in the developed industrialized countries of the West and in the so-called transitional economies in the East. In its single, concluding chapter (Chapter 7), Part IV focuses on the following questions: Will the economic developments in the West lead to further limitations of the role of the state with regard to public ownership and welfare, or will they rather tend to combine further limitations on the public sector with an expansion of the role of the state in other directions? And in the East, will further privatization, economic restructuring, reshaping of the legal and institutional setup, and growth of market relations lead to the emergence of free market economies of the U.S. type, or rather to dirigiste-type economies in which the state continues to play a critical role as owner, regulator, manipulator of market relations? The chapter indicates why, in the West, the insecurities brought about by rapid structural shifts in production and employment, widespread and decisive technological changes, and expansion of a transnational production system and of global ties, along with rises in unemployment and/or drops in real wages, increase the uncertainties and the unease of a large part of the workforce with respect to its future prospects. With regard to the East, the chapter examines the complex and contradictory tendencies at work in the continuous processes of transition from command-and-control to broad market relations and points out the difficulties ahead after the terribly trying critical first phase (1989/1991 to 1995).

The chapter delineates the potential differences ahead between, on the one hand, the Russian Federation and, on the other, the East European groups of countries that engaged in the transition process at initially different levels of development, namely the Central European countries (the Czech and Slovak Republics, Hungary, and Poland) and the Southern European countries (Albania, Bulgaria, and Romania).

Because the book addresses questions of the size and scope of the state in general and the state's particular role in the growth of the public sector and welfare, as well as the state's possible evolution – in developed and developing countries – following the changes brought about in the West and in the East since the 1980s, it will be, I believe, of interest to students in many disciplines. These discussions should draw the attention of economic students concerned with the state and the economic process (and especially with macroeconomic policies and decisions and with the economics of transition to market relations); they should prove of use for students of history preoccupied with the long-term transformations of the state and of the forms and rationale of the public sector; last but not least, they should solicit the interest of students of political science and sociology who aim to glean some of the main long-term policy lessons of the events preceding and following the great transmutations of the 1980s and after.

The research on which this work is based was funded in part by generous grants-in-aid kindly extended to me by Professor George Walker, Vice-President for Research and Dean of the Graduate School, Indiana University. For helping shape the final form of this book, I am in debt first of all to my colleagues, Professors Robert A. Becker and Michael Kaganovich, who read the early draft of the manuscript, and to Professors Eckhaus Janeba, Tom Kniesner, and Elyce Rotella for their advice and for the useful materials they put at my disposal. I am further deeply grateful to Professor Domenico Mario Nuti of the University of Rome for detailed, invaluable comments on the prepublication draft of this work and to the publisher's two anonymous referees for their appropriate and extensive comments, which incited me to develop further and to clarify various crucial points presented in this book.

Finally, I am much in debt to the Indiana University librarians – of the Reference Department, Government Publications Department, and Inter-Library Loans Department – for the continuous and useful help they kindly extended to me during the preparation of this work. My debt is also great to Ms. Suzanne Hull of the Graphic Department of Indiana University for carefully crafting the tables and figures in the text, to Ms. Ruth Fishel for her patience and intelligence in typing the various versions of the manuscript, and to Ms. Peg Hausman and Robert Racine for their extremely helpful editorial changes. I am responsible for all remaining errors.

Part I

Rationale for the State's Expansion

Why should a private enterprise economy be subjected to any kind of government intervention and not be left entirely to the guidance of the "invisible hand" of the market? The answers to this often-repeated question have varied enormously through time under the impact of intertwined economic, social, and political considerations and of power relations within the society. Modern conservative politicians, and certain economists, contend that the more limited the economic role of the state, the better off the economy and the population at large. Other economists dismiss this contention and its theoretical underpinnings as unrealistic (as we shall see in Part II). These economists point out that the market cannot perform all the socially necessary economic functions – moreover, that it could not consistently discharge all of them efficiently. As a matter of fact, the state's (i.e., the government's) interventions in the economy have developed historically in a number of ways that could be grouped into the following basic categories: legal and regulatory, allocative, growth-oriented and/or stabilizatory, income distributive.

Building on the foundation of property laws, the first category of activities has consisted of determining the market's legal structure and regulating its processes involving coalitions and bargaining among consumers and firms. As Professor Milton Friedman, an ardent defender of individuals' freedom to choose, has pointed out (in *Capitalism and Freedom*), government is essential for achieving something that the market cannot do for itself, namely to act both as "a forum for determining the rules of the game" and as "an umpire to interpret and enforce the rules decided on."

Other government activities have arisen from the necessity of supplying various collective types of goods and services – referred to as social goods in contrast with private goods – which the market fails to properly price and provide either entirely or in an efficient way. This may concern the handling and impact of "externalities" (namely, pollution's neighborhood effects) or the provision, say, of spacecrafts and military hardware – that is, goods whose benefits are not limited to the one consumer who purchases the good, as is the case for private goods. (But the production of certain social goods could

1

of course be carried out directly by state-owned enterprises or by private ones selling their products to the state.)

It is in particular the growth-oriented and income-distributive groups of state interventions in the economy that have brought forth the increased disagreements of modern conservatism (discussed in Part II). This group of activities – aiming to affect notably aggregate demand, employment, output levels, and prices – has involved recourse to a variety of measures, including deficit spending (often leading to vast expansions of state expenditures at given historical junctures), purchases of failing private firms, and a host of subsidies, grants, and joint (public–private) partnerships. Finally, the income-distributive group of state interventions has embraced activities involving adjustments and "corrections" of the market-conditioned distribution of income and wealth, aiming to help the unemployed, the aged, the disabled, and the disadvantaged in general, and thus bring the income distribution in line with society's apparent current ideas about ethical standards and a "fair" social distribution.

The ways in which any and all of these functions have been interpreted and discharged by states – whether from deep-rooted causes or under the influence of passing circumstance – have of course varied over time and have called forth reinterpretations, criticisms, corrections, and even policy reversals. As I indicated in the Preface, in this work I am drawing the reader's attention mainly to certain states' approaches to state ownership and to income transfers for social welfare. In Western Europe and in the United States, the latter activities have tended to grow concurrently (particularly in the interwar period and after World War II) and have eventually called forth powerful reactions against their growth, as we shall see.

In Chapter 1 I point out the ways in which state ownership has developed in Britain, in France, and then in divided Germany during the so-called epoch of "merchant capitalism," that is, from the seventeenth through the eighteenth century, under the predominant economic philosophy of mercantilism. I then examine the special conditions supporting the further growth of this kind of ownership in the nineteenth century and up to World War I – that is, during the early years of "industrial capitalism" in Great Britain and France, and afterward during the period of the spread of industrialization, notably to both the United States and Germany under the guidance of mixed mercantilist–liberal approaches. I then focus on the creation in World War I of the first "command economy." The command economy is up to a point the model implemented, with various adjustments, first by the Soviet Union, on the basis of a centrally directed, fully nationalized economy, and then by the Nazis, on the basis of a vast and thorough network of regulations and controls of an economy predicated on private ownership. Afterward, I draw attention to the eventual expansion of the role of the state, state ownership, and welfare measures, first in the United States during the Great Depression and then in Western Europe after World War II until the 1980s, in the form of (so-called) nationalization and the creation of "welfare" states.

Again, as I indicated in the Preface, a number of post–World War II economic changes in the West reflect in a delayed, ambiguous, and remote fashion the trajectory of the Soviet Union's drives for expanding state ownership and for directing its economic processes in a "planned" style. In Chapter 2, I sketch only the ways in which the communist party-state was put together on the ruins of the tsarist empire and on the latter's economic legacy. I indicate how, under the guidance of the Marxian theory as interpreted by Lenin, the new state transformed the economy, modified its structure, expanded state ownership, and attempted (ineffectually) to direct all its input–output operations. After examining as well the nature and extent of the Soviet income transfers for its social "safety net," I show that the sought-after complete centralization of the hierarchically structured Soviet economy could not fend off the quasi-market relations seeping into its state complex and distorting its central commands. Nor could it eliminate the deformed market relations surrounding it. I then present in broad outline the various historical phases of the Soviet regime and the nature and scope of the various reforms attempted there and in its satellites, showing their eventual impact on the collapse of the Soviet party-state. It is in Parts II and III that I consider the problems of the transition from that system to a capitalist one.

1 Public Ownership and Welfare

1.1. Mercantilism and State Ownership

The emerging and then consolidating European monarchic states of the seventeenth and eighteenth centuries inherited from the powerful examples of the medieval city-states such as Milan, Florence, Bologna, Genoa, and Venice a tradition of continuous interventions of the central power in the economic and social life of their communities, along with a strong impulse toward an incessant warfare of competition and aggression. In many respects some of these policies, which began to assert themselves forcefully also in England and France from the sixteenth century on and which came to be known as "mercantilist policies," were actually extensions to the limits of the newly developing monarchical states of the traditional preoccupations and practices of the late Middle Ages.[1] The modern states shaped themselves into strong and wealthy economic bodies by means of both internal and external conflicts. The internal conflicts pitted the central state power against the church, the nobility, the medieval parliaments, the districts, and the towns in a vast attempt to transform and reorganize society's economic and social structures. The external ones involved the newly rising states seeking a dominant place among the European nations and in trade (which henceforth included America and India). State making and state power were thus intertwined. The essential means of power, wealth, was increasingly viewed as indispensable for security, aggression, and eventual conquest. States sought to attain wealth by avoiding the export of bullion (gold and silver) and by securing a favorable balance of trade. The latter was achievable first via the subsidization and strict regulation of production (in England with regard primarily to manufacturing, but also up to a point to agriculture, along with the management of shipping); second, via the restraint of imports through high duties and, if necessary, through absolute import prohibitions and the encouragement of exports using drawbacks, bounties, treaties of commerce, and the establishment of colonies. It was implicitly assumed that the entire country should identify its production with exports and its consumption with imports and, like a provident individual household, should avoid consuming more than it produced by its export earnings.[2]

In Britain, during the reign of Queen Elizabeth, as well as of James I and Charles I, the Crown tried to obtain an interest in every industry. Moreover, the Crown exercised a considerable royal prerogative in granting patents for carrying out highly remunerative operations in a wide variety of industrial fields, including the manufacture of saltpeter and gunpowder, alum, and soap.[3] The attacks of Elizabeth's sailors and privateers against the ships and colonies of Philip II of Spain were simultaneously a religious, a nationalist, and a profitable mercantile enterprise. The power of the country was heavily dependent upon shipping. The policy of encouraging native shipping as a means of bringing in wealth, which had engaged British attention since the time of Richard II, was embodied in very strict regulations by the Rump Parliament. Parliament promulgated these rules not only to encourage English commerce, but also to strike a blow against prosperous Holland.[4] Foreign trade was viewed as subservient to state power – that is, meant to bring in the wealth needed for the strength and security of the realm. However, the trade operations themselves were let out to chartered and regulated companies (the East India Company, the Levant Company, the Eastland and the Muscovy [since 1698] Companies), all operated entirely by London merchants. It was in the financial district of the City of London, in its money market, its privately run Bank of England, and the East India Company, that the country's economic power was concentrated. The weight of state-owned assets was limited. The Crown directly owned only the army and naval establishments, armories, military ships and dockyards, public buildings, the mint, and the post office (since the reign of Charles I). The Parliament was the "authorizer and constitutary" of canal companies and turnpike trusts.[5]

It was rather in the France of Louis XIV that the idea of vesting enormous economic powers in the state and an absolute monarch received its fullest application during the period under review. It was in France that the so-called mercantilist concepts were accepted as axioms. It was there that the following propositions were viewed as compelling: the prosperity of a state can be achieved only at the expense of its neighbors; bullion must be attracted into the country and prevented from getting out; and a nation must crush its enemies in order to achieve economic supremacy. The powers of the Crown to direct the economy, to control and support industry and mining, and to regulate the country's commerce were far larger in France than they had ever been in Great Britain. The French king had control of saltpeter and gunpowder manufacture and the right to administer all defense industries, which became a vast royal enterprise. (Persons making arms or ammunition without royal approval were considered criminals punishable by heavy fines or death.) The country recognized the Crown's ownership rights over all subterranean wealth; over a share in the revenues from mining and metallurgy; over the disposal of certain national products (in particular, ores and mineral resources); over salt production, which yielded great financial returns to the royal treasury; and over the granting of monopoly rights to certain persons in various branches of manufacturing. Further, the Crown had the power to foster new arts and crafts and manufactures in any and all fields. Not one manufacturing branch or foreign trade operation escaped the king's intervention and exigent protection. The apogee of French economic statism was reached in the seventeenth century under the rigid mercantilist administration of Jean Baptiste Colbert (1619–1683), King Louis XIV's subservient minister. Following the royal tradition already established in the sixteenth century, Colbert held that France could achieve enormous riches if it were to produce goods of the highest quality in profusion and if it were to secure their transport and delivery abroad by its own means. At the height (1664–1669) of his career, Colbert established and rigidly controlled numerous royal manufacturing facilities – true state enterprises – for the production of fine tapestry, soda and coal tar, thread and cloth, dyes, leather goods, porcelain, and soap, as well as cannons and anchors. In addition, he extended subsidies, loans without interest, and direct and indirect bounties to various industries – in particular, to encourage the production of iron, coal, and fabrics of all kinds.[6]

Colbert's legacy of exacting regulations concerning industrial production and trade were not without perspicacious critics. Among the latter, Pierre de Boisguilbert asserted (in his works of 1695 and 1707) that wealth depended neither upon the regulatory minutiae of manufacturing and commerce nor upon the overvaluation of precious metals, but rather on a "natural harmony" of industry, the supply of necessities, and the abolition of export duties, particularly on grain. Richard Cantillon, in his famous essay of 1755 on the nature of commerce, pointed out that as the supply of bullion increases in a country, prices go up, which discourages the foreign buyer, thus leading to an unfavorable balance of trade; but then as bullion declines, prices go down, and the process starts all over again. It was toward the middle of the eighteenth century that the revolt against Colbertism reached its peak (particularly under the impulse of the new Physiocratic economic school). However, while the perpetual Colbertian hindrances did call forth seminal ideas from the opposition, the latter remained for a long time ineffectual. In practice, Colbert's regulations not only continued in force; they were even reinforced by further regulations.[7]

Meanwhile, with diverse adjustments and national adaptations, mercantilist ideas continued a triumphal march into Prussia (and afterward even into far-off Russia). A specific German derivative of mercantilism known as "cameralism" (from the word *camera*, designating the place in which the royal income was stored) was an all-encompassing theory in which any problems of internal or external security resolved themselves primarily into the question of the princely revenues. Originally focused on efficient administration, specifically on the rules and practices of domanial and royal administration, cameralism eventually expanded to include broader economic issues and, in particular, finance problems. In this larger framework it envisaged managing a country's resources in a way that would yield the most for the absolute monarchic ruler, in order to enable him to fulfill his duties, increase his power, and pursue his interests (allegedly coinciding with the interests of a prosperous population). In time, cameralism became the discipline used for training officials in handling the various economic problems that beset the German states from the sixteenth to the nineteenth century. Theories on tariffs and taxes, allegedly the best guarantors of wealth, on the promotion of industry and trade, as well as on the sources of international rivalry and differences in development, figured prominently in this broadly defined doctrine. From 1729 on, the study of cameralism developed in so many directions that it finally had to be divided into three disciplines – introduction to economics, policy sciences, and cameralist sciences – a division that subsisted for a long time in Germany's universities.[8]

The promotion by the state of industrial enterprises, even those whose ownership and direct use often belonged to the fiscal authorities, did rely on the advice and help of commercial firms. Such firms were eventually entrusted with the management of some of these enterprises, particularly those concerned with munitions, metals, cutleries, and sugar refining. Frederick the Great (1740–1786) contributed appreciably to pioneering investments in a number of crucial state-initiated enterprises, including the Silesian Malapane ironworks, endowed with the first blast furnace on German soil; the Berlin iron foundry, in which the entire Berlin manufacturing industry had its origins; and the manufacture of silk in Krefeld, the weaving industry in Eberfeld and Barmen, and the linen industry in Bielefeld. In regard to maritime trade, Frederick established a joint-stock company (the Overseas Trading Corporation) in which he held the lion's share and to which he granted numerous privileges – including the monopoly on buying and selling wax and salt. Before as well as after Germany's unification, Prussia became the most important German industrial state, whose manufacturing regions (Silesia, Westphalia, and the Rhineland) eventually dominated the German economy. As Clive Trebilcock has pointed out, the interest of the state, however narrowly defined it might have been, did introduce new technologies and achieved significant results through their development. The Prussian war-related industries outlived other types of "protofactories" and thus, from a developmental point of view, provided a useful apprenticeship in industrial affairs for the Prussian state in a number of strategic industries.[9] According to Albion

W. Small, the author of a detailed work entitled *The Cameralists*, from the cameralist point of view ''the state was a magnified family with a big farm as its property'' whose citizens ''may, can, and should exist only in function of the state.''[10]

At the close of ''the epoch of merchant capitalism'' in Western Europe, many of the mercantilist emphases – on comprehensive economic regulations, the forceful determination of the direction of industrial development, state ownership of mines and factors of production, state financing of manufacturing enterprises, and elaborate state controls on trade – started to be increasingly questioned. Here and there they eventually fell into disuse, notably in rapidly developing Great Britain. But they continued to play a critical role in other countries, where they were viewed as the necessary state instruments for changing the economic structure of economically lagging states, accelerating their industrialization and helping them to ''catch up'' with Great Britain.

1.2. Mercantilist–Liberal Mixtures and Industrialism

From the late eighteenth century through the nineteenth century the critique of mercantilism became insistent, though it was still not necessarily readily accepted and applied. The leader of the Physiocrats, François Quesnay, and his followers asserted that the role of the government was to protect ''life, liberty, and property,'' while production and trade should be left alone to be pursued freely. Hence their famous motto: *laissez faire, laissez passer.* While the mercantilists viewed as indivisible the ideas of state unification and state power, the Physiocrats separated the two. On the one hand, they were in favor of national unification in all respects, while on the other hand they were indifferent to ''considerations of power.'' Concerning the ends, mercantilism had been preoccupied with wealth as a basis of state power; physiocracy regarded laissez-faire as valuable to the individual and, therefore, desirable on that account.[11]

The classic critique of mercantilism and state interventions in the economy, along with the most cogent case for free trade, was devised by Adam Smith in the late eighteenth century, in the increasingly industrializing Great Britain. In his well known and widely influential work, *An Inquiry into the Nature and Causes of the Wealth of Nations,* Smith opposed a radically new approach to the old mercantilist ideas about the importance of protectionism for ensuring a favorable balance of trade, as well as mercantilism's emphasis on domestic manufacturing to secure the state's wealth and power. Smith stressed instead that consumption constituted ''the sole end and purpose of all production'' and that the interest of the producer ought to be attended to ''only so far as it may be necessary for promoting that of the consumer.'' In the mercantilist system, he noted, the interest of the consumer was "almost constantly sacrificed to that of the producer" – and with regard to the management of colonies, he added, the interests of the home-consumer had been sacrificed to those of the producer with even a more "extravagant profusion" than in all other commercial regulations.[12] While, as we shall see later, from the early to the late nineteenth century Smith's liberal critiques greatly influenced British economic thought and policies, in most other developing countries, including the United States, their practical impact remained for a long time marginal.

Yet the processes of industrialization that had begun in Great Britain on the basis of limited notions of science and engineering grew and spread in depth through increasing applications of sciences to production. This was the case in Britain itself, as well as in its former colony, the United States (particularly from the middle decades of the nineteenth century on); eventually, it was also the case in the Western European countries. In the early nineteenth century, the main characteristic of industrialization was expansion in the use of the machine into a limited number of industrial branches. In the second half of the century, accelerated industrialization produced not only diversified uses of new and increasingly complex machines in numerous industries, but also a vigorous expansion of science-based technologies, new industrial methods, and new products. In its earlier phases in Britain (from the mid-eighteenth century on), industrialization had involved empirical breakthroughs affecting textile machinery, textile chemistry, iron making, and coal mining. Up to around the 1830s, textiles in fact remained the undisputed leading industrial sector. A decade later – when Great Britain became the recognized "workshop of the world" – machine tools speeded up and standardized the output of looms, spinning machinery, steam engines, and other critical equipment.[13] Simultaneously, the development of railroads pushed many-sided metallurgical industries and the new, science-based industries to the forefront in the newly industrializing countries.

Until the early nineteenth century, the British "mercantilist panoply" (as Sidney Checkland has called it) had been an extensive one. After the American colonies broke away from Britain and after the defeat of France at the end of the Napoleonic Wars, much of the scope of the laws that had been formulated in regard to British shipping and British imports from France fell into disuse. As industry increased in wealth, and eventually in political power, the Corn Laws were repealed (in 1846), thus eliminating the barrier to a general extension of trade and giving the great factory towns the advantage of a cheaper food supply. The obsolete Navigation Laws were repealed (in 1849), and various other measures (in 1853 and 1860) made free trade a reality in the full sense of the term at least until the 1870s.[14] Yet, late in the Victorian days, as trade patterns started to change, the British suffered with increasing discomfort the forceful competition resulting from the rapid and manifold industrialization of numerous developing countries, above all the United States and Germany. It was then England's turn to wonder what measures might be necessary to defend its markets and avoid lagging behind the advancing United States and Germany.[15]

Within its liberal, nonmercantilist framework, however, direct ownership by the British central government remained confined to defense establishments, the post office (which from 1912 on had an effective monopoly over the telephone system), and the telegraph (which had been added to the public sector in 1869). In addition, the government acquired a majority of shares in the Suez Canal Company (in 1875) and the Anglo-Persian Oil Company (in 1914). However, while at the central level the basic idea of state ownership was acceptable when a clear national interest was at stake, at the local level, communal interests drove in other directions. They pushed toward the expansion of municipal responsibilities and ownership in many new fields. From the 1890s on, after various battles with private companies, the municipalities acquired the right to go into business to provide not only water supply and sanitation, but also various new services, notably gas, electricity, and the tramways.[16]

Meantime, the evolution of the former British colony, the United States, as well as the main European countries, paralleled only in some respects the British developments. In principle, it was thought that in the newly independent United States, the federal government would play only a minor role in relation to the states and local governments. For a long time it was also assumed that in contrast with experiences elsewhere, government ownership and operation of business-type activities would not play "a major role in the American economy."[17] But these contentions depend on how one chooses to interpret the terms *business-type activities* and *major role*. Laissez-faire doctrines (which as I recalled imply free trade and therefore only minor state interventions, along with close attention primarily to the needs of the consumer rather than those of the producer), while widely accepted in principle, particularly during the last quarter of the nineteenth century, had only a rather limited impact on government policies. Certain authors (Thomas K. McGraw, for instance) have pointed out that in the promotion of selected industries, the subsidization of exports, the limitation of imports, and the maintenance of an overall favorable balance of trade, U.S. policies actually paralleled certain forms of mercantilism dominant in the preceding centuries in Europe, though a coordinated industrial policy "has always been a hard sell in the United States."[18] From around 1816 to the onset of World War I, tariffs played their usual role in protecting and promoting U.S. domestic production. Behind its walls, many U.S. industries secured a domestic market free of foreign competition, under the pretexts of sheltering "infant industries," protecting critical national defense industries, contributing to general prosperity, and maintaining a high standard of living. Before the War of 1812, U.S. tariffs were only mildly protective: they varied between 8 and 18 percent ad valorem. But after that war, the situation changed rapidly. Between 1816 and 1832, tariffs were considerably raised; after 1832, except for a respite between 1842 and 1846 when protectionism came under agrarian opposition and the duties were lowered, tariffs started to rise again. From 1861 on, with minor interruptions, the trend of tariffs was sharply upward. The average tariff rate on dutiable imports rose from 20 percent in 1860 to more than double that by 1864; it then fluctuated between 42 and 57 percent until 1897, when it started to decline, falling by 1913 to 30 percent. Besides protecting domestic industry, tariff duties were also the backbone of the federal revenue system. Finally, they probably helped the pursuit of a favorable balance of trade, a useful thing for a major debtor nation (as was the United States at the time).[19]

Furthermore, direct government ownership of vast assets and businesslike governmental activities were hardly of secondary significance in the United States. To start with, one should not forget that, after the Revolutionary War, the original states relinquished their claim to Western lands and ceded them to the national government. The latter's holdings were further expanded twenty years later with the Louisiana Purchase. Thus, the federal government became the owner and administrator of hundreds of millions of acres of land, "the biggest real estate operation in history" (before the creation of the USSR). In a series of land ordinances starting in 1784, the Americans surveyed and settled a sparsely inhabited continent in about a century. Besides land sales and grants of vast tracts of land to settlers moving West, the U.S. government also made extensive grants of public land to the railroads. It is estimated that a block of lands larger than the state of Texas – 130 million acres west of the Mississippi, equaling about one-tenth of the entire public domain – was transferred to the railroad companies. This gift, highly criticized by some and defended by others, accelerated the economic growth of the West, reduced the charges for transporting government goods, and increased the price of the lands adjacent to the railroads that remained in the government's hands. It is true that only a few railroads were built by the public authorities. However, up to 1870 the government supplied three-fifths of the original cost of railroad construction. Government was active also in promoting other forms of transportation: the federal government provided large subsidies to the merchant marine, particularly until the Civil War, and the state and local governments subsidized the private construction of turnpikes, canals, and other means of transportation.[20]

The federal government owned and operated various assets, much as other industrial nations did, that is, the postal service, water supply, and armories and arsenals, as well as the adjacent establishments needed for maintaining the army (supply depots, kitchens, repair shops, etc.). In the country's early years, it also subsidized two national banks. But unlike the situation prevailing in the other leading industrial countries, in the United States the impulse for colonization (in China, Hawaii, and the Philippines) played only a minor economic role. With an immense unified territory, vast resources, increasingly skilled immigrants, a total population rising between 1790 and 1910 from less than 4 million to close to 92 million, and vastly growing industry after the Civil War, by the beginning of the twentieth century the United States could aspire to assert its industrial superiority over that of any other country in the world.

With respect to state policy the other main developing countries, France and Germany, also refrained from following Britain on the antimercantilist path. In fact, revolutionary as well as postrevolutionary France remained ruled by resolutely protectionist principles. This policy was forcefully upheld against the "British enemy," notably in 1791 (under the Constituent Assembly), in 1793 (under the Convention), as well as in 1814 (during the last year of Napoleon's Empire). Under the Restoration of the monarchy – specifically under its tariff of 1816–1818 – protectionism again reached the high levels attained during the Empire. The same policy continued virtually unchanged during the so-called July Monarchy (1830–1848) with some exceptions only (notably with regard to shipping, then the main means of carrying on foreign commerce). The customs policy relaxed somewhat under the Second Empire (in 1860) but eventually regained strength under the Third Republic, especially in 1892, in 1897, and after 1910.[21]

The French state continually intervened in favor of manufacturing, particularly in support of the textile industry, metallurgy, and mining. The results of these interventions were, however, far less felicitous then those obtained through private initiative in Great Britain. To start with, the Revolution of 1789 did not set the goal of a new economic basis for the country, nor did it result in the creation of one. The Revolution did liquidate the innumerable and apparently inextricable old territorial divisions, strengthened the centralization of the state, and took over the totality of the properties of the church and of émigré nobles (properties that it eventually sold to private owners). But postrevolutionary France remained, with respect to the economy, very similar to the France of the ancien régime, except with regard to certain aspects of agriculture. Industry and commerce were carried out in 1815 in the same way as in the latter part of the eighteenth century. By and large, public ownership in metropolitan France expanded little, except in transportation. As in other European countries, the public sector included notably the postal system (nationalized in 1839 and 1851), the mint (1879), and the government printing office (1902), accompanied by the monopoly on tobacco

(1811) and matches (1872) – along with the usual expansions at the municipal level. With regard to the Bank of France, which was created in 1800 independent of the state, the latter eventually placed it under a powerful governor appointed by it (especially from the 1820s on).

While private initiative centered its attention, from the 1850s on, on the development of big banks and the great Parisian department stores, France continued to remain, on the threshold of the twentieth century, a country of small private enterprises. It is particularly with regard to the system of railroads – and abroad, with regard to the colonies – that the French state carried out important economic transformations, significantly expanding its ownership and control. Concerning the railroads, the main policy was for a long time that of granting to private companies the right to provide these needed "public works" – since only the private companies could mobilize the enormous capital needed for the purpose. The state's first intervention involved taking over the least profitable lines. Then, after 1840, it began to engage more or less methodically in the construction of a centralized national network. With this objective in view, the state assumed responsibility for covering the least profitable expenses – those involving the purchase of land and the building of roadbeds, bridges, and tunnels. The state then leased these properties for ninety-nine-year terms to private companies, which committed themselves to providing the rails, ballast, stations, and rolling stock. French railroads would not be nationalized until the 1930s, but by 1914 the public treasury had paid out 5.7 billion francs for France's rail network, while the private companies, through the sale of stocks and bonds, had mobilized more than three times as much. The French network was then smaller than that of Germany, but much more extensive than that of Britain. In the foreign sphere, citing the necessity of enhancing the country's overall economic and political power, France rapidly achieved a remarkable expansion of its colonial empire. Indeed, from 1880 to 1912 its empire increased from less than 1 million square miles to over 6.3 million, placing it second only to that of Great Britain. From the early 1880s on, a policy of "assimilation" of the colonies into the French custom union became the watchword and was methodically applied from Algeria to Indo-China.[22]

Germany, France's closest neighbor and a historical enemy, rose to the highest industrial power status during the last quarter of the nineteenth century, a fact that seems almost incredible when one recalls its inauspicious conditions at the dawn of that century. A highly divided country, Germany had consisted of over 300 states after the Westphalian peace of 1648. Even as redefined by the Congress of Vienna of 1815 (which retained the partial consolidations introduced by Napoleon during his occupation of that area), Germany still comprised a total of 39 states. The primary impetus toward unity came from Prussia, the foremost German state, which controlled the crucial industries of Rhineland and Westphalia, as well as the far-reaching German commercial routes from north to south and from east to west. It was Prussia that pushed resolutely toward the 1834 formation of a German Customs Union (Zollverein). The Zollverein's creation, however, was followed by many interstate rivalries and discords, and it was only as a result of Prussia's defeat of Austria in 1866, and then of France in 1871, that a united Germany finally emerged under Bismarck's leadership.

Early in the century, influential German speculative philosophers and politicoeconomic writers rejected the Western "individualistic-cosmopolitan" free trade doctrines and emphasized instead the need of "nationalist" (supermercantilist) policies to strengthen Germany militarily and economically and to overcome its developmental lag behind Britain. Johann Gottlieb Fichte affirmed in *The Closed Trade-State* (1800) that nations must be independent and autarkic, each supplying its own needs. Friedrich List, who had resided in the United States in the 1820s and had been influenced by the writings of Alexander Hamilton, decisively rejected free trade in his *National System of Political Economy* (1841) – except in the case of the Zollverein – stressing the importance of a highly protectionist national commercial policy; List advocated an active industrial policy to promote long-term growth and change. Indeed, except for the specific case of the Zollverein, the idea of free trade had a rather limited impact on this country. The German liberal tradition remained weak: while it eventually achieved some intermittent periods of success in the 1850s, 1860s, and 1870s, liberalism was easily overcome when it seemed appropriate to the decision makers. High protectionism was finally made the rule in Germany from 1879 on (indeed, protectionism triumphed in most developing countries in that period of generalized industrial depression).[23]

Against this background it may be interesting to recall that, throughout the nineteenth century, the most direct contrast between Germany and Britain was the German emphasis on universities and technical schools for training a highly skilled labor force. In contrast to Britain, which relied on private initiative, inventiveness, and skills acquisition, and in direct opposition to France, which had also developed outstanding institutions of higher learning but steered its trained scientists and engineers toward employment in the state machine, Germany was the only country systematically directing its technicians toward its newly developing industries. Also in contrast to Britain, Germany's industrialization proceeded at an extraordinarily rapid pace, thanks to a unique combination of factors: the rapid assimilation of what had been done elsewhere; the accelerated expansion of the coal and steel industry (particularly after the acquisition of Lorraine iron ore in 1871), machinery construction, the railroads, and its highly advanced chemical, electrical, and optical industries; and the enormous concentration of its production into large industrial establishments due to open financial and technological understandings among its industrialists and to the formation of monopolistic cartels (*Konzerne*).[24]

The German Reich (or the federal states) managed most of the railroads, ran various nationalized enterprises and mines, and in various ways assisted the private establishments. With regard to railroads, in some German states railroad construction had been undertaken by the state from the very beginning; in other states, part of the railroad system was purchased by the public sector; in Prussia, the state exercised first an extensive control over the railroads and then nationalized them (in 1876). By that time Germany had by far the largest railway network in Europe; however, only the post–World War I Weimar Constitution was to provide that all state railroads were to be transferred to the Reich.

In 1906, Prussia operated thirty-nine nationalized mines, twelve ironworks, and five saltworks and managed extensive land estates and forests as well. The stock of the Reichsbank was in private hands, but its president and officers were appointed by the kaiser. At the local level the state had taken over businesses and enterprises formerly owned by the nobles, as was the case notably for porcelain factories in Meissen and Berlin, breweries in Munich, and tobacco factories in Strassburg. Further, the municipalities usually owned and operated – either alone or in mixed ownership with private capital – the waterworks, as well as the gasworks, electrical power plants, slaughterhouses, and various systems of transportation. According to 1907 estimates, the mines and other industrial establishments owned by the Reich, federal states, local authorities, and other public bodies employed more than 1.5 million persons. These public enterprises employed about one-tenth of the workforce in industry, trade, and transport alone. As Gustav Stolper perceptively remarked, "The foundations were already laid on which later the war economy, the experiments of the [Weimar] Republic, and finally the National Socialist system could be built.[25]

1.3. Framing the Command Economy

World War I brought into existence the first modern model of a "command economy," a model that was to be emulated in peacetime – first by Soviet Russia and later on by Nazi Germany – with equally disastrous consequences for their countries and the rest of the world as well. Let us now see which particular steps were taken by the Great War's main belligerents in order to meet the requirements of a total war, and how and why the German war leadership, steeped in the Prussian tradition, succeeded in creating a truly integrated war economy – their so-called *Kriegswirtschaft*.

From its beginnings, the war forced the belligerents to reorient their human and material resources into new channels. This shift introduced a number of experiences and ideas about industrial organization and management that were to reshape for years to come the economic policy frameworks of belligerents and nonbelligerents alike. Finally, it annihilated the lingering laissez-faire tendencies that had started to prevail in some countries, replacing them with state controls and centralized state programming.

A state's "real war fund" is drawn from four principal sources: increased production, reduced personal consumption, reduced investment in new forms of capital, and the depletion of existing capital. What a government wants for war differs from the peace needs of the civilians. What it wants is to quickly mobilize its economy in order to produce the greatest volume of goods and services needed for essential military uses. To achieve this, it needs to transfer production resources from some uses to others, as if private ownership did not exist or were not relevant. Means must be created for rapidly "commandeering" productive instruments and agents and for directing them according to the estimated war needs. The great advantage of such commandeering is that it facilitates the rapid transition from peacetime production to a war economy.[26] These orientations may involve the use of either specific measures or the entire gamut of direct government controls, affecting businesses, branches and sectors, and foreign trade, as well as the instruments of public finance and of money and credit. The controls may also entail changes in the institutional framework itself, affecting not only the means but also the legal framework of production, including the extent of public ownership and the frontiers between public and the private domains.

How exactly did the measures taken during World War I bring about the structural transformations suggested above? The patterns of belligerents' adjustment to the war, while tending over time toward certain similarities, differed as a result of numerous complex factors. These included the traditional relationships within the respective states between civilians and the military, as well as between government and business; the decision makers' perceptions about the appropriate pace and scale of mobilizing of human and material resources; and the structure of production and availability of material supplies and foodstuffs. Controls also varied in accordance with each country's specific constraints – namely the extent of voluntary (or involuntary) cooperation from labor and management, the patterns of industrial specialties, the peculiarities of the geographic conditions, and, last but not least, the time of entrance into the war, along with the extent of participation in it.

Consider now the case of the main belligerents, starting with Great Britain. That country entered the war on August 4, 1914. Since, as everywhere else, the entire process of mobilizing and concentrating armed forces had to be effected by rail, by August 5 the British government took over the railways of Britain, Scotland, and Wales for the entire period of the war, placing them under the Railway Executive Committee. Its controls with regard to the rest of the industrial machine remained tentative and undecided for the first ten months of the conflict. However, the early assumptions that British naval might, economic power, and a small "expeditionary force" would be all that was needed to defeat Germany turned out to be erroneous. Equally erroneous proved the assumptions about the ammunition needed, the speed at which military orders could be fulfilled, and the demands of coordination ensuring production and procurement targets. The nation's needs in men and supplies became far more pressing and involved magnitudes far bigger than those originally assumed. It became also clear that "business as usual" was not winning the war. By May 1915, the old government collapsed, opening new opportunities for an innovative "Ministry of Munitions" that would bring under one control all the procurement and production activities of the government. Unfortunately, the new period – which was to extend over one and a half years and during which the scope of government regulations was to increase sharply – also brought numerous labor strikes, ever-expanding production demands for the army, and menacing price increases. Finally, during a third phase opened at the end of 1916, which did bring about a large expansion of the activity of the Ministry of Munitions, the government had to resort to even more stringent controls, involving on the one hand woolens, leather goods, and other materials needed for military production and, on the other hand, the production, distribution, and consumption of foodstuffs (which were largely supplied from abroad). The growing assertion of state power with regard to possession, control, direction, and regulation – in every sphere of production and trade where the basic needs of the army and the public had to be taken care of – is attested to by the existence at the beginning of 1918 of some 220 boards and committees overseeing all kinds of activities and products. These included acetylene, coal, cotton, diamonds, electric power supply, fish, grain, insurance services, labor of all kinds, leather, liquor, lubricants, machinery, munitions, oats, petroleum, rubber, and more. Yet, except for the universally known emphasis on munitions production, no coordinating mechanism was put into place to ensure some kind of conformity with a central policy for the activities of this intricate assemblage of boards and committees.[27]

Like England, France had made almost no preparations for the war and had no prearranged elements that could be rationally brought together either when the conflict started or as it unfolded. Yet, as in the case of the other belligerents, the war promptly raised critical problems of mobilizing the available resources, marshalling transport capabilities, coping with the inadequacy of the production structure, and finding and allocating labor. The latter issue became especially crucial, since France immediately had to draw some 63 percent of all its male workers into a vast army. The military mobilization itself, however, went smoothly, since the state established immediately its control over the entire railway system. Other pressing issues arose rapidly. It became obvious that French industry was not capable of producing many of the materials indispensable for the war. Moreover, after the German invasion in the north, France lost not only a large amount of its human resources, but also control of close to 75 percent of its coal and over 60 percent of its steel and iron metallurgy. Finally, the other countries' introduction of new technologies brought about by the war hampered France's ability to catch up with and surpass its rivals in the production of modern armaments.

As the war grew in scope and intensity, French industry lagged further behind the vanguard and, as C. J. Gignoux noted, "got accustomed to working for the state and depending on the state" as far as the purchase of most of its supplies and the sale of most of its products was concerned. By 1916, a number of so-called industrial partnerships, or consortiums, comprising all the industrial firms using a given raw material, were formed – first in the armament industries and later in a large number of other industries. The state, soon the sole authorized buyer of any raw material, would turn it over to the respective association for distribution to its members, at an administratively fixed price. The price of the final product was also determined by the state. Lacking any and all appropriate means for knowing the market, the state was in fact entirely dependent on the advice and recommendations of the leaders of the consortiums. Thus, R. Pinot, the secretary of the powerful Comité des Forges (the metallurgical consortium), became, as a French historian noted, "the unofficial minister of armaments," enjoying both a real purchasing monopoly and a fixed-price system of payment for commercial operations. Thus, the war reinforced the nearly monopolistic position of certain larger enterprises in various "strategic" economic sectors, thanks to their close cooperation with the state. On the other hand, cooperation among the state's own offices, committees, and commissions – developed in response to the accumulating scarcities brought about by the war – grew only little by little, without of course eliminating numerous bureaucratic overlaps and duplications.[28]

Germany's approach was in strong contrast to the British inability (or unwillingness) to create a central coordinating mechanism for the numerous boards and committees supervising their economy's production activities. It was in contrast, too, to the French reliance on the leaders of industry themselves to guide the industry's war production. The German military leadership methodically and consistently prepared the way toward the creation of an integrated war economy administered like a single great factory under its full control. As Friedrich Hayek reminds us, long before 1914 the Prussian state had been organized like no other country, as a single factory. The Prussian poet Novalis had already deplored this situation by the end of the eighteenth century.

A number of factors pushed German policies forcefully in this direction. As soon as Britain entered the war, the fear of a British blockade became obsessive in Germany. Moved by the idea that Germany's ability to carry out the war depended to a large extent on its capacity to secure an adequate supply of raw materials for war production, Walther Rathenau, the leader of the German power industry, and one of his engineers, Richard von Mollendorf, alerted the war minister, von Falkenhayn, about the immediate importance of this problem. On August 14, 1914, von Falkenhayn accepted Rathernau's suggestions and created a War Raw Materials Section (the Kriegsrohstoffabteilung, or KRA) in the War Ministry. The KRA's goal was to funnel requisitioned materials to the firms contributing to the war effort. Under Rathenau's own direction, the KRA developed into a vast apparatus whose detailed surveillance and control embraced the flow of all commodities circulating in the economy. To carry out its assignments, the KRA organized and supervised a number of associations for raw war materials (Kriegsrohstoffgesellschaften), grouping together the appropriate private companies, and encouraged them to draw up yearly plans on the supply and distribution of their raw materials (a precursor of some of the French war arrangements and many postwar planning organizations). By August 1916, Germany took a decisive further step. A Hindenburg Program set Germany the goal of doubling its munitions output and tripling the production of all other defense materials. On the basis of this program, the war economy expanded to include not only the supply of raw materials, the production of arms, and the production and distribution of foodstuffs, but also the total mobilization of the labor force. By November 1916, the totality of the war machine, including the KRA and its associations, were integrated into the War Emergency Office under General Wilhelm Gröner, the former chief of the Military Railway Service. According to Gröner, the new War Office headed Germany itself "as a colossal firm which includes all production of every kind, and is indifferent to the kind of coat, civil or military, which its employees wear." The new measures, added Gröner, were intended "to mobilize all effective labor, whereas up to the present we have mobilized only the army and industry." To a large extent, detailed state economic control and planning now embraced the basic operations of the entire German economy. It was this "colossal firm" encompassing the entire wartime economy – the fully developed German *Kriegswirtschaft* – that became, as I have indicated, the model of the Soviet economy, as well as that of the Nazi economy.[29]

As the integrated German economy was thus mobilizing its coordinated forces to the utmost for total war, the Allied positions were increasingly endangered on the Eastern front by the collapse of Russia and the disintegration of its armies. Facing this impending disaster, the United States decided to enter the war on the side of the Allies, on April 6, 1917. From the beginning, the major U.S. problems were the reorientation of production, the restructuring of its industrial output, and the cutting of nonessential imports and exports, but also the methodical building of a bridge of ships to send men and materials over the Atlantic in minimum time.

As in the other belligerent countries, the president eventually took control of the country's railways (on December 26, 1917), though compensation was provided to the owners for each year or fractional part of the year during the period of federal control, including provisions for the maintenance, repair, renewal, and depreciation of property. With regard to the crucial question of shipping, the U.S. Shipping Board, and an Emergency Fleet Corporation created by it, focused their efforts on the tasks of increasing U.S. tonnage as fast as possible and seeing that it was utilized fully and effectively. By July 1918 (not long before the war's end), the ships built under contract for the Fleet Corporation – 233 new vessels with an aggregate tonnage of 1.4 million – were still relatively few in comparison to those requisitioned. But the combined tonnage of the British and U.S. fleets' newly built ships already exceeded those lost through unrestricted submarine warfare (2.6 million tons), and U.S. construction under government contract was continuing to grow rapidly.

The biggest and most complex problem, that of reorienting the entire nation's production, brought about various interesting efforts to centrally coordinate certain functions normally left to private uncoordinated decision making. Already a few months before the U.S. entrance into the war, in August 1916, a Council of National Defense and an Advisory Commission were set up to survey and analyze the country's industrial and transportation system and to ascertain how they might be appropriately utilized in case of war. However, the Commission was fully organized only by March 3, 1917, and by then what was needed was not a survey, but detailed instructions for bringing about effective cooperation between the government bureaus and agencies and the war industries, taking account of the latter's requirements for restructuring and expanding their output. Though the Commission had not been meant to be an executive body, it did divide itself into seven committees focused on munitions, manufacturing, raw materials, engineering, labor, and other supplies. In effect, the Commission became a kind of informal advisory industrial cabinet. But as the war developed, this arrangement proved unsatisfactory. The need to plan production of numerous forms of munitions led the War Department to suggest creating the General Munitions Board, which would assume coordination of the activities of all the appropriate governmental bureaus and departments. This board began its work on

April 9, 1917, but functioned only until July 28, 1917, when it was also found inadequate for the purpose. (Notably, it was said to have been more of a clearing house than the needed commanding directorate.) Its replacement was the War Industries Board (WIB), which was supposed to improve the administration of the war program and become an agency of effective national economic coordination. However, both because of its status as a subordinate and advisory agency of the Council of National Defense and because of a lack of cooperation from the military services, it found it impossible to fulfill its July mandate. Finally, by March 1918, the president had elevated Bernard Baruch to the chairmanship of the WIB and redefined his functions, as well as those of the board. The latter functioned until November 30, 1918. According to Robert D. Cuff, who devoted an extensive study to the WIB, the search for "some middle way" to integrate individualistic groups and a centralizing state – a new compromise between traditional free enterprise and the national planning required by the war – ended, as might have been expected, in "a bundle of paradoxes and contradictions which cannot be described as either free enterprise or public planning."[30]

Thus, except for Germany, no major power managed to fully resolve the paradox pitting pressures for economic centralization in the service of total war against the innate decentralizing tendencies of the private economy, accustomed to centralization only within the limits of certain companies, branches, or industries. What Germany's central command set out to do and did was to disregard the rights of private firms to structure their inputs, outputs, and prices according to their own ideas about demand and supply. As I indicated, the German high command ran the economy as a single, integrated, nationalized firm, even though the old owners continued to maintain their proprietary titles. Neither the British, the French, nor the U.S. government could take this path. While all the central governments did intervene to oversee the key industries needed for the pursuit of the war, these interventions did not culminate in the creation of a single fully centralized British or U.S. mechanism; and though in France requisitions, priority claims, restrictions, and rationing were centralized, the actual guidance of most war production and distribution was left in the hands of the private leaders of the appropriate industrial cartels.

Obviously, the war's most crushing economic effects fell on the defeated and humiliated Germany. However, neither this nor the stumbling nature of the victors' wartime attempts to centralize means that the war had only a limited or temporary impact either on the expansion of the role of the state in the other countries or on the ways in which the economic sectors of the belligerent nations responded to the immediate needs for complex postwar adjustments. Actually, the vast dislocations caused by the war and its aftermath – the enormous shifts in the patterns of demand and supply and in workforce utilization; the great needs for reconstruction, reorganization, modernization, and development; and the pressures of an intensified international competition – pushed all the industrialized countries toward rapid and massive extensions of the states' economic interventions. These interventions combined controls, subsidies, credits, tariffs, quotas, and price manipulations in a variety of ways, along with particularly complex changes in the scope of state-owned enterprises and the structure and reach of state-implemented social policies. I consider some of these issues in the next section.

1.4. Nationalization and Welfare

Let us turn our attention now to the expansion of state ownership and the related changes in social policies during the six decades from the early post–World War I years to the early 1980s. I believe that this entire period has been strongly affected in the West by two sets of closely interrelated factors. The first set may be viewed as encompassing the successive instabilities engendered by the difficult postwar economic readjustments and their repercussions, leading eventually to World War II and then again to a highly unstable international situation. In the wake of World War I came the dramatic rise and consolidation of the Soviet regime, the breakdown of the international market and the Great Depression, the ascent of Nazism, and its preparation and then launching of World War II (in association with Italy and Japan). That terrible war was followed by the new and menacing Soviet–Western nuclear rivalry. The second set of factors marking the West's policies during these six decades reflected misconceptions, both about the strengths and prospects of the Soviet Union and about the vigor of labor's political and trade union organizations in the West. These misconceptions jointly affected the pace of Western nationalizations and a number of its social policies. Let me consider first the questions relating to the expansion of state ownership in the countries of our focus, and then the special results in the same countries of the drive to create the so-called welfare state.

In Great Britain, the post–World War I years were dominated by the experiences of war controls and the rising influence of socialist and trade union ideas about the alleged usefulness of "common ownership of the means of production." While before that war the Fabian socialists had stressed the idea of an incremental broadening of industrial democracy, the Labour Party put forward in the famous Clause IV of its 1918 constitution (discarded only in 1995!) the idea that the national government should take over the country's "commanding heights," that is, its key industries and its institutions of banking and finance. Though, from the late nineteenth century on, the Fabians had encouraged the expansion of municipal ownership – dubbed by some as "municipal socialism" – they, as well as many liberals and conservatives, viewed municipalization as an alternative to nationalization and a preferred method of public ownership. While ultimately rejecting socialist ideas, the British governments had to resort to all kinds of administrative improvisations and experiment in order to cope with the critical problems posed by the needs for rationalization and consolidation of various industries. One of the innovations of the time, with many later offsprings, was the launching of the public service board, a new type of industrial concern for organizing activities in certain industries tending toward monopoly. Modeled in part on earlier organizational patterns, for example, the Port of London Authority of 1908, the new type of concern was first established in the fields of broadcasting and electricity. Thus were instituted in 1926 the British Broadcasting Corporation and the Central Generating Electricity Board (which assumed national responsibility for electric power generation, leasing the distribution of power of some 600 municipal and private undertakings). The establishment of these public corporations was followed in 1931 by that of the Agricultural Market Boards and in 1934 by the last successful case of global municipalization, the London Passenger Transport Board. This latter took over the whole complex of transportation in that city, including the underground railways, the metropolitan railway, and the bus, trolley, and tram services.[31]

By the end of the interwar period, publicly owned concerns consisted notably of (a) public undertakings operated directly by various departments of the central government – the post office, telegraphs, telephones, dockyards, ordinance factories, Commissioners of the Crown Lands, Stationary Office, and Mint; (b) national undertakings operated by ad hoc bodies, such as the British Broadcasting Corporation and the Central Electricity Generating Board; (c) local undertakings operated by the local authorities for community needs, mostly public utilities and municipal housing; (d) local undertakings operated by ad hoc bodies, such as the Port of London Authority, the Metropolitan Water Board, and the London Passenger Transport Board.[32]

The greatest push in British history toward nationalization took place after World War II with Labour's accession to power from 1945 to 1951, and then again during Labour's successive returns to power form 1964 to 1970, and finally from 1974 to 1979. As soon as it came to power in 1945, the Labour Party stressed its commitment to both nationalization (for the control of the commanding heights) and the welfare state. Concerning nationalizations, let me note – without entering into the innumerable changes involving nationalizations, denationalizations, and renationalizations (e.g., in the case of iron and steel) – that during the period immediately following World War II, Labour secured the nationalization of the Bank of England (1946), the mines (under the National Coal Board, in 1947), the electricity and gas utilities (under the British Electric Authority, which took over a vast number of undertakings of the haphazard electrical system then in operation, and those of the Gas Council along with twelve area gas boards). In addition, Labour pushed toward the nationalization of large sections of the transport industry. Thus, to the British Overseas Airways Corporation, which had been run as a public concern since 1940, Labour added in 1946 the British European Airways. It also established the British Transport Commission entrusted to provide "an efficient, adequate, economical, and properly integrated system of public inland transport and port facilities." Last but not least, it nationalized the iron and steel firms with a certain output capacity (denationalized in 1954 and renationalized in 1965). Paradoxically, before the second return of Labour to power, the conservative governments themselves added other national corporations to the list – the Atomic Energy Authority (1956), the Independent Television Authority (1957), the Sugar Board (1957), the Electricity Council and Central Electricity Generating Board (1958), the British Railway Board (1963), the British Waterways Board (1963), and so on. Upon its return to power from 1964 to 1970, Labour added as a public corporation British Steel (1967), the Post Office (1969), and the National Bus Corporation (also in 1969). Finally, after a rather short conservative intermission during which the government further nationalized a significant number of public corporations (involving the ports, civil aviation, oil, and gas) and rescued certain ailing corporations (e.g., Rolls Royce in 1961), Labour continued the expansion of public corporations to other ailing companies (e.g., Leyland in 1975), as well as to major shipbuilding, ship engineering, and ship repairing firms and to regional development boards. This erratic expansion of public corporations resulted by 1979 in the existence at the national level – that is, excluding local or regional bodies – of some fifty public enterprises, predominantly in fuel and power and in the transport and communication industries.[33] But 1979 also turned out to be a decisive year in the affirmation of the most broad-based opposition to the entire philosophy of public ownership – an issue I address in detail in Chapter 3.

The evolution of public ownership in France also registered important fluctuations during the era under review. In the years immediately following World War I, the industrial establishment tried to put an end to the vast state interventions in the economy that had developed in various directions during the war. But the impact of this campaign remained ineffectual. The state continued to impose its control over private industry, notably in the fields of electricity, petroleum supplies, transportation, communications, and housing. It provided subsidies and created joint companies for the development of hydroelectricity, engaged itself systematically in the reconstruction of railways through the provision of compensatory funding for the losses occasioned by reorganization, pushed the private aviation companies toward concentration and subsidized their growth, framed an oil policy aimed at reducing France's dependency on British oil companies, and, through the post office (PTT), stimulated a program for the automation of telephones. At the same time, it also encouraged the intervention of local governments in the creation of public companies, notably for the provision of cheap housing (*habitations à bon marché* [HBMs]).

The Depression forced the state to reduce its expenditures between 1930 and 1934. Starting in 1934, however, it began to rearm, as the German war menace was rapidly increasing under the Nazis. The French left coalition, the Popular Front, elected in 1936 on an antifascist platform, pushed successfully toward the nationalization of the armament and aircraft industries (in 1936), as well the railways (in 1937), and secured for the state a controlling interest in the Bank of France. Though the nationalization of the armament industries eventually became an instrument for their modernization and reorganization, the immediate effects of the change tended to be slight. Thus, twenty aviation firms were regrouped into seven nationalized companies, but in the short run their output continued to remain absolute, as their factories were poorly equipped, their machinery was out of date, and their production was heavily dependent on manual work. As the danger of war intensified, a 1938 law placed the economy under a generalized state control (dirigisme), blocked wages and salaries, and established the control of foreign trade and of capital exports. By August 1940, an "organizational committee" under state surveillance was set up in each industry with the task of establishing its production program, distributing its raw materials, determining its conditions of production, and proposing its sale prices to the appropriate authorities. France's defeat by Germany led to the splitting up of the country into a German occupation zone and a subservient so-called free France under the Vichy government. The latter enacted a number of industrial organizational measures and methods of economic control that to a degree influenced subsequent national planning and its supporting statistical systems.[34]

After the liberation of France, the new government of General de Gaulle emerged from the French military liberation forces and from the Conseil National de la Resistance (CNR – French National Resistance Council). The de Gaulle government launched a vast process of nationalizations, aiming both to punish companies that had collaborated with the Germans and to expand the state's control over the economy's commanding heights, including certain strategic positions involving major industries and the country's main banks. (These goals, set in March 1944 by the Center–Left CNR, expressed at the time the joint position of its membership, consisting of the Catholic social movement, the socialists and communist parties, and the trade unions.) The first industries to be taken over as a punitive measure were the car manufacturing company Renault, the Northern Coal Mines, and the Gnome et Rhône transport company. These were followed by the nationalization of the Bank of France and other major banks (in December 1945), some 60 percent of the insurance companies, certain mines, and the gas and electric companies (in April 1946). At the time, the new state incarnated the very idea of Liberation: it was the cement of a France torn and exhausted by the war and the embodiment of the national unity of the Resistance. As a French writer then put it, "The state of 1945 was celebrated as national sovereignty had been celebrated in 1789."[35]

In the then prevailing conditions, the nationalizations of 1945–1946 were perceived by the trade unions' chief organization, the Conféderation Générale du Travail (CGT – National Confederation of Labor), as an instrument of social progress. Socialist politicians and some high state employees saw the nationalizations as an instrument of reconstruction and industrial moderni- zation. It is with these latter considerations in mind that the French govern- ment launched the first National Plan of Modernization and Equipment (1947–1953), centered on the production of electricity, coal, metals, cement, agricultural machinery, and transport equipment. (It was the second plan [1954–1957] and especially the third [1958–1961] that turned France's atten- tion decisively toward the future, aiming in particular toward a balanced development of the country's regions.) The nationalizations of 1945–1946 were followed by some further nationalizations in 1948 (of the Transatlantic Company) and by the creation of Air France, as well as by increased state participation in metallurgy and in airplane production (namely, the Dassault firm). The resulting array of public entities constituted the virtually un- changed framework of the public sector until 1982, when the socialists, re- turning to power, launched a new and massive process of nationalizations. In other words, the state sector – as conceived and realized at the Liberation and functioning independently of detailed parliamentary influence – endured and served various purposes, not only of the Left but also of the conservative governments, in the quarter century from de Gaulle's return to power in 1958 to François Mitterand's victory in 1981.[36]

At that point, through its expansion in 1982, the public sector absorbed all the large banks, five predominant industrial groups, and many other industrial enterprises, along with the main insurance companies. This empowered the state to exercise control over 30 percent of the sales, 25 percent of the in- dustrial labor force, and 50 percent of total investments in the country. Through the 1982 nationalizations the state took over no less than thirty banks, two key financial companies (Paribas and Suez), and five predominant industrial groups (Thomson-Brandt, Compagnie de Saint-Gobain, Pechiney, Compagnie Générale D'électricité, Rhône-Poulenc), and increased its partic- ipations in various large firms (Dassault, Havas, Matra, Roussel, Elf), as well as in three main insurance groups (including the key Assurances du Groupe de Paris Vie).[37]

The 1982 nationalizations, planned by the socialist and communist parties since 1972 in the then prevailing conditions of a prolonged economic crisis, were sternly denounced by the conservatives as out of step with the process of denationalization that had started to take place by then in Great Britain, Japan, Canada, and Germany. It was indeed paradoxical that the French public sector should become, at such a time, the most important among the market-directed economies. And even before the return to power of conservatives in 1986, the socialists had found themselves obliged to revise or discontinue many of their 1982 policies, as I shall point out further on (in Chapter 3). For now, let me note that according to the 1986–1987 data, the French public sector consisted then of not less than 650 enterprises with 2.2 million people gainfully employed, accounting for large shares of the electronics, automobile, pharmaceutical, and glass industries, as well as nonferrous metal firms, household equipment production, and insurance. It also controlled half of the basic chemical output, the entire electrical, coal, steel, and armaments industries, the railways and air transport, and the post office services.[38]

Consider now the special situation of the public sector in Germany, the last country in our review of developments in Western and Central Europe. In the early post–World War I years, during the short-lived German communist revolution, there were strong impulses toward massive nationalization. However, as the momentum of this revolution was rapidly lost, few of its programs could not be enforced, except with regard to coal and steel. Yet, given the country's large historic heritage of public ownership, during the Weimar Republic in the mid-1920s the public sector – federal, state, and local – still accounted for a substantial number of diverse enterprises, with some 1.9 million gainfully employed (i.e., 9.8 percent of the country's labor force). The federal government directly controlled some 530 large enterprises and the states, some 1,520. In addition there were some 4,920 public sector corporations, and the local authorities accounted for 15,120 communal enterprises providing the usual communal services – sanitation, water, gas, electricity, and so on. The public sector as a whole comprised some 10.1 percent of the national income in 1927. While before the Depression of the 1930s this sector held relatively minor positions in banking and finance – except for its own bank, the Reichskreditgesellschaft, which soon ranked with the four biggest private banks – in 1931 the government acquired an undisputed dominance of that entire field. At the same time, the government established a number of stock companies that took over the administration of formerly state-owned arsenals, power plants, and various other enterprises founded after the war. The stocks of these companies were concentrated in a Reich-owned holding company, the Vereinigte Industrie-A.G. (VIAG), which was to be scheduled for partial privatization only in the 1980s.[39]

The Nazi regime did not attempt to nationalize businesses or to expropriate agricultural lands, except for those of the Jewish and other "enemies." Moreover, quite soon after their accession to power, the Nazis gained sufficient strength to place each and every piece of property and each and every important economic decision under their command, in many respects as in the framework of the *Kriegswirtschaft* of 1916. Without any interference, the centrally administered Nazi system geared the economy's activities toward the needs of a totalitarian state. As Ludwig von Mises noted in his famous 1919 study, *Nation, State, and Economy*, while an economic structure like the command economy of World War I cannot be called a "socialist economy" – since socialism means the transfer of the means of production out of private ownership of individuals into public ownership – it does involve the socialization of production, since within its peculiar framework it is no longer up to the owner "to determine what should be produced, to acquire raw materials, to recruit workers, and finally to sell the product." The main difference between the Germany's increasingly centralized economy of World War I – fashioned to respond to war needs and to pressures of blockades – and Hitler's Germany is that the latter, from its beginnings, intended to rely for its supplies not on autarky but rather on the invasion and conquest of what it claimed to be its "vital space."[40]

Germany's defeat in World War II led to its eventual splitting into two separate states – the Federal Republic of Germany (FRG) and the German Democratic Republic (GDR). I refer to the latter's development in Chapter 5. For now, let me note that from its inception the FRG opted decisively in favor of a market-directed economic order, but this federal state continued to be, on the basis of its heritage of public ownership from the Weimar Republic and from the Third Reich, the largest owner and entrepreneur in the country. Besides its monopoly in railways, postal services, and telecommunication systems, it occupied crucial ownership positions in mining, metals, electricity, gas, shipbuilding, and automobile production, as well as an important share in banking and credit. While the federal government did not attempt to expand its holdings and while it started a process of partial privatization in the late 1950s – about which more will be said in Chapter 3 – as of the early 1980s its industrial assets remained considerable. It then held majority assets in VIAG (embracing electricity, gas, aluminum, metallurgy, and chemicals), Salzgitter (steel – the former metallurgical company Herman Göring), Saarberg (coal), and IVG (transport equipment and oil), which together employed some 112,000 workers, and minority assets in the former Nazi holding company VEBA (energy and chemicals) and Volkswagen (VW automobiles), with 309,000 gainfully employed. Also at the time, besides the federal reserve bank, Deutsche Bundesbank, the federal government had holdings in numerous other banks that jointly occupied the third rank among the German financial institutions, as well as considerable holdings in electricity. Four large state banks (the Westdeutsche, Bayrische, Norddeutsche, and Hessische Landesbanken) acted as crucial channels of industrial and regional policies. In the early 1980s, among the country's 500 largest enterprises, some 90 involved large capital holdings by the public sector – namely, 45 by the federal government, 15 by the states, and 30 by local authorities.[41]

The extent and importance of the public sector in the United States – the last country on which we focus in this section – are less clearly ascertainable than in the European countries that we just examined. From the outset, the critical problem is what exactly is to be included in this U.S. public sector. Since the 1920s the most common form of government enterprise was the public authority, whose characteristics included independent corporate status, no direct power to levy taxes, power to raise funds in the money markets, and full government ownership. Unfortunately, at the federal level there is no generally accepted definition of the federal corporation, so the figures given for them may vary from one source to the next. As in the case of the federal enterprises, the state and local enterprises are not clearly defined and categorized by law and administrative practice. The U.S. Census Bureau counts some public authorities in the category of "special districts" and others in the category of "dependencies of state or municipal governments," so that, in this case also, wide variations may occur among the totals listed for these enterprises.[42]

During World War I, in order to meet certain production needs and provide for the autonomy and flexibility needed in carrying out a business enterprise, the federal government had created various government corporations (the U.S. Emergency Fleet Corporation, the U.S. Grain Corporation, the War Finance Corporation, the U.S. Housing Corporation, the Sugar Equalization Board, the Spruce Production Corporation, the Russian Bureau, Inc.). Most of these were liquidated before 1930. In the early 1920s the United States established Federal Intermediate Credit Banks as an adjunct farm-financing instrument, along with the Inland Waterway Corporation, which was concerned with interstate transportation. In 1930, during the Hoover administration, the federal government established the Reconstruction Finance Corporation (RFC) – modeled on the War Finance Corporation of 1918 – whose principal goal was to make emergency credits available to banks, financial institutions, insurance companies, and industrial corporations in difficulty. The RFC functioned until 1954. During the New Deal the federal government launched a number of critical corporations created to fulfill needs unsatisfied in various sectors. Some of these corporations are still extant, though not necessarily in their original form, notably the Commodity Credit Corporation, the Export–Import Bank, the Federal Home Loan Bank, the Federal Housing Administration Fund, the Federal Insurance Corporation, the

Federal National Mortgage Association (FNMA, familiarly called "Fannie Mae"), and the Federal Savings and Loan Insurance Corporation. To these were added that unique government–enterprise complex, the Tennessee Valley Authority (TVA). Besides the development of flood control and navigation facilities along the Tennessee, the TVA's mandate included generating electric power and fostering growth and change in an entire region.[43]

A miscellaneous number of ephemeral corporations were set up during the U.S. involvement in World War II. Immediately after that war there were some 110 federal corporations, but by 1948, only 75 were said to remain, of which 12 were then in the process of liquidation. In addition to these, there were some 38 mixed-ownership federal corporations. Forty years later, in 1988, according to a study by the U.S. General Accounting Office, there still existed 45 federal corporations with the common characteristics of "budget status, legal status and purpose." These corporations were authorized or established by the Congress to serve "a public function of a predominantly business nature." Besides the 7 corporations listed above under the New Deal, the study includes 38 additional corporations, 35 of which are subject only to federal decisions and 3 of which do not meet all of the criteria (namely, the Corporation for Public Broadcasting, the Legal Service Corporation, and the U.S. Postal Service). Among the 35 corporations subject to federal decisions, the biggest grouping comprises some 23 banks and financial institutions concerned primarily with agriculture, housing, savings, pensions, education, consumer cooperatives, and regions. Among the remaining 12 corporations, the most notable are the Communications Satellite Corporation, the Saint Lawrence Seaway Development Corporation, 2 rail corporations (Conrail and Amtrak), and the National Fish and Wildlife Foundation.

According to a different type of account, there were in existence "at least fifty major federal enterprises" playing a major role in the provision of credit and finance throughout the economy and producing "15 percent of the nation's electric power, most of the freight rail service in the northeast quadrant of the country, all intercity rail passenger service, and residential along with the major part of commercial mail delivery." Among the additional holdings cited by this second source are the Alaska Railroad Company, the U.S. Government Printing Office, the National Capital Airports, the Upper Colorado River Water Storage Corporation, and the Lower Colorado River Water Storage Corporation.[44] For completeness, we should add to the federal public sector the vast public domain, which in the mid-1970s encompassed 33 percent of the total U.S. land area of close to 2.3 billion acres. (The state governments held an additional 6 percent of the total, the county and municipal governments about 1 percent, while the Indian lands covered 2.3 percent.)[45]

The state governments operate many businesses in transportation, power, and insurance, as well as canals, bridges, ferries, and harbor facilities. One of the largest public enterprises in the nation is the Port of New York Authority, established in 1921 by an interstate compact between New York and New Jersey. As in the other developed countries, the local governments conduct an array of activities, including water supply, electricity, passenger transport, and housing. According to certain estimates, at least 1,000 state and interstate authorities and 6,000 local and regional authorities are currently in operation.[46]

A crude approximation of the weight of the federal versus the state and local business enterprise, as well as of the total government fixed nonresidential capital versus total private fixed nonresidential capital, may be obtained from data from a U.S. Department of Commerce study, the *Fixed Reproducible Tangible Wealth in the United States, 1925–89*. According to these data (computed in 1987 dollars), federal fixed nonresidential capital, which consists of structures (excluding military facilities), accounted in 1989 for $211.4 billion, of which $36.5 billion represented the value of industrial buildings, electric and gas facilities, transit systems, airfields, and so on. State and local fixed nonresidential capital in structures amounted to a total of $1,562.9 billion, of which sewer systems, water supply, electric and gas facilities, transit systems, airfields, and the like accounted for $400.9 billion – respectively, over seven times and close to eleven times the federal holdings. (It would be rather inappropriate to assert that these data reflect a ''high'' federal concentration of such capital – though of course these data cannot take account of the crucial federal role in the allocation and distribution of credits played by its corporate banks and financial institutions.) The total publicly held nonresidential net stock of capital in structures came to $1,774.3 billion (i.e., the federal government's $211.4 billion plus the states' $1,562.9 billion) – a figure reflecting, besides the industrial structures detailed above, publicly owned office buildings, highways and streets, and educational and hospital buildings. By contrast, total fixed nonresidential private capital in structures amounted to $9,650.2 billion, or five and a half times as much. Put another way, the total government's share amounted to slightly over 15 percent of the country's fixed nonresidential capital stock (of $11,394.5 billion [$1,774.3 plus $9,650.2 billion]).[47]

As can be expected, comparative data on the size of each country's public sector and on its ratios to GNP, to total employment, and to capital formation are not always consistent, given vast differences in the underlying definitions. (I return to the issues in Chapter 5.) Let me note for now only that as far as the public enterprises are concerned, all the European countries we have considered displayed, in the early 1980s, high concentrations of such enterprises in telecommunications, electricity, and transportation. Thus, for instance, in the twelve countries of the European Economic Community, the share of public enterprises in total value added amounted to over 13 percent, in total employment to over 11 percent, and in capital formation to over 20 percent. Sectorally, the percentages ran as high as 60 percent for telecommunications and transportation and 73 percent for electricity; small shares were displayed in banking and finance and in commerce.

Consider now the problem related to the main changes in the orientations of social policies in the countries of our analytical focus. During the sixty-year period from 1920 to 1980, all these countries saw a critical expansion of the state's functions with regard to adjusting the distribution of income and wealth, particularly with regard to building comprehensive public systems of social protection into what came to be known as the "welfare state."

Poverty has always been the condition of very large parts of the population in all societies. Traditionally, its mitigation has depended on charity from family and neighbors, professional or religious organizations, or charitable institutions. An early interesting historical exception is the 1601 Elizabethan Poor Law Act, which ceased to exist under this name only in 1948, when, as we shall see later on, it was superseded by the National Assistance Act. The Poor Law had provided for a kind of residual safety net for pauper children, the aged, the sick, and the disabled.[48] Eventually, as industrialization and urbanization developed, with the continuous growth of organized labor, new social problems and social debates were brought to the fore – problems and debates that had not existed when agricultural activities were predominant or when such problems had not affected growth and economic fluctuations as deeply as they started to do from the 1870s on. In all the advanced countries, debates gained momentum either about the social causes and social responsibilities for poverty or about the ways to minimize its growth and impact on social stability and economic growth.

During the critical half century preceding the methodical articulation of social insurance systems in most developed countries (c. 1920), various piecemeal schemes of social protection were enacted, particularly with regard to pensions, unemployment, and (limited) health insurance. Thus, apart from its Poor Law, Britain enacted in 1897 the Workmen's Compensation Act, which first applied to a number of specified occupations and then was made general in 1906. In 1908, it enacted the Pensions Act, which granted noncontributory pensions from age seventy on, subject to a means test. Also in 1908, it passed the Children's Act, extending the state's responsibility for children and aiming to prevent deprivation in early life. In 1912 a Health Insurance program was applied to those thought to be in need because of a loss of earnings and the expenses associated with sickness. Finally, also in 1912, Britain adopted a plan of unemployment insurance, first restricted to certain industries, then made general in 1920.[49]

Toward the end of the nineteenth century, in 1898, the French passed the

Employers' Liability and Compensation Law, which made employers liable for all the occupational accidents of their workers. The French state assumed in 1905 the liability of a modest old age pensions system, subsequently expanded (in 1910) and made compulsory to cover all wage earners. Finally the state subsidized the trade unions' unemployment funds from 1905 on and provided direct aid to the unemployed from 1914 on, through the municipalities and the counties (namely, "departments").[50]

It was, however, Bismarck's imperial Germany that was the first to try enacting a consistent system of compulsory workers' insurance against sickness, accident, disability, and old age. Most of Bismarck's proposals were debated and finally adopted between 1883 and 1889. The first to emerge from the parliamentary struggles was the Health Insurance Law, providing insurance for a large segment of workers on the basis of both employers' and workers' contributions, along with the Accident Insurance Law, with the insurance provided by the employers. Finally, in 1889 the Old Age and Disability Insurance Law extended pension benefits to industrial workers, agrarian laborers, artisans, and servants, with the government making a contribution to each pension. While Bismarck had hoped that an integrated social legislation would tie labor to the state and check the growth of revolutionary tendencies in its political and trade union organizations, the 1883–1889 measures were disappointing in that respect. Subsequently, the above laws were codified (in 1911) in a uniform body of legislation (the still valid Imperial Insurance Code) extending social insurance across a wide range of social strata, from industrial and agricultural workers to civil servants, as well as white-collar workers.[51]

Yet it was only during the deep social and economic crises and changes registered between 1920 and 1980 that comprehensive public systems of social protection finally took shape in all the developed capitalist countries. At the heart of what came to be known as the "welfare state" were, on the one hand, social security programs, aiming to stave off the poverty cycles menacing the employed population in various ways and, on the other hand, public assistance arrangements for the needy. Broadly defined, the first group of programs concerned old age, survivor, and disability insurance, as well as unemployment aid, yielding retirement benefits, survivor benefits after the death of the breadwinner, and invalidity benefits over extended periods and, over short periods, unemployment compensation. The second have involved means-tested programs focused on target groups (e.g., children, single-parent families, the poor) and various forms of cash assistance for housing, transport, food, and health care. Certain countries added universal benefit systems, either separately or in some combination with the social security scheme. These covered either the entire population or large segments of it under diverse programs concerning health (e.g., with pluralist systems of provision and fee-for-service payments) and education (for various groups and at various levels); such programs often also considered critical components of broader strategies for economic growth and development. The processes of coalescing the laws and regulations shaping both the social security and the social assistance systems and defining the modern welfare state developed, however, along different paths in each of the countries we are studying because of differences in their respective backgrounds, their economic and social conditions, and their particular political power balances and ideological biases.

Consider first the case of Britain. That country took the decisive step toward a programmed welfare state in June 1941 when the Inter-departmental Committee on Social Insurance and Policy Services was appointed under the chairmanship of Sir William Beveridge to survey the existing national schemes of social insurance and make appropriate recommendations for the future. After the publication of the crucial Beveridge Report, the government made its proposals for a comprehensive scheme of social insurance in September 1944. Subsequently, under the Labour government (1945–1951), a comprehensive set of measures were passed into law: in 1945, the program of Family Allowances (for every family with more than one child); in 1946, the Industrial Injury Act against employment accidents; also in 1946, the National Insurance Act, providing various payments for unemployment, sickness, maternity, and retirement pensions; and in 1947, the National Health Service Act, providing for free medical treatment (including dental, ophthalmic, and hospital services) for the whole population. And, in 1948, the crucial, separate National Assistance Act brought into a single comprehensive scheme the then-existing assistance programs (including those of the Poor Law), concerning all kinds of assistance (for unemployment supplementary pensions and for persons in real need and not qualified for assistance under the national insurance schemes). The Labour-programmed welfare state also continued its support for new town and municipal housing and opened access to secondary education for all children. Finally, the main structures of all welfare services and benefits were brought together in 1964, and the consolidated system continued its further expansions up to the end of the 1970s,[52] when the underlying conception of the welfare state became the center of a number of pressures for great changes, including the political conflicts that I examine in Chapter 3.

In France, also after World War II, the entire system of social insurance (which had become compulsory on July 1, 1930) underwent deep transformation – first in 1945–1946, and then in 1974–1978. The original plan conceived by the CNR (the National Council of the Resistance) envisaged guaranteeing a sufficient income for the entire population so as to ensure the family's subsistence under all circumstances. In its broadest sense, the French system of social protection was supposed to ensure job security and the liquidation of unemployment, income security for the worker and compensation for his family charges, health security through adequate access to medical care and through prevention of industrial accidents, and sufficient allocations in cases of sickness, maternity, disability, and old age. In practice, given various social resistances, market pressures, and the demographic situation, the heart of the social protection system, namely social security, had to focus primarily on the questions of health, as well as on pensions and family benefits. First the laws concerning sickness, maternity, disability, old age, and death were revised and expanded. Eventually, the national statutory health insurance scheme covered virtually the whole population, with the largest fund (CNAMTS – Caisse Nationale d'Assurance Maladie des Travailleurs Salariés) insuring most employees, including dependents and pensioners. And second, a truly new charter was established concerning family allowances. The ultimate system of social insurance accordingly comprised the social security scheme, involving insurance coverage against the risks of sickness, old age, and family-related problems; an unemployment insurance scheme, concerning unemployment compensation; and an ensemble of social assistance schemes, disbursing various forms of benefits to the indigent members of the society. In time, the rising social security contribution rates have, however, driven a large wedge between before- and after-tax income, as virtually all social protection programs are financed by the social security contributions leveled on wages.[53]

The German social insurance system also crystallized eventually into a sharply differentiated dual system of social security and social assistance. As I indicated above, the Bismarckian legislation codified in 1911 provided that country with a more comprehensive system of public protection than existed anywhere else in the world at the time. After World War I the Weimar Republic extended that system further through a number of measures concerning children and the family, housing and health (1924–1925), and unemployment insurance (1927). Paradoxically, the Nazis did not deeply modify that system, and some of their additional war regulations remained in effect after the war. The main modifications of the then prevailing system undertaken from 1949 on concerned, in particular, pension adjustments – war pensions, the so-called equalization of burdens for the war veterans, war invalids, war widows and orphans, and the integration into the system of the refugees from the East. Other significant measures concerned coverage and rates of allowances for children.

The German social security system as it functioned throughout the period considered has consistently emphasized status differences, family priorities, and the role of voluntary bodies (mainly churches). It has been predicated on the principle of joint insurance: both employers and workers co-insure against loss of income due to sickness and unemployment, contribute to retirement pensions, and insure against the cost of medical treatment. Taxes and compulsory social security contributions account for a significantly high proportion of taxpayer income, putting Germany near the top of the European Community countries in this respect. (Note, however, that the funds that the private sector administers are autonomous; i.e., they are not included in the total of public expenditures.) The German Constitution stresses the principle of universal social security for those active in the economy. With regard to women, who may be noneconomically active, the system emphasizes the rights associated with marriage and maternity. (But increasing divorce rates are deepening the conflicts over benefits and entitlements.)

The second markedly separate system of benefits is the social assistance scheme (*Sozialhilfe*), financed by both local and federal funds. The "social rates" for assistance are drawn up by the German Association for Public and Private Relief, an association of religious and voluntary bodies, whose rate proposals are not, however, binding on the states (*Länder*). According to certain estimates, in the German assistance system the average benefit of the assisted – which represents Germany's poverty line – is roughly equal to about half of the net average earnings.[54] Naturally, claims for social assistance tended to increase sharply in the difficult years of the late 1970s, and they, rather than the fully funded social security scheme, have become the subject of contention within the country's welfare system, as we shall see in Chapter 3.

Finally, consider the vast changes in the U.S. system of relief and social protection, with the first wave carried out in the Great Depression years and the second in the 1960s. During the 1930s, Congress, at the urging of President Roosevelt, adopted the Social Security Act, comprising an employment insurance scheme funded by a payroll tax on the employers; an old age pension scheme for the retired aged 65 and over and their survivors, funded by a tax on both employers and employees; and a system of assistance to the needy through grants to the states and/or federal funds for the aged and the blind, dependent children, and the crippled and disabled, as well as for maternity and child-health services. This system was expanded notably in the 1960s through President Johnson's program for the Great Society, aiming to fight poverty, equalize opportunities for all Americans, and broaden the nation's health, educational, cultural, and artistic frameworks. Successively, Congress provided funds for the country's poorer high school districts, set up a rent supplement for low-income families, and established foundations for subsidizing artists and scholars. After various subsequent measures, the U.S. social security system has come to refer to the original 1935 statute of social security, concerning old age insurance (OAI), which was extended by Congress in 1939 to include survivor benefits (then designated OASI); disability benefits were added in 1954 (thus changing OASI to OASDI); and finally Medicare added health insurance in 1965 (hence, OASDHI), creating

the largest government program in the United States. The old-age and survivors and disability insurance funds have been financed though the Federal
Insurance Contributions Act and the Self-Employment Contribution Act, both
funded through payroll taxes. In addition, two trust funds were established
for Medicare: the Hospital Insurance Trust Fund (for hospital insurance, Medicare Part A) and the Supplemental Medical Insurance Trust Fund (for physicians' services, Medicare Part B). As of 1995, the total OASDI combined
employer–employee contributions amounted to around 15 percent. On the
other hand, the U.S. social assistance system has come to refer, though not
always consistently, to the needs-related programs for those who are needy,
elderly, blind, or disabled, for families with dependent children, and for other
categories of the disadvantaged. These programs included, until 1996, Supplementary Security Income (SSI; created in 1972 and focusing on the elderly
and the disabled, subject to certain income and asset limitations), transfers in
kind for housing assistance, Food Stamps, school lunch programs, and the
health insurance program for the poor, Medicaid, and Aid to Families with
Dependent Children (AFDC) (which since 1935 has provided federal benefits
for single-parent families).[55] The latter program was often asserted by some
critics to be "the worst part of the welfare system," wasting appreciable
resources for the support of nonaged, able-bodied, nonworking people and
perpetuating rather than diminishing the scope of poverty. Finally, in 1996
the management of AFDC was transferred to the states, and its recipients
were put under stricter requirements and obligations, as we shall see in Chapter 3.

Given the diversity of the programs involved in what has come to be
known as "social protection," that is, social security plus social assistance
(including health and family care programs), the data available must be
viewed as yielding only broad orders of magnitude. In any case, according
to OECD data, the social protection transfers per unit of GDP increased
significantly from the early 1960s to the early 1980s. (I return to these issues
in Chapter 5.)

1.5. Concluding Comments

The role of the state in the structuring of public ownership and of the systems
of social protection has varied according to political and economic circumstances and the ideologies predominant during given historical periods. Mercantilism, which became, from the seventeenth century on, the guiding
doctrine of the absolutist states – under Cardinal Richelieu as well as under
Oliver Cromwell – viewed absolutism as the appropriate instrument of political unity. And it was this unity that was assumed to render the state strong
and capable of securing both conquests and riches.

With the industrial revolution, however differentiated its impact, the increasing transformations of England and France, and then of Germany and the United States, as well as with the concomitant growth of political freedom, governments began to either abandon or amalgamate to various degrees the principles of mercantilism. From the eighteenth century on, as private banking and finance, manufacturing, and commerce grew in strength and political influence, the state lost its absolutist role in shaping the economy's activities. Increasingly, the state became an auxiliary force in the spread of industries, the consolidation of their achievements, and the creation of the appropriate means for their development. In its new, adjunct role, the state discharged many new functions, whether in providing the means for importing, adapting, and "indigenizing" foreign models; for supporting (via subsidies) the growth of certain industries; for contributing to the spread of scientific information and training the workforce; or, last but not least, for owning when needed – directly or jointly with the private sector – crucial instruments of development (such as the railway system). In time, to the inherited regional differences – or to differences among federated states in Germany and the United States – urban growth and the development of municipalities added new elements of differentiation between the functions and scope of public ownership at the levels of federated regions, or states, and municipalities.

Paradoxically, as we saw, major wars tended to limit rather than expand the establishment of new public enterprises. Already, the first total war allowed the belligerent powers to expand to an extraordinary degree the scope of government's economic commands, surveillance, and control without expanding government ownership itself. Total war gave the state leave to move at the macro or micro level virtually in any new direction it chose without necessarily increasing state enterprises or expanding their scope. Total war allowed the state to "socialize," or virtually "expropriate," the private owners' rights without taking away their nominal ownership titles.

Contrariwise, the state's functions have tended to grow again concomitantly with the growth of relief policies and the organizations of industrial workers pushing toward nationalizations. This has proved especially true after major wars and major depressions, which leave a country with a disjointed industrial matrix, a legacy of obsolete technologies and unnecessary production, and potentially high unemployment. Remarkably, even moderately conservative parties may tend to pose little resistance to such policies, if they perceive that indeed one private sector may be lacking at that moment the capacity and necessary will to surmount its difficulties. Relying increasingly on either direct or indirect methods of supervision and control of the crucial directions and operations of the economy, not only liberal (in the twentieth-century sense) but even conservative governments may then resort to creating all kinds of state enterprises and corporations outside the legal or administrative frameworks of the existing government agencies, whose old rules may have prevented them from properly adapting to and discharging the needed new tasks.

Under a "liberal" government, the New Deal brought about a powerful thrust toward modifying the then-prevailing parameters, pushing to the fore emphases not only on consumption and aggregate demand, but also on the creation of certain state enterprises, income redistribution, and debt reduction, and raising the working population's "purchasing power." After World War II, in France, during a liberal–conservative coalition headed by General de Gaulle, and in Britain during the socialist accession to power as well as under subsequent socialist–liberal coalitions, growing public ownership and expanding welfare measures became key instruments in the shaping of the structures of what became known as the modern "welfare state."

The continuous increase and diversification of state functions – in particular with respect to the resources that it has been able to mobilize for its expanding goals and services – and the broader impacts of ideologies and illusions about the state's capacity to overcome nationalization market imperfections, technological lags, the persistence of unemployment, as well as the menace and the consequences of poverty, have started to run into increasing doubts and oppositions everywhere from the early 1980s on. The reversal of the 1920–1980 trends in recent times has been due to a fascinating intertwining of causes, including economic reasons, administrative expediency, ideological assertions, political strategies, and a dash of new illusions – to which I return in detail in Part II.

2   An All-Encompassing Party-State

2.1. Marxism and State Ownership

The verb *to nationalize*, coined during the French Revolution, meant "to return to the nation" the properties of various "estates," namely those of the clergy and nobles. From the middle of the nineteenth century on, its derivative, *nationalization*, acquired various extensions, connotations, and interpretations. One such extension referred to bringing under "the control of the nation" banks and railroads (even foreign capital holdings) that were supposed to be "renationalized" for the purpose. Another extension of the term referred to the "socialization" (or nationalization) of the means of production and to the centralization of all production activities in the hands of the state.[1]

In order to understand the rationale and scope of nationalizations carried out by socialist and/or communist parties, one must first explore the meanings assigned by the founders of Marxian socialism to private property and to the state. Also, one must attempt to understand the ways in which these parties – which often, though not always, claimed allegiance to the same Marxian theories – have come to diverge in their interpretation of Marxism or how they have come to combine Marxian ideas with different – and at time flatly opposed (or, contradictory) – practical considerations. To start with, let me note that in the *Communist Manifesto* (1848) Karl Marx and Friedrich Engels asserted that communist theory "may be summed up in the single sentence: Abolition of private property." For them, private property was in essence "modern bourgeois property . . . the final and most complete expression of the system of producing and appropriating products that is based on class antagonisms," which in its development continually destroys other forms of property (e.g., those of the petty artisan and the small peasant). The alleged existence of this type of property in the hands of "one-tenth" of the population is thus due to "its non-existence" in the hands of the remaining "nine-tenths." The goal assigned by Marx to the revolution of the working class was "to wrest by degrees, all capital from the bourgeoisie, to centralize all instruments of production in the hands of the state, i.e., of the proletariat organized as the ruling class."[2]

The European socialist movement, which began to develop vigorously from the last quarter of the nineteenth century on, started soon to break up into two main currents stressing different interpretations of the Marxian theoretical heritage. One current, the social democratic one, which gained ascendancy first in Germany and in Central Europe, and then in France and in England, asserted that the number and power of the workers were bound to increase to such an extent that they would eventually be able to achieve a power shift in the state in their favor. A strong tendency within the social democratic camp held that the shift could occur peacefully, through parliamentary means. In due time, a gradual growth into socialist society would thus become possible. However, within the same socialist current and within the same basic frame of reference, the socialist theoretician Karl Kautsky and his followers criticized this "idyllic reformist" tendency, asserting that the growth of the working class was necessarily concomitant with the "development of capitalism and the concentration of capital." This, added Kautsky, meant that the antagonism between workers and capitalists was bound to grow into a gigantic battle, a battle whose outcome was not in doubt since the working class was "indispensable for society," while the capitalist class had increasingly "become superfluous."[3]

The second main socialist current, the Bolshevik one (subsequently called also "communist"), rejected as of the early twentieth century both the reformist and the Kautskian social democratic theories. It set instead as its primary goal the total destruction of the capitalist state. As Lenin, the leader of the Bolsheviks, asserted in 1916 in his *The State and Revolution*, the "imperative questions of the present day" were the "expropriation of the capitalists, the conversion of *all* citizens into workers and employees of one huge 'syndicate' – the whole state – and the complete subordination of the whole of the work of this syndicate to the really democratic state, the state of the Soviets of Workers' and Soldiers' Deputies."[4]

Consider closely the rationale and the implications of the Bolshevik positions, which led, shortly after these statements were made, to the Communist Party's conquest of power in Russia. In the communist scenario, the workers under the leadership of their "avant-garde," the Communist Party, must simultaneously discard the capitalist state, abolish bourgeois property, create a new kind of integrated economy (a huge "syndicate" with all the citizens converted to its workers and employees), and establish a new state (that of the Soviet Deputies). In this frame of reference, the abolition of "modern bourgeois property" – a property that allegedly embodies the "exploitation of the many by the few" – crowns a long historical process. In fact, according to Marx, the process of "socialization" of private property had started under capitalism with the dissolution of scattered properties based on the labor of their owners and has continued incessantly with its expropriation of various capitalists "exploiting many laborers" by other capitalists with still larger holdings, leading finally to an enormous concentration of capital. Likewise, under capitalism, the state – a "separate entity, beside and outside civil society" – has become "nothing more than the form of organization which the bourgeoisie [the capitalists] necessarily adopt for both internal and external purposes, for the mutual guarantee of their property and interests."[5] Hence the communist disdain for social democrats of all branches, who have been ready and willing to operate within the framework of the existing production relations, property relations, and the state, whether they considered that they could shift the power in this state in their favor peacefully or whether they believed that such a shift could only follow a protracted conflict that they would eventually win.

Singly or in coalition with other parties, the social democrats have been in favor of nationalization for a wide variety of reasons. They have advocated such measures in order to let the state care for certain ailing mines or industries and thus secure the jobs they provide; help in the concentration, rationalization, and modernization of certain lagging industries, thereby accelerating technological progress and the transformation of the entire economy; take over certain industries in order to facilitate carrying out a "coherent" industrial policy; expand the direct controls over banks and credit institutions in order to cope with pressing problems concerning large investments, levels of savings, the national debt, and commercial relations; and extend the scope of nationalization with a view of ushering in a new type of industrial relations, and, in the process, consolidate the socialist trade union political base in the nationalized sector. As we saw in the preceding chapter, the socialist parties in France and England resorted to nationalizations whenever they acceded to power, even when there were significant intervals between periods of rule.

By contrast, the communists, following Lenin's interpretation of Marx, long opposed nationalization within the framework of market-directed economies, as their foremost goal was the destruction, rather than the mending, of the bourgeois state. However, this policy underwent deep changes, notably in France after World War II. Characteristically, in the pre–World War II years the program of the Popular Front – elaborated by the middle-class radical socialists, socialists, and communists and published on January 12, 1936 – had put forward no comprehensive nationalization projects. In fact, the communists at the time had asserted their opposition to any "structural changes" in the capitalist system.[6] The significant change in this respect took place only after the liberation of France. During World War II, the Conseil National de la Résistance had put forward the idea of the "return to the nation of the large means of production,'' and on October 1, 1944, General de Gaulle announced "the takeover by the state of the management of the country's common riches.'' At that point a large consensus existed in France in favor of nationalization, a consensus from which the communists could not easily break away. From then on, the French communists participated along with the socialists in formulating programs favoring nationalization, even though they diverged with the socialists as to the methods of managing the nationalized properties.[7] For communist parties in other countries, nationalization was a measure to be taken only after their accession to full political power.

As I indicated above, Marx had contended that by the action of the immanent laws of capitalism, incessant expropriations "of the petty artisan and of the small peasant,'' and then of the increasingly large capitalist firms themselves, would lead to an even higher "concentration of capital" in fewer hands. Then at the inevitable downfall of capitalism, all that the communists would have left to do was the less protracted operation of expropriating the remaining handful of expropriators. In prerevolutionary Russia, relations with respect to ownership clearly moved in different directions than those envisaged by Marx – a point I return to later.

Let me recall briefly the evolution of that country with respect to property and the state. Russia at the beginning of the seventeenth century had no cameralist theoreticians of its own, but that school's ideas perfectly fitted Russia's historical development. Under Peter the Great (1682–1725) Russia's absolutism plunged its roots deep into the autocratic medieval tradition of the Moscow state, a tradition in which the state was the *votchina*, that is, the ancestral "patrimony of the sovereign.'' The people inhabiting a feudal *votchina* – a veritable estate owned by its great landowner – came to be regarded as belonging to that estate and to its owner. Similarly, the Russian land and people came to be viewed as belonging to the sovereign. The real structure of the society was perceived by everyone as a kind of "household filled with servants to whom were assigned obligatory duties.''[8] Peter mobilized his patrimony with the goal of achieving a vast and powerful army for war and expansion, building the necessary supporting factories, remodeling up to a point the country's immensely backward hierarchy, and educating at least some of the country's future leaders – all this while keeping in place the system's two medieval supporting pillars: autocracy and serfdom.

For its feeding and clothing, its armament and shipping, the permanent army created by Peter required large factories and an enormous amount of resources. Most of the factories' workers were bonded to the state (so-called serfs of the Treasury) or possessed by private owners. Thus, when the state established what was, for the time, a modern factory, its labor had to be drawn from the state's peasant-serfs; and when the state handed over this factory to a private entrepreneur, the bonded workmen were also handed over to him. The Russian factory workforce was thus based at its inception upon the same system as that of agriculture, namely upon bondage, and its wage rates were established by imperial edict.[9] After Peter's death, some of the industrial establishments he had created were leased to private persons or closed, and only under Catherine the Great (1762–1796) was a broad industrial impetus again given by the state, primarily to the development of consumer goods manufacturing. At the same time, the deeply degrading and increasingly desperate condition of the peasant serfs was brought into sharp focus by a bloody rebellion led by the adventurer Emelian Pugachov, who proclaimed, inter alia, "the abolition of serfdom." Pugachov was executed in 1775, but the social unrest that had fueled his rebellion continued to affect, in many damaging ways, the troubled historical development of that country.[10]

Economic development in the next century remained weighed down to a large extent by the miserable situation of the peasantry. Around the middle of the nineteenth century, the largest single class of people in European Russia (representing 38 percent of the population of the European provinces) was the 21.5 million serfs. In addition, there were 19 million treasury peasants and peasants without landlords, settled on state lands (i.e., 33.5 percent of the population of the European provinces) and 2 million "appanage peasants" living on the lands of the imperial family (i.e., 3.5 percent of the population of those provinces). Though not subjugated to the landlords, the peasants on the state lands were under the control of the office of State Domains within the Ministry of Finance. These peasants were viewed, as in the past, essentially as a source of revenue for the treasury and were living in conditions as dismal as those of the other peasants.

The Peasant Emancipation Act of 1861 and the "allotment" of land to the peasants eventually changed the traditional land ownership patterns in the countryside. Thus, by about 1905, according to various estimates, 39 percent of the total available land was owned by the state and by public bodies, while the remaining balance was in private hands. Of the latter lands, 70 percent were accounted for by the allotted lands. Yet the agricultural system was technologically so backward that the emancipated peasantry remained plagued by high debt, crop failures, and recurrent widespread famines.[11] Moreover, the absence of significant indigenous capital and the disastrous lack of communications significantly hampered the pace of the country's industrial development in comparison with the pace then prevailing in other European countries.

Throughout the period under review and the beginning of the twentieth century, the state – the decisive economic owner, investor, manager, and controller – continued to be the biggest entrepreneur in banking, mining and metallurgy, the armament industry, the sugar industry, the timber trade, and the critically remunerative sale of vodka. The state controlled the Bank of Russia (founded in 1860), as well as numerous public municipal banks that exercised extensive controls on the flow of credit to industry, agriculture, and trade. The supervision by the state of the limited private industry – still small even after the generous stimulus given to it by the famous statesman and financier Sergei Witte – continued to be extensive and annoying. An attempted revolt of the private manufacturers of the metalworking and machinery industries against generous advantages the state granted to its own industries in the field (in the form of enormous subsidies and tax exemptions) was unsuccessful.[12] The extent of the direct role of the state in the economy on the eve of World War I is documented in part by the budgetary data for 1913. According to these data, the largest share of state expenditures, namely 31.1 percent, was earmarked for the state enterprises, then including the railroads, the crucial liquor monopoly, and, of course, the post, telegraphs, and telephones. In addition, 26.5 percent was designated for defense. On the revenue side, 26.5 percent was coming from the state properties, including the railroads, and over 34.0 percent from the state royalties, also covering the state liquor monopoly.[13]

If during World War I Germany became the embodiment of organization for total war, tsarist Russia provided an example of just the opposite. After the declaration of war on July 19, 1914, its disproportionate mobilization of manpower, poorly equipped transportation system and industry, its problems with regard to foreign trade, and incapacity to formulate a coherent economic or military program for a prolonged struggle severely affected its overall performance. The induction, equipment, and transportation of some 20 million soldiers constituted a heavy drain on its supplies of manufactured goods of all kinds. Its poorly equipped and antiquated industries were further handicapped by the expulsion of many managers and skilled workers of German origin, as well as by its shrinking relations with the foreign suppliers whence much of its capital equipment had been forthcoming. Its railway system, not particularly efficient in peacetime, had broken down almost entirely by the end of the first year of the war, because the rolling stock deteriorated as the railway repair shops were hastily converted to the manufacture of war supplies. The disastrous defeat of the Russian armies and their retreat from Galicia and Poland from April 1915 on further worsened the situation. While the private industrialists were trying to assert their claims to their share of state orders of war supplies and new state industries, the disoriented government bureaucrats were trying haphazardly to assert the state's controlling functions – all this without much success for either group of contenders.[14] Finally, the collapse of tsarist Russia in 1917 and the success of the Bolshevik revolution engineered by the Communist Party set the foundations of the

Soviet-type model on the ruins of the least developed of the great European powers.

In Section 2.2 I present the specific elements of this model, which was subsequently implemented in many other countries not necessarily more developed than Russia. In Section 2.3 I detail both the ways in which the creators of that centralized system, akin to the German *Kriegswirtschaft*, combined it voluntarily and/or involuntarily with market mechanisms, and the problems that such combinations generated. In the same section, I present the legacies of this system with regard to ownership and employment patterns. In Section 2.4, I focus on the nature and scope of the "safety net" in a system supposedly guaranteeing full employment, a problem also crucial in the questions of privatization and the transition to a capitalist framework. The chapter's concluding comments are presented in Section 2.5.

2.2. The Party-State and Its Economy

The foundations of the Soviet system were laid during the first phase of the Soviet regime, which began on November 7, 1917, with the seizure of power by the Communist Party and ended in March 1921 with the inauguration by that regime of a set of measures known as the New Economic Policy (NEP). The first phase, called "War Communism," evolved during a bloody civil war combined with a war on many fronts against foreign intervention. It had as its framework a chaotic economy, virtually disintegrating while the revolutionary communist government was trying to consolidate its hold on the new state power, restructure property relations, and radically reshape the ways of running the economy. In the 1920s, Soviet writers traditionally viewed War Communism as a "heroic" period, a crucial "experiment" in the transition to socialism, even though influenced by the exceptional circumstances in which it had to take place. During Stalin's era, War Communism was downgraded by official accounts to a "dispensable" stage in the process of transition and, as the pro-Soviet Western economist Maurice Dobb put it, as only "an empirical creation, not as the *a priori* product of theory."[15]

Contrary to Dobb's contention, I believe that War Communism was in many respects a product of Marxian theory (in Lenin's interpretation). I believe, moreover, that its leaders' approaches to state power, property relations, and centralized administration and planning set the basic frameworks within which all Soviet-type regimes have tended to operate since then whether in Russia, in its satellites, or the countries associated with it – and during all their evolving phases.

Consider first the forms of state power engendered under War Communism. The second All-Russian Congress of the Soviets Workers and Soldiers Deputies (i.e., the Congress of the Councils of Workers' and Soldiers' Representatives) proclaimed in its Decree No. 5 on November 7, 1917, that "all power now belongs to the Soviets. The commissars of the former Provisional Government have been eliminated." Before dispersing on the morning of November 8, the Congress elected an All-Russian Central Executive Committee as "the highest organ of state power in the interval between All-Russian Congresses of Soviets" and confirmed as the center of power the first "Council [Soviet] of the People's Commissars," as it had been decided to call the ministers of the new revolutionary government. This Council was headed by Lenin and consisted entirely of Communist Party members. According to one of the principal architects of Soviet legal theory, Decree No. 5, which destroyed the old state and its civil service, constituted "for a long time the whole proletarian law of the state." The Congress's decisions thus involved the theoretical transfer of power to the councils of workers' and soldiers' representatives and the practical transfer of real power throughout the country to the Communist Party. The autonomy and the supremacy of the party – the absolute leader of all state structures – became from then on the immutable characteristic of the Soviet-type system, be it during the so-called dictatorship of the proletariat or subsequently, when this "dictatorship" was supposed to give way to various stages of "developed socialism." The party alone retained the privilege of defining its own goals and strategies from then on, for itself and for the entire system, as long as this system remained in existence. As the last constitution of the Soviet Union put it (in Article 6), "The leading and guiding force of Soviet society and the nucleus of its political system, of all state organizations and public organizations, is the Communist Party." The party "determines the general perspectives of the development of society and the course of the domestic and foreign policy."[16]

Consider next the question of property and its relations – first to production, and then to the market. A rapid succession of decrees established total state ownership of land, industry, banking and insurance, and domestic and foreign trade.[17] With regard to land, an official decree of February 19, 1918, abolished "forever" any private property rights (including that of the peasants) to the soil, subsoil, waters, forests, and all animal herds, and transferred these rights to "the entire working people." In fact, the agrarian revolution was then following its own impulses. The peasants took over the estates of the landowners, but then refused to give up their new possessions to the government. The land was distributed and redistributed among local peasant populations without regard to the official Soviet decrees. While in principle the possession of land was settled legally, in practice the disputes and the redistribution of land within and between villages kept socialist experiments in this field in check. Further, the government's attempts to be the sole distributor of all commodities, including agricultural products, and its efforts to rigidly enforce the principle of a government monopoly on all trade in grain led to numerous peasant uprisings and sharp conflicts with the new authorities.

Because of its complex character, industry also raised many difficult issues. A decree of November 27, 1917, first instituted labor control over management in order to avoid the collapse of production. The Supreme Economic Council (Vysshi Sovet Narodnogo Khoziaistva – VSNKha) was established on December 15, 1917, and was granted extensive powers to confiscate private enterprises. A decree of June 28, 1918, provided specifically for the nationalization of certain large "commanding" industries whose capital exceeded a specified limit. Finally, an order of the VSNKha of November 29, 1920, officially extended nationalization to all industrial firms employing more than five workers if they used power-driven machinery. In practice, here, too, complete and unrestricted confiscations and/or nationalizations spread within many branches of industry and in many parts of the country, not necessarily in accord with the dates of the official decrees.

The banking and insurance sectors were monopolized soon after the Bolshevik takeover. A decree of December 17, 1917, nationalized the banks, merged the private banks (excluding the cooperative ones) into the State Bank, and established the state monopoly in banking. The insurance sector was nationalized by a decree of November 28, 1918. Various decrees "annulled" stocks and bonds, confiscated practically all savings, and abolished inheritance, while others abolished the private ownership of urban buildings exceeding a certain value.

The nationalization of the domestic and foreign trade sector resulted from a number of measures that dovetailed with those concerning the nationalization of industry and banking sectors. Thus, a decree of January 26, 1918, nationalized the merchant navy and proclaimed a state monopoly in maritime inland water transport, and a decree of June 28, 1918, nationalized the railway system. Commerce by private persons was practically suppressed, and the People's Commissariat for Food Supplies, created on April 2, 1918, was charged later that year with the responsibility of trade in all articles of personal and domestic use. Concomitantly, the state's monopoly on foreign trade was proclaimed by a decree of April 18, 1918, and a decree of January 11, 1920, created a Special Commission for Foreign Trade charged with controlling all foreign trade operations.

Along what lines was this party-led nationalized system supposed to work, produce, and develop? Were there at the time an economic plan and effective centralized organs of coordination? What functions were left in this system to market relations, commodities and money, prices and wages? The analysis of the early Bolshevik approaches to the hierarchical party-led organization and administration and to its relations to the market is indispensable for understanding its modus operandi throughout the entire life of the Soviet system. Indeed, the early Bolshevik ideas about the nature and functions of the market were deeply embedded in the system, continually influencing the ways in which market problems have been tackled and their possible impacts evaluated.

To grasp the underlying Soviet concepts concerning the functioning of its economy, one has to recall Soviet leaders' views about the German economy before and during World War I. A crucial book by the leading Bolshevik theoretician of the time, Nikolai I. Bukharin, gives us invaluable clues about these ideas. This book is *Economics of the Transformation Period*, written in 1920 and carefully annotated by Lenin. According to Bukharin, the modern capitalist economies had supplanted the "anarchy" in production typical of earlier "commodity-producing societies." Modern capitalism has allowed the appearance within its economies of various forms of organization of production: "The monopolistic associations of producers, the combined enterprises, and the penetrating of bank capital into industry have created a new type of production relations, by transforming the unorganized system of commodity capitalism into an organization of finance capitalism." Theoretically, added Bukharin, the trusts, cartels, employers' associations, corporations, and bank consortia could provide "maximum stability" to the bourgeois system through coordination under the state's power. At the "mathematical limit" the entire national economy could be transformed into "an absolutely closed combined trust" in which all enterprises "have transformed themselves into mere individual workshops, into branches of this trust" and where "the entire economy has become an absolutely unified enterprise."[18]

This idea of a vast economy organized as a single "unified enterprise" – which advanced finance capitalism had allegedly virtually created and which the Russians were ready and willing to operate – remained the cornerstone of the Soviet system. However, within this system – at each level, within each "module," and in each activity – the party organization would represent the nucleus of command and control in conformity with the central government's decisions. During War Communism the party assigned to the VSNKha the overall task of directing the nationalized branches of the economy through its bureaus (known as *glavki*, from the Russian *glavnyi komitet* – chief bureau). The VSNKha was supposed to draw up a general economic plan and the *glavki* were supposed to supervise the key operations of the branches under their control. While subsequently the party criticized, discarded, and then reinstated "glavkism" again, its operation under War Communism certainly remains the first example of the Soviet attempt at centralized management of the main activities of its nationalized branches and their enterprises.[19] In this connection it is appropriate to recall that Bukharin stressed the existence of an alleged formal similarity between Marxian communism and what he called "the finance-state capitalism of the war period," namely "state capitalism, the most perfect species of capitalism," in terms of "social rationality." But he was careful to add that socialism was still only "incomplete" communism and that the Soviet system was certainly not a form of state capitalism, since the social contents of the two were different.[20]

These peculiar ideas about so-called finance-state capitalism and its capacity to transform its economy into a single unified enterprise were accompanied by equally odd Bolshevik ideas about the nature of market relations and what Marxians call market "categories," namely, commodities, money, values, prices, and wages. As I recalled above, Bukharin contended that modern capitalism had entirely (Lenin noted, only up to a point) supplanted the anarchy of the earlier commodity production relations. In any case, since commodity relations and monetary transactions were typical of capitalism, the Soviet processes of nationalization were supposedly bringing about their radical transformation and would eventually lead to their total elimination. Indeed, noted Bukahrin, when the Supreme Soviet steps forward as a conscious regulator of a unified economy, "the commodity is transformed into a product and loses its commodity character." To this Lenin approvingly added the crucial remark: "a product designed for social use and not through the market." The contention that the party-state economic system – "unified" as it were in a single enterprise and directed from above by a single organ (the VSNKha) – produced not commodities bought and sold through markets, but rather products exchanged without direct connections to value and price, became the foundation of Soviet planning concepts and an insuperable barrier to an effective reliance on market relations. As Bukharin put it, "Value, as a category of the capitalist commodity system in equilibrium," is the least useful for the transition period, "where commodity production disappears to a major degree and where equilibrium is absent." In this transition period, typically "price is not based on a value relation." This phenomenon, in turn, is tied to the collapse of the money system. Money becomes in this transition era an imperfect symbol of the circulation of products, while prices and wages become "illusory quantities" without content; wages are replaced by a "special share" in the total product. Thus, in the early Bolshevik frame of reference, the centrally managed economy tends to become a "naturalized" moneyless economy (in which resources are allocated and "products" are created and interchanged according to a plan).[21] As N. Kovalevsky recalls in his 1926 analysis of War Communism, at the time the People's Commissariat of Finance deliberately aimed at doing away with money in the long term, in the short term transforming it "merely into a tool for the expropriation of private economy, into a tax levied on the not yet socialized economic relations."[22]

According to the jurist Vladimir Gsovski, the basic principles of War Communism were "the exclusive ownership by the State of basic economic resources (land, water, industry, etc.), government monopoly over major economic activities (banking, insurance, foreign trade), and the ultimate control of private property rights admitted within this scheme."[23] To this cogent summary must be added, however, the principle of the party's supreme control over these resources and activities and the party's crucial notion that the entire economy – or rather the state's economic complex – could be run "rationally" by its hierarchical organization as a unified enterprise. Yet, as we shall see in detail in the next section, while the leaders of the Soviet party-state continued to pretend until its collapse that within its nationalized complex, interindustry relations took place only in products (not reflecting "values") and in noncash transactions, actually the system had to attempt continually to adjust itself in a more or less coherent fashion to both administrative decisions and market influences. However, the administrative price changes could not stop prices from being almost random numbers: prices tended to be multiple according to transactions or transactor. Market influences arose from the very existence of commodity exchanges and cash transactions between the state complex and its components, as well as between the latter and the free labor market, the agricultural sector organized in cooperative farms, and the population at large. While all the direct and indirect commodity and money relations would influence costs and price calculation (value considerations) in a variety of ways within the state complex, until the end Soviet leaders showed confusion and lack of familiarity with both market relations and the concept of property and nourished deep apprehensions toward them. These leaders continued to claim that the tools of the socialist planner were material accounting and engineering rather than economics (which in its Soviet version had, indeed, little to offer). The official publications continued to assert that as long as market relations subsisted officially – only within agriculture and in the connections between the state complex and the population at large – the "blind" forces typical of commodity-producing societies would affect only these interdependencies. Only in these areas, they added, would the "law of value" hold sway – that is, the "internal" law subsuming the interaction of all elemental forces that regulate allocation of resources, production, and trade in commodity-producing societies. Thus, according to the official sources, the Soviet system would continue to remain a combat ground between a "voluntary," party-defined "planning principle," operating coherently within each nook and cranny of the state complex, and the old, "blind" law of value operating outside it in often completely uncontrollable ways, in the opposed, commodity-producing and -consuming areas.[24]

2.3. Centralism and Reforms

In practice, how did the Soviet party-state attempt to adjust both to the market relations surrounding the state-run complex and to the innumerable influences and impacts of market "categories" within this complex itself? To what extent and in which way did the Soviet leaders fight off private initiative – or, if needed, encourage it and utilize the impact of market forces? In what measure did the various combinations of hierarchical centralism and decentralized market relations hinder the subsequent attempts at transition from a centrally administered economy to a market-directed one?

In order to handle these issues appropriately and to understand how the Soviet system continually attempted to combine fundamentally conflicting elements, one must carefully delineate the successive main periods following War Communism (i.e., from 1921 to 1991) during which crucial changes took place or were seriously considered with regard to the framework within which the relations between collective and private property, between the hierarchical plan and the diffuse welter of market relations, were scheduled to develop.

Following the War Communism period, the party inaugurated the New Economic Policy (NEP) amid the economic chaos brought about by the civil war and by disastrous party policies concerning the peasantry, grain confiscations, property rights, production and trade, money, and prices. Lenin proclaimed the need for a "temporary retreat" and affirmed that in order to save the Bolshevik-led system, the regime had to grant concessions to private initiative, private property, and private rights. As Lenin explained subsequently (on November 5, 1921), "We have been adopting . . . a reformist method" not to break up the old social system, but to revive trade, small property holdings, petty proprietorship, capitalism "while cautiously and gradually getting the upper hand over them, or making it possible to subject them to state regulation only to the extent that they revive."

The "temporary retreat" actually had to last, with ups and downs, until 1928. It was officially opened on March 21, 1921, with a decree changing first the policy of brutal and arbitrary confiscation of grain surpluses (prodrazverstka) into a taxation policy, that is, into the establishment of a tax in kind (prodnalog) calculated according to the size of the crops, leaving the surplus in the hands of the peasants. As of May 24, 1921, free barter was allowed, and on May 28, free trade in grain, bread, and forage. The factual possession of land resulting from peasants' land redistributions was stabilized by a decree of May 22, 1922, and attempts to equalize acreage between individual villages were banned. The Land Code of 1922 offered the new collectivist forms of land tenure to the free choice of the peasants. (Some 70 percent of the communes organized during War Communism had come to an end by 1921.) Small-scale private industry was legalized on May 17, 1921, employment of 10 to 20 workers in such enterprises was authorized on July 7, 1921, and certain small establishments in the state's hands but not officially nationalized were returned to their owners on the basis of a decree of December 10, 1921. A subsequent decree of May 22, 1922, granted private rights for the purpose of production and prohibited any new property confiscations. The Civil Code, which took effect on January 1, 1923, embodied the new policy framework created by the NEP: it left in the hands of the party's hierarchy the land and the commanding heights of the economy – that is, large-scale industry, banking, insurance, transport, and trade; allowed private capital in certain economic activities (small-scale industries, special concessions to foreign capital and mixed corporations); and authorized free trade in agricultural products and in small-scale industrial commodities. Sustained efforts were made in addition, from November 27, 1922, up to 1924, to straighten out the confused and disorganized monetary and fiscal situation through the introduction of a new parallel monetary instrument issued by the Central Bank, the *chervonets*, with a nominal value of 10 rubles convertible to gold. By 1924, the old "soviet currency" successor of the prerevolutionary ruble was withdrawn from circulation.[25] In the meantime, a crucial reform was also carried out with respect to the operation of the state's industrial enterprises, officially called "trusts." While the VSNKha continued to be recognized as the directing and controlling organ, beginning from 1921 on, each trust was enjoined to operate on the basis of so-called commercial accounting (*khozraschot*), taking into consideration all the elements of its production and aiming at increasing its income, all calculated at prices arrived at by agreement with suppliers and customers (or in special cases only) fixed by the central organs. However, from 1923 on, the state's intervention in pricing started to increase substantially, with particular attention to the interrelations between industrial and agricultural prices.[26] According to official data, by mid-1925 the state sector accounted for some 72 percent of industrial output, the cooperative sector for 9 percent, and the private sector for close to 19 percent, the highest point that the latter was to reach during the NEP. By that time, the new Gosplan (State Planning Commission) was drawing up its first advanced balance sheet of the economy for 1925–1926 – while vehement discussions were taking place in the party, the administration, and the economic journals about the then prevailing food shortages and the principles that should guide the country's industrialization and should underlie the drafting of a comprehensive five-year plan.[27]

Recognition of certain private property rights and reliance on private initiative in agriculture and in small-scale industry and trade, as well as the shifting of the state's own industry to economic accounting and "market" prices (even if at times sharply manipulated from the center) within the NEP's framework, brought about the country's economic recovery. But even as the NEP was unfolding in the mid-1920s, the Communist Party was trying to figure out when and how it could again transform the nature of private property, shrink its compass, and end the cohabitation between the party's administrative control of the economy's commanding heights and the private economy's market relations. Finally, after deep internal conflicts, the party fashioned from 1928 on, under Stalin's full control, a highly centralized hierarchical economic management system, launched its first Five-Year Plan, and moved to liquidate private property, notably in agriculture.

The first Five-Year Plan, which inaugurated the USSR's forced industrialization drive, also set the stage for vast reorganizations in other domains – in particular, for the brutal liquidation of small and scattered peasant holdings' and for the spread of "collective farming." To start with, the party-state apparatus (the so-called nomenklatura, i.e., the party-"nominated" administrative machine) again began the forced collection of grain, proceeded to close village markets, and abrogated rights previously conceded to the peasants to dispose of their own produce (after tax). The peasants began to be herded into collective units, in an accelerating process beginning in early 1930 with a view to its completion by 1934. Concomitantly, Stalin discarded the idea of any reliance on private commercial enterprises and small-scale private industry. The Soviet state proclaimed the abolition of the private ownership of the means of production and asserted that socialist ownership signified the ownership by the state of the totality of such means. The sale of one's own small products was still allowed, but private trade in the sense of buying for resale was prohibited as not adding to "value." In the new Soviet definition, public property was declared to consist of "government property, property of collective farms and property of cooperatives." The Civil Code of 1923 did not even mention ownership of collective farms and linked the ownership of cooperatives to private ownership. (The producer cooperatives [*promyslovaia kooperatsiia*] met their end only in 1956.) In its turn, private ownership acquired the new name of *personal ownership*, namely, something akin to but not identical with private ownership. This personal ownership was defined by the Soviet Constitution of 1936 as consisting only of "earned income and savings, dwelling houses, and articles of personal consumption and comfort," except in the case of the peasant household in a collective farm, which was allowed to hold additional "ancillary husbandry" on its house and garden plot, as well as certain types of livestock.[28]

Centralized economic administration and control, based on a unitary plan for the economy as a whole, relied in its functioning on the following principles: (a) the party leads the economy as a single, huge, multibranch, multiplant corporation, appoints its managers, and sets its overall and sectoral production growth targets; (b) the party and its centralized administrations decide the division of the national product between investment and consumption, as well as the composition of each of these categories; (c) the party-state's central plan specifies in physical terms the distribution of scarce raw materials, intermediate products, and capital goods; (d) after priority provisions for the production of producers' goods, the remaining physical resources are left for the output of consumer goods and services; (e) product prices are set centrally, while the state agencies control the circulation of products from producers to users. In this framework, the state enterprises are production units that, under the surveillance of their respective party nuclei, must act according to the central directives of government's ministries and agencies. Each enterprise is assigned mandatory production targets and receives most of its material inputs through administrative supply allocations; the investment and working capital of each enterprise are financed by grants from the government budget or loans from the banking system, according to plan; enterprises must transfer most of their profits to the state budget.

In principle, market mechanisms were set to operate, though only subsidiarily, mainly through the following channels. For the planned implementation of central commands, the centralized system of allocation was scheduled to rely as well on various financial and monetary instruments, in order to encourage or discourage the use of certain inputs, orient the labor resources in selected directions, and distribute the goods produced. However, as managers were compelled to fulfill certain key plan targets in physical terms within specified constraints, they necessarily tended not only to avoid various other specifications of the compulsory plan, but also to develop illicit ties with the authorities involved in procurement, technology, and marketing and to corrupt them by bribes or other means in order to reduce their own tasks, accelerate their own deliveries, and meet their own main assigned targets. Controlled markets expanded to most of the available workforce, with the wage scale set centrally as the determinant element of both income distribution and price structure. (In its actual use and distribution of labor, the system also relied on a vast network of concentration camps.)[29] Eventually, the failures of plan production and coordination led to the development of innumerable market channels within or alongside state enterprises, illegally nourishing a banned "shadow" or "underground" economy.[30]

As of the mid-1960s, the Soviet state sector accounted officially for almost all of the gross value of industrial output; only a small fraction was stated to be produced by workshops and other enterprises of consumers' cooperatives and the collective farms. State farms and institutions controlled over 57 percent of the agricultural land; the collective farms, 41 percent; the subsidiary plots of the collective farms, less than 1 percent; and the plots of workers and employees, roughly 0.5 percent. At this time the top party bureaucracy attempted to improve central planning via the administrative rationalization of prices and the use of certain economic indicators in preference to others (namely, prices and sales instead of gross outputs and profits) for evaluating enterprises' performance. But all this had to coexist with the enterprises' unbending obligation to complete "planned contractual deliveries in physical form with respect to quantity, quality, and assortment." The results were disappointing, and eventually the principles of the reform were circumvented.[31]

The real trials and judgment of Stalin's Soviet system and its legacies were carried out with enormous difficulties in Eastern Europe. The first actual attempt to disentangle the party-state's top administration (the top of the nomenklatura) from the direct management of the economy and the enterprises was attempted and partially carried out in Yugoslavia, a country that had not been under the direct control of Soviet troops and that had openly broken with Moscow in 1948. The Yugoslav departures from the Soviet model and procedures – strongly condemned by the Soviet apparatus as dangerous "revisionism" – underwent many changes over time, and the direct impact of that country's experiences remained for a long time limited. One commanding desire determined the course of the Yugoslav experiment: the will to create an alternative to the fully centralized economic management *à la russe* and to replace it with a decentralized form of enterprise management – still under party surveillance – combined with "socialist market relations." Within this alternative, the Yugoslav party-state initiated a so-called workers' self-management system. In this kind of organization, the workers (actually all the employees) of an economic enterprise (whose physical assets remained the property of the state) were called upon to manage it through a workers' (employees') "management council." The latter's activity was to be supervised by the commune, a unit of municipal government controlled by the party (rebaptized in Yugoslavia as the Communist League). Central planning institutions were replaced with a view toward indicative planning only, while market relations between the enterprises were encouraged to expand. The state's instruments were to consist essentially of a variety of taxes, subsidies, and regulations. In time, however, it became evident that the official term *workers' self-management* overstated the reality. The directors of the enterprises played the decisive role in regard to such formerly centrally determined decisions as output mix, pricing, plant sites, and investment outlays. The Communist League continued to control the state administration and influence the trade unions and municipalities responsible for appointing the enterprises' managers. As before the reforms, the League did not relinquish the role of selecting, controlling, and manipulating the managerial elite at the level of the federation or the consistent republics. Thus, what the Yugoslav communists succeeded in doing was creating a non-Stalinist market-oriented economy using the Stalinist methods of shifting and appointing the leadership cadres – a method that would influence the reforms of the Soviet system in various ways, particularly during the early years of Mikhail Gorbachev's regime.[32]

In the meantime, even before the breakdown of the Soviet regime (which I examine in detail in Chapter 4), numerous other Eastern European proposals to modify the Soviet party-state system were discussed or partially implemented after bloody uprisings in Poland, Hungary, and Czechoslovakia. These events offer useful insights into the operation of the USSR itself throughout its history, as well as into Soviet attempts at specific reforms, notably during the last years of that party-state system. Certain courageous economists of these three countries developed valuable in-depth analyses of the ingrained shortcomings of the Soviet system, including the party's strategy of development and its emphases; the physical plans and centrally administered prices; the awkward mix of rigorous directives and poor incentives; the concept of a centralized "single firm" and systematic party control at each level of the firm's hierarchical structure; the idea of introducing "enterprise methods into the 'unified' economy," rather than of "economic methods into the enterprises"; and the widespread misconceptions about the market and the clumsy use of so-called market mechanisms. Hungarian writers critiqued efforts to promote growth through rigid plans relying on a combination of penalties and rewards that were intended to stimulate the enterprises to fulfill and surpass certain planned targets. According to the Hungarians, the result was the transformation of the party-state economies into huge Kafkaesque factories producing and using "nothing but rejects" while the managers were doggedly resisting the introduction of new technologies and the development of new products. The socialist economies, these critics pointed out, tended to acquire only the semblance of the features of developed countries, while differing from them as far as results were concerned. In fact, these were only "quasi-developed" economies whose basic characteristic was a marked discrepancy between form and substance.[33]

Most of the East European reforms (other than those in Yugoslavia) did not involve in practice more than various reductions in the scope of party-state controls on plan implementation, along with various other improvements in the methods of directing the economy. In Hungary, in particular, the reforms reduced the scope of the central plan and delegated a significant role to the enterprises in the preparation of their programs, as well as in their trade relations. Nowhere, however, until the late 1980s, were fundamental alternatives suggested with regard to the "guiding" role of the party in the economy. In the Soviet Union itself, from the mid-1980s on, the reforms projected by Mikhail Gorbachev – the so-called perestroika – were set to run along certain East European lines and certain planning-cum-market combinations and devices of the NEP era. But the underlying economic situation was by then far more critical than one could have inferred from the officially distorted Soviet statistics and analyses. As Gorbachev himself finally indicated in an important piece of testimony at a meeting of enterprise executives held in December 1990 – when the entire system was already collapsing – "Even before 1985 . . . we talked about the fact that the economy was beginning to reach a critical state, that a crisis was knocking on the doors and windows. Growth rates were falling, national income was dropping, everything was supported by spending." They were coping, added Gorbachev, thanks to the high price of oil and vodka: that's how the USSR achieved "balance." Specifically, he went on: "We made ends meet using money and got people so drunk on vodka that the question of genetic consequences arose, the question whether we were undermining the nation, the people, above all the Russian people. The raw materials branches were the basis of the economy . . . an economy excessively militarized." After recognizing that, at the time, he and his associates had bought a way out by "using the old methods of rigid planning and rigid programs," Gorbachev mused about the possible changes in the direction of the market, stressing the importance of "property relations . . . the core of radical economic reform" and the need for "bringing order into the financial system." But he still added, as in the past, that "without the effective functioning of executive power along the entire vertical hierarchy, no progress will be made."[34]

It is with this sad balance sheet that the USSR and each of its republics entered the early 1990s, descending into the maelstrom of the final disintegration of the Soviet Union and of the changeover to uncharted and uncertain waters. I shall examine these changes in Chapter 4. For now, let me point out that on the eve of its collapse, the USSR, and within it the soon-to-be sovereign Russian Federation, displayed the interrelated patterns of ownership and employment presented in Table 2.1. The official data show that, by industries and branches, the patterns of employment were closely similar in the USSR and in the subsequently independent Russian Federation. In both, the highest concentration of employment was in industry and, within industries, in manufacturing. The Russian Federation's legacy of industries and services eventually required it to provide employment to some 65 percent of the former Soviet labor force (including also a good part of the former scientific workforce).

As can be seen from Table 2.2, on the basis of data of the late 1980s we can conjecture that after the disintegration of the USSR, the Russian Federation must have inherited in manufacturing some 25,240 of the largest firms out of the total 46,840 Soviet firms – that is, some 53.8 percent. Undoubtedly the Federation inherited the core of the military–industrial complex, but no detailed data have been made available on the defense industry. At the col-

Table 2.1. *USSR and Russia: Distribution of Employment by Ownership Structure, 1990 (Millions and Percentages)*

Ownership Structure	USSR	Percent	Russia	Percent	Ratio 2:1
State enterprises	109.6	79.1	61.3	82.3	55.9
Leased enterprises, joint-stock companies, joint ventures	4.7	3.5	3.1	4.2	65.9
Cooperative sectors	19.2	13.9	8.1	10.9	42.1
Collective farms	(11.6)		(4.0)		
Consumer cooperatives	(3.4)		(1.5)		
Cooperatives for production and services	(4.2)		(2.6)		
Private sector	4.9	3.5	1.2	1.6	24.4
Other	0.1	—	0.8	1.0	8.0
Total	138.5	100.0	74.5	100.0	53.7

Sources: USSR: computed from Goskomstat, *Narodnoe Khoziaistvo SSSR v 1990s*, Statisticheskii ezhegodnik (National Economy of the USSR, Statistical Yearbook), Moscow, Finansy i statistika, 1991, p. 97; Russia: computed from World Bank, *Russian Economic Reform: Crossing the Threshold of Structural Change*, New York, World Bank, 1992, p. 288 (Goskomstat data).

lapse of the regime in 1991, the share of the state continued to be dominant (namely, 98.5 percent in manufacturing, 98.3 percent in construction, 100.0 percent in transports, 90.8 percent in the economy as a whole).[35]

Yet, while the state remained in principle the exclusive owner of the means of production, in fact a critical, complex, and tortuous process of transfer of powers and assets, from the collapsing party-state center to nomenklatura's leaders of ministries, branches, and enterprises, was well under way. After the collapse of the system, the process of "grabbing" state assets in a variety of ways accelerated. The constitutive and operational elements of the centralized commanding system – the recognized scope of state ownership; the state's authority in target setting for sectors, branches, and enterprises; and the forms and connections of the productive and distributive sectors, together with the centralized financial institutions – all started to be transformed and replaced, whenever possible, with informal contacts and arrangements between the top economic members of the officialdom, previously subservient to the central party's higher-up political leadership. The formerly highly cen-

Table 2.2. *USSR and Russia: Energy and Manufacturing Sectors, 1987 (Number of Firms)*

| | Number of Firms | | Ratio 2:1 |
Sector	USSR	Russia	
Fuel	1,179	352	29.8
Electrical energy	1,424	982	68.9
Metallurgy	711	379	53.3
Engineering	9,238	5,306	57.4
Chemical	1,072	561	52.3
Wood processing	5,547	3,885	70.0
Construction materials	4,336	2,161	49.8
Light industries	7,960	4,034	50.6
Food industries	9,554	5,480	57.3
Glass, ceramic, and other industries	5,819	2,100	36.0
Total	46,840	25,240	53.8

Sources: USSR: computed from Goskomstat, *Promyshlennost'*, statisticheskii sbornik (Industry, statistical collection), Moscow, Informatsionno-izdatel'skii tsentr, 1991, p. 11; Russia: computed from World Bank, *Russian Economic Reform: Crossing the Threshold of Structural Change*, New York, World Bank, 1992, p. 83 (Goskomstat data).

tralized Soviet machine thus started to disintegrate through uncoordinated, chaotic metamorphoses in uncharted directions. I examine the complex process in detail in Chapter 4.

2.4. Income Transfers

According to Soviet writers, the basic differences that existed between the Soviet Union's and the capitalist states' social insurance systems were all clear evidence of the superiority of the former in comparison with the latter. Allegedly, the development of capitalism had engendered "a whole series of previously unknown dangers," including notably "the threat of unemployment, occupational disease, death, disability, premature aging, and injury." In short, both the need for social security and the capitalist mode of production had "emerged together," but the capitalist states granted social security only when "compelled" by class struggle. Contrariwise, the demands for a "rational" social security system were clear to the Soviet Union from its beginning, thanks to Lenin. According to the principles he laid down, social security had to be established "for all wage-earners and their families," and provisions for benefits had to be made for all cases of incapacity – accidents, illness, old age, permanent disablement, pregnancy, and unemployment.[36]

Actually, capitalism did not engender all the "dangers" attributed to it, nor did the Soviet social security system stick to all of Lenin's recommendations. The Soviet system evolved in practice through a number of stages from 1918 on. The legacy of tsarism was in this respect quite limited. Before the revolution, two basic laws defined the scope of social insurance: a law of 1866 required that free medical care be provided by factory owners to all their workers, and a law of 1912 specified that benefits be paid by employers in cases of work-connected accidents, general illness, maternity, and death. Unfortunately, all these measures applied specifically to large establishments and mines only and covered less than one-fourth of the labor force. Old age pensions existed only for government employees, a category that included, beside those of the state hierarchy, the employees of the state's large enterprises and railroads as well.[37] Under the Soviets, the social insurance system changed at each important historical juncture, and both scope and actual application were often uncertain.

In 1918 a decree of the Council of People's Commissars, signed by Lenin, stipulated that social security should include all types of medical aid for those who needed it and compensation for unemployment and for loss of earnings due to a disability for whatever reason, including old age. But its application under the conditions of civil war and foreign intervention remained only theoretical. At the beginning of the NEP, the new social insurance system anchored in the Labor Code of 1922 provided for the obligatory insuring of all employees by the state or by the private enterprises then in existence. This insurance was to cover illness, maternity, disabilities, and unemployment. These measures were, however, in practice treated as subsidiary to the party's real interests, and from 1928 on focused increasingly on industrial production, productivity, work discipline, and the rapid return to work of the temporarily disabled. This implied attention to disease, accidents, work injuries, and rehabilitation, as well as care for pregnant women and the young, and far less concern for the aged and the permanently disabled. It is these kinds of priorities that shaped the development of health care and medical and rehabilitation institutions. Moreover, rights to pensions for the retired were treated separately, with a special law for each specific category, for example, for teachers (in 1924–1925) and for army officers (in 1924–1928). It is not at all certain that by 1937, when Stalin proclaimed that "socialism has been completed in the USSR," pension rights had been extended to all the important categories of workers and employees.[38] In the meantime, Stalin declared, in 1930, that socialism had succeeded in "completely eliminating unemployment,'' and until the collapse of the USSR no provision was made for losses due to any form of unemployment. In sum, the safety net consisted of insurance linked to employment, available medical care, certain family benefits, and the guaranteed employment at low wages in an economy with scarce consumer goods and with variously subsidized prices and services.

After Stalin's death, Nikita Khrushchev's Pension Law of 1956 established the foundations of the Soviets' new social insurance system, which remained in effect until the USSR's demise. This law provided for payments to retirees, as well as for various other transfer payments, and, combined with the autonomous system of medical assistance and with various laws that eventually extended benefits to the collective farmers (in 1964), built the first integrated Soviet safety net. This system viewed the population as consisting of two groups: those who could work and those who could not (namely, the aged, the permanently disabled, and the young, as well as women and/or families with small children). For their primary needs, the first group received wages; the second group, payments and services through social security funds. In addition, the entire population was provided with education, health care, housing subsidies, and cultural needs through a so-called social consumption fund. The distinct social security funds were also included in this all-encompassing social consumption category.[39] Computed on the basis of the official national income figures for 1970 and 1985 (285.5 billion rubles and 568.7 billion rubles, respectively), Table 2.3 indicates the volume of various income transfers involved.

While the main types of expenditures for the population as a whole involved free education for the young, vocational training, medical care and treatment, and housing subsidies, the social insurance funds primarily concerned pensions and grants-in-aid for temporary disabilities, rehabilitation, maternity, and special family needs. Given the structure of the Soviet social consumption fund, it is difficult to draw an appropriate comparison between Western and Soviet expenditures on welfare. Obviously, neither the total social consumption fund nor the social insurance fund were fully adequate for the purpose. The closest approximation could involve the Soviet social insurance fund, plus the health care expenditures – that is, a total income transfer on the order of 11 to 15 percent of the national income.

Social insurance was in principle funded by the state. Soviet factory and office workers were exempt from social security contributions, but in fact the latter were paid by the enterprises or organizations as a percentage of the total wage bill, with evident repercussions on the wage levels. The rates for these contributions were established by the government by agreement with the trade unions, which also contributed some additional funds. The social security system was managed through two administrative systems – one involving the republics and regional agencies, the other the trade unions, which

Table 2.3. *Structure of the Soviet National Income and the Soviet Social Consumption Fund, 1970 and 1985 (Percentages)*

National Income	1970	1985
Investment and other	29.5	26.4
Consumption	70.5	73.6
Social consumption	(22.4)	(25.8)
Education	(6.5)	(6.9)
Health care	(3.5)	(3.7)
Social insurance	(8.0)	(11.6)
Pensions	(5.7)	(8.7)
Housing subsidies	(1.2)	(1.7)
Unaccounted for	(3.2)	(1.9)
Total	100.0	100.0

Source: Computed from *Narodnoe khoziaistvo SSSR za 70 let, Iubileinyi statisticheskii ejegodnik* (The national economy of the USSR for 70 years, jubilee statistical yearbook), Moscow, Finansy i statistika, 1987, pp. 430–435.

controlled many of the medical and recreational facilities and dispensed much of their favors to bureaucrats and to bureaucrats' friends. The main forms of social security for the aged and the disabled were pensions and monthly allowances. The pensionable age was fixed at sixty years for men with a work record of twenty years and at fifty-five for women with a work record of twenty years. Pensions were on the order of 50 to 75 percent of the former wage level. Given the low levels of pensions older people were encouraged to keep working, in which case they received both the full pension and their usual wage. In the 1980s some 45 million persons were pensioners.

The development of the medical system, in the context of incessant pressure to meet the economic plan's production targets, called for the use of increasing quantities of simple medical facilities, low technology, modest material inputs, and cheap labor. The Soviets kept the growth rate of health expenditures low compared with those in the West. Building space, equipment, and medicines, however, were always of poor quality. In addition, poor and inadequate housing, poor sanitation, unchecked chemical pollution, the deterioration of nuclear facilities, urban road traffic, and other chronic environmental problems had negative impacts on health, nutrition, and general living conditions.[40]

A disastrous situation in housing was a basic characteristic of the Soviet regime throughout its existence. In the 1950s, Nikita Khrushchev attempted to improve the prevailing conditions by way of massive investments in new construction, but by the end of the 1980s Gorbachev was still stressing the existence of an "acute housing problem" due to inadequate quantity and quality of apartments and dwellings, shortcomings in housing allocation, and an inefficient system of housing rents. Private housing represented ideologically the least acceptable form of housing ownership, and numerous disingenuous legal restrictions were placed on it. On the other hand, low rents – heavily subsidized through the social consumption fund – combined with the limited stock of residential housing, constantly led to excess demand for scarce state-owned housing and generated all kinds of rationing mechanisms, as well as methods for circumventing them. According to the official Soviet data, in the mid-1980s only 85 percent of all urban families (97 percent in rural areas) lived in separate apartments or houses, then forcing many households to reside in so-called communal apartments and dormitories under distressing conditions. The massive investments needed for building new homes, the appropriate improvements in the performance of the construction industry, and a systemwide and methodical reliance on cooperative and private construction were all by then well beyond the capacity of adjustment by the collapsing Soviet regime.[41]

In all the Soviet-type economies the existence of widespread poverty was systemically overlooked: only rudimentary social assistance provided means-tested benefits of last resort. By 1989 the first official data on poverty in the USSR put the number of poor at the low level of some 14 percent of the population, that is, at 40 million people with a per capita income below the official subsistence minimum. A considerable number of the poor consisted of aged persons with low pensions. Even on the basis of official data, it has been estimated that four out of ten old age pensions of former workers and employees – particularly those of former collective farmers – were below the official subsistence minimum. It should also be noted that striking differences existed in the incidence of low incomes among the republics; the highest percentages of poverty were concentrated in Central Asia.[42] Yet the increasing unemployment and harsh poverty that followed the collapse of the Soviet Union made some of the conditions prevailing in certain areas of that union under the communists seem to be more attractive than they had really been – as we shall see in Chapter 4.

2.5. Concluding Comments

It is neither sufficient nor accurate to view the Soviet "socialist" models as having implied only "an economy without private property and without the capitalist profit motive." The Soviet party-state and its satellites in fact generated a number of combinations and variants transgressing their original Marxian principles. None of these experiments, however, was able to lead to stable, workable results. Yet it is not just the capitalist model and its standards of performance that finally brought the Soviet rule to ruin. Rather, a number of unavoidable constraints, as well as the increasing internal corrosion of a system led by a single party and its rapacious bureaucracy, finally convinced even some of its leaders of the incapacity of such a system to achieve balanced, harmonious growth and change.[43]

Recall briefly some of these combinations and variants. Given the early conditions of the civil and foreign wars, famine, and its own obvious incapacity to assert effective control over the peasants, the Soviet party-state could not immediately apply its ideological schemas. During War Communism, no matter how much it legislated, it could not assert its full power in the villages, integrate a collapsing economy into a coordinated single enterprise, impose an economic plan, and achieve the elimination of market relations – notwithstanding its debasing of the currency and its allocation, with the help of "balances of resources and distribution," of the key available inputs to its shattered, nationalized industries.

The collapse of War Communism brought about the first official "temporary retreat," namely the NEP. The need to adapt sacred Marxian principles concerning the scope of state ownership, centralized management, and operational commands and controls, along with the necessity of reviving market relations and the "market categories" (commodities, prices, wages, profit, and money), shaped the new policies. The state's direct controls were, in principle, confined henceforth to the boundaries of the "commanding heights," while small private property was let to regain strength along with the cooperatives – peasant cooperatives, cottage craft cooperatives, and consumer cooperatives. As the economic situation improved, the drive within the party for returning to the principles set forth during War Communism regained strength, particularly from 1925 on.

By 1928 Stalin's command economy – the model emulated and faithfully implemented from Prague to Beijing – began to extend the party's grip over all the country's capital assets, forcing the collectivization of the peasantry and proclaiming the leader's will to run the state complex as a single unified enterprise submitted to a unitary plan. But Stalin and his henchmen could not avoid distorted market relations, either in hiring labor or in trade relations between the state producer complex, the collectivized farms, and the population at large. While the masters of the system continued to entertain the illusion that they had eliminated the market – at least in the relations between the state enterprises – by substituting bookkeeping accounts for money transfers in their transactions, they eventually became aware that market relations were seeping in. In a variety of forms, market forces were penetrating the state complex and the state's plans, and the Communist Party's vision of a single, fully integrated, centrally administered socialist economy functioning as an engineering servomechanism started to disintegrate little by little – not in 1991 but from the late 1950s on. Carrying out the plans involved increasing "illegal" transactions – barter or market exchanges. The failures became evident, not because the system was failing to "catch up and surpass" the highest capitalist levels – it reached some of these levels in military hardware – but because it was running increasingly into diminishing returns and unbearable internal difficulties.

Without envisaging the necessity of a real transition to a market economy, communist leaders from Eastern Europe to the USSR and China were compelled to attempt, clumsily and not very effectively, to increase the scope of market relations. They did so in a variety of ways, either along the lines laid down during the NEP or along new ones – namely, by reducing the extent of the central control over the commanding heights; supporting small private property in the countryside, in trade and distribution, and in small industry and crafts; increasing the use of foreign capital in the form of concessions and of jointly owned companies, and reducing if not abandoning planning altogether. But the NEP solutions and like reforms proved, as in the past, too restrictive and finally unviable. Ultimately, the entire set of fundamental principles had to be first questioned and then abandoned in order to open the way to broader, more "real" market relations. If there is a compelling and lasting lesson in the disintegration of the Soviet hierarchical party-state, it is that one cannot enclose for long, and without valid results, badly truncated NEP-type market relations within a single, unitary, party-controlled and -mismanaged economic framework. I return to the disintegration of this system and the problems of its transition to a market economy in Chapter 4.

Part II

Methods of Remodeling the State

This part focuses on the policy reversals brought about in the industrial and transitional economies by critical changes concerning the role, size, and structure of the state. In the industrial countries, particularly since the late 1970s and early 1980s, debates, crucial elections, and key policy decisions have centered on the complex problems of the nature and tasks of public and quasi-public enterprises, on the scope and consequences of welfare programs, and on state policies with regard to income redistribution. On the other hand, in the former Soviet countries, multiple conflicts and confrontations – generated within Russia proper, its imperial provinces, and its satellites – have centered inevitably on the complex, interlocking issues brought about by the rapid disaggregation of the main structures of the all-encompassing Soviet party-state.

The debates for or against dismantling public and quasi-public state-owned or -supported enterprises and the actual liquidation or privatization of the most outstanding among them, notably in Great Britain, have had a great impact throughout the world. In Chapter 3, I indicate how these debates throw light on the multiple forms and purposes of public companies and off-budget statutory agencies, as well as on their use as devices for circumventing certain constraints, as alternative ways of asserting control in certain sectors and branches, as channels for moving credit in selected directions, and as instruments for coordinating government programs and plans. The debates also show the difficulties encountered at times in attempts to disentangle the frontiers between the public and the private sectors – for instance, in the case of government-oriented corporations with long-term capital supplied by the state or that are integrated into state-determined planning frameworks. Particular attention is then given to the questions of planning and performance of such companies and to possible impacts that state-set objectives and controls have on them. Their performance is further evaluated with regard to the existence or absence of any "general rules" concerning their management. A later section focuses on the real objectives involved in their liquidation, namely extending the sphere of the market, achieving greater efficiency, and/or, more simply, raising badly needed cash and unloading the state's excessive financial burdens involving subsidies, servicing, and management. After examining the nature and operation of these public enterprises, the discussion turns to the analysis of the welfare system. In particular, I shall stress the similarities of welfare reform with the dismantling of certain public or quasi-public enterprises, as regards the limitation of government functions at various levels and, more generally, the downsizing of the state.

In Chapter 4, I turn to the processes of transforming the collapsed Soviet party-state economy into a system oriented toward expanding market relations. I show that one of the crucial factors shaping the amplitude, diversity, and uncertainty of these processes is the disintegration of, and the vacuum left by, the former party-state center of command and control. The collapse of that center has led to the consolidation of autonomous, self-centered fiefdoms in all the economy's sectors and branches, fiefdoms led by the former second-in-command ministerial heads, directors, and managers. The new central political power has not yet succeeded in assuming the full conduct of public affairs. The efforts of Russian leaders and economists to devise methodical programs of transition and/or to rely on the concepts and plans of Western advisers proposing the application of "shock therapy" to the disorganized Russian economy – namely immediate and simultaneous price liberalization, financial stabilization, and privatization – have floundered. The processes of transformation have followed chaotic, unstable, and often uncontrollable paths, leading to massive inflation, reductions in output and employment, and general poverty, along with deep political conflicts preventing the establishment of a truly coherent and effective center in full control. The price liberalization inaugurated in Russia in January 1992 forced increasing distortions and adjustments in production and distribution. Stabilization proved very difficult to achieve in a country in which interfirm relations, firm–bank connections, and firm–government ties often obeyed rules and patterns of behavior typical of the former disintegrated system. Privatization in its "first phase" (1992–1994) led deliberately to the entrenchment of the managers and the workers' collectives as the new owners in about half of the former state-owned patrimony. The kind of capitalism that emerged out of these processes has been called "nomenklatura capitalism," that is, capitalism of the former officialdom – a system afflicted by widespread crime, pervasive poverty, and a lacerated safety net for the old, the unemployed, and the disabled.

In the West and in the East, the issue of privatization is tied to the question of the scope of the state's agenda – both of which are, as we shall see, at the heart of the problem of downsizing the state. Privatization itself has no necessary limits: it can target not only public enterprises, but all budget-financed activities in all the economy's sectors. In Part III, I turn to the options and dilemmas connected with privatization, the rationale of the certain choices and alternatives, the dynamics of state divestiture, and the basic issues that it necessarily raises in relation to the state's agenda – in the key industrial economies within the broader framework of the G7 and in the transitional economies in both Russia and its former East European satellites.

3 Limiting the State's Size and Scope

3.1. A Critical Upheaval

Starting in Great Britain and the United States in the late 1970s and early 1980s, a political and ideological upheaval has vigorously reaffirmed ideas, once widely held but long since forgotten, about the state's "excessive," "inappropriate" expansions and the need to reduce it to a more "suitable" size and ambit. Let me recapitulate briefly the tenor of these issues and the ways in which they were again propelled into the foreground. In this chapter, I outline the developments involved only insofar as they throw light on the rationale for downsizing the state by reducing public ownership and shrinking the compass of its welfare programs.

The arrival in power of Margaret Thatcher and Ronald Reagan, at the end of the 1970s and the beginning of the 1980s respectively, portended crucial changes in the last quarter of the twentieth century. In Great Britain, Margaret Thatcher brought to an end the era of the "postwar settlement" that had emerged there out of the wartime suppression of party politics and that embodied acceptance by both socialist and conservative parties of the goals of full employment and the maintenance of the welfare state. This agreement had set not only the framework but also the agenda for postwar economic policies, "for neither full employment nor the Welfare State could be maintained without an expanding economy" – as a British analyst rightly put it.[1] In the United States, Ronald Reagan brought to an end an era of economic policy begun almost fifty years earlier, namely the Roosevelt era, which, though losing ground for a number of years before Reagan's triumph, had still provided a broadly accepted national agenda concerning full employment, government controls over the allocation of the national output among different uses, and the specific composition of the nation's social programs. While Thatcher's and Reagan's new priorities displayed a number of cardinal similarities, they continued to retain significant divergences due to the differences in the economic and sociopolitical settings of the two countries. Let us consider in detail these likenesses and dissimilarities.

The common basis for Thatcher's and Reagan's programs was their strong personal conviction that all damaging trends and failures of the past could be reversed and surmounted, and a bright future ensured, if the frontiers of the state (in the United States, of the federal government) were rolled back while a new market environment emerged within an appropriate framework of monetarist discipline and supply-side policies. According to Thatcher, the "corrosive and corruptive effects of socialism" had to be decisively brought to an end. The "socialist, statist" British government, she stated, represented a "centralizing, managerial, bureaucratic, interventionist style of government," which had levied high taxes on work, businesses, consumption, and wealth. It had relied on planned development at every level and had taken a high-handed approach to managing the economy, with Keynesian methods of fiscal manipulation and with subsidies to regions and industries. As for the Conservatives, until her timely triumph they had "merely pitched camp in the long march to the left" and had "never tried seriously to reverse it."[2]

Similarly, in his crucial *Economic Report of the President*, transmitted to Congress in February 1982, Reagan stressed that the first steps of his administration had been taken toward the "long overdue redirection" of the role of the federal government in the economy and that his foremost objective was to improve the economy's performance "by reducing the role of the federal government in all its various dimensions." This, he added, involved commitments to reduce federal spending and taxes as a share of the national product, to balance the budget eventually, and to curtail substantially the "vast web of regulations" spun over the past decades by the government – regulations that had interfered with "almost every aspect of every American's working day." In short, while the past Democratic governments had increasingly meddled with "individual initiative and freedom," a new environment would emerge through the combination of a reduction in incentive-stifling taxes, the slowdown in the growth of federal spending and regulations, and the gradual control of the money supply.[3] With regard to U.S. spending, taxing, and deficits, it should be remembered that after World War II budgetary policy had been viewed as the key instrument for maintaining high employment and stabilization. The prescription was the Keynesian one: an increase in government spending and a decrease in revenues (in a recession) would sustain aggregate demand and thus reverse the situation, while deficits as such would be discouraged in "normal" times. But in the 1970s, various policy failures, along with the fear of substantial increases in the ratio of national debt to GNP, caused the Keynesian-inspired deficit rule to fall into disuse, thus leaving both parties and Congress without guidance as to the desirable size of the surplus or deficit.[4]

The common Thatcher–Reagan policies thus involved a radical departure from the Keynesian focus on full employment, aggregate demand, and fiscal instruments. The emphasis was now on antideficit, anti-inflation measures (rather than avoiding unemployment), financial management and monetarist discipline (rather than fiscal manipulation), and ad hoc supply-side incentives (rather than aggregate demand), along with the curtailing of subsidies and "wasteful" income transfers. However, the particular conditions prevailing in their respective countries and different political necessities pushed the Thatcher government and the Reagan administration in different directions and toward the use of different practical measures.

Thatcher saw her main task as that of reversing the possible advance of "collectivism." Accordingly, she directed her attacks against the bastions of Labour power, namely the trade unions, the so-called council estates (locally managed public housing), the socialist local authorities, and the critical nationalized industries. She concentrated her efforts on curbing the unions, selling the council houses to their tenants, and curtailing the funds provided by the central government to local governments. At the same time, she pushed an expanding privatization drive that rapidly gained increasing support both at home and abroad. According to Thatcher, nationalization had been at the heart of the collectivist program by which Labour governments sought to remodel British society, so, naturally, privatization was at the "centre of any programme of reclaiming territory for freedom." Thatcher's deep conviction was that a government's performance in running any business or in administering any service was inevitably so lamentable that one should always demonstrate "why government should perform a particular function rather than why the private sector should not." Yet, while the crisis of the system that brought her to power was in part a crisis of the welfare state and while she claimed that welfare benefits had been distributed with no consideration of their impact on behavior – namely that they had "encouraged illegitimacy, facilitated the breakdown of families, and replaced incentives with perverse encouragement for idleness and cheating" – she did not place the reform of the welfare state at the top of her agenda. Public support for antiwelfare measures was weak, and in addition, as I said before, her attention was focused on demolishing Labour's strongholds. For this purpose she relied not only on battling unions and public property, but also on diminishing the power of local authorities, the result being higher centralization rather than decentralization. Hence, all in all, under her direction "the state was rolled back in some areas and rolled forward in others."[5]

President Reagan did "roll back" the state's frontiers, but not via liquidations of public assets. Rather he aimed to downsize the federal government through shifting power in favor of the states, along with shrinking welfare and downgrading federal responsibilities toward social problems. As he explained it in his *Second Inaugural Address* on January 23, 1985, one of his "fundamental goals" was to "reduce dependency and upgrade the dignity of those who are infirm or disadvantaged" by relying on a growing economy in which "support from family and community offer our best chance for a society where compassion is a way of life, where the old and infirm are cared for, the young and, yes, the unborn, protected, and the unfortunate looked after and made self-sufficient."[6] Meanwhile, Congress went partially along with his specific proposals on reversing certain "entitlements" in order to eliminate "unintended benefits." Notably, it agreed to restrict eligibility and reduce benefits in the key welfare program, Aid to Families with Dependent Children (AFDC), to limit eligibility for food stamps to households with certain incomes (130 percent of the poverty level), to cancel subsidies to state and local governments for hiring poor people, and to cut back extended programs for workers who are unemployed more than twenty-six weeks. Congress did not, however, agree to impose a limit on federal spending either on Medicare or on certain Supplemental Security Income programs.[7] As I point out in detail later on, the entire Reagan program – that is, the downsizing of the federal government via various means connected with "balancing the budget" and involving taxes, spending, power restructuring, and, last but not least, curtailment of welfare – has been reasserted in the 1990s by Republican leaders Newt Gingrich and Dick Armey in their "Bold Plan to Change the Nation" entitled the Contract with America.[8]

My purpose is not to draw a balance sheet of the Thatcher or Reagan regimes, but only to show how and why, notwithstanding their cardinal ideological similarities, they came to emphasize within their different national socioeconomic settings two major – and different – clusters of issues and solutions to their common objective of redefining the state. Thatcher brought to the center of the stage the issues of public ownership, nationalization, and privatization; Reagan, the issues of social dependence, social insurance, welfare, and income transfers. Both groups of problems continue to exercise a decisive impact on policy decisions worldwide, and it is to their implications that I shall devote the coming pages. In Section 3.2 I focus on the nature, scope, and framework of the public corporation, its frontiers with private enterprises, and the factors that shape their respective economic activities. In Section 3.3 I present the debates on the logic and purpose of privatizing public properties and on the role of such privatizations in downsizing the state. In Section 3.4 I turn to the issues involved in reforming social security and social assistance and their implications with regard to the size and functions of the state. I offer my concluding comments in Section 3.5.

3.2. Frameworks of Public Corporations

In Chapter 1 I traced the process of expansion over time of public and quasi-public ownership within the different historical settings of Great Britain, France, Germany, and the United States. As I noted there, such expansions may involve inter alia vast landholdings, various forms of takeover of private enterprises (i.e., nationalization), and the creation of all kinds of companies or off-budget agencies by statute (or under statutory authority) set to pursue a particular public purpose in different markets.

Consider now in detail the range, functions, and operational frameworks of the public corporation. To start with, it should be noted that public corporations have been used for a wide variety of purposes: as alternative devices for bypassing legal debt limits, for circumventing various budgetary pressures and requirements, and for asserting public control in areas in which the private sector could not provide services considered of "public interest." Further, such corporations have operated in different settings and in all kinds of fields, from utilities to industries to credit institutions, at all levels of government – local (municipal), provincial or regional (the state level in Germany and the United States), and national (federal in the United States) – with a view to combining managerial autonomy with public service accountability and control, as well as to coordinating a wide variety of government programs and plans. Government corporations have also channeled credits to certain industries and satellite financial institutions, improved access to credit markets for certain borrowers, stabilized certain sectors' and branches' incomes and prices, controlled and advanced urban housing and infrastructure developments, and encouraged trade relations. The variety of institutional alternatives has been further increased by the growth of complexly intertwined public relationships with the private sector, using both mixed (public–private) corporations and purely private organizations under government influence, direction, and control. The flexibility and range of this public tool has overlapped with several other policy instruments shaping the behavior of the private sector – such as the contracting out of government functions, grants-in-aid, loan guarantees, and special benefits involving deductions or tax exemptions for certain activities.[9]

The term *government corporation* turns out to be a kind of loosely defined catch-all category, since one cannot find anywhere a definition fully and unequivocally applicable at all times to all cases. The European Center of Public Enterprise, for instance, in the 1960s defined as a public enterprise "any enterprise in which the state, or public collectivities, or other public enterprises, directly or indirectly hold a capital share substantial enough to exercise effective control over that enterprise." A directive of the EEC of June 25, 1980, specified that a public enterprise "is an enterprise over which the public authorities may exercise a dominant influence because of their financial participation *or* because of the rules guiding that enterprise." A subsequent definition of the EEC asserted in 1987 that in the EEC "a public enterprise, or an enterprise with public participation, is one in which the public authority disposes of effective power, whether it holds a majority or a minority share in its capital."[10] Yet in France, for instance, the term *établissement public* (usually translated as "public corporation") covers two kinds of entities whose capital belongs in whole or in part to the government or other public agency: *établissements publics industriels et commerciaux* and *établissements publics administratifs*. The latter can hardly be likened to public corporations.[11] In the United States, a 1981 *Report of the National Academy of Public Administration* distinguishes a "government enterprise" from a "government corporation." The first is defined as a government instrumentality or program "which generates revenue from a commercial type of activity," which may or may not be incorporated, and which is intended to be self-sustaining. The second is said to be created as a separate legal person – by legislation or pursuant to it – which is financed by appropriations and which can use and reuse its revenue and its assets. The report adds that besides this "government-owned corporation," other government corporations are the mixed public–private corporation and "the private corporations established by federal statute but privately financed and owned." Yet, as knowledgeable commentators have pointed out, this "threefold division" does not entirely capture the "complexity of the instrument." Moreover, even the official Government Control Act is not of "much assistance" in sorting out this reality.[12]

In fact, the differences between the public and the private sector are in some respects ill defined in the United States, and in other countries as well. In awarding contracts, the government can bring into its employ business firms, nonprofit organizations, and even individuals, all lodged in the economy's private sector. Via grants-in-aid, the central governments can construct an even wider network involving state and local governments and nonprofit organizations, as well as individuals. Moreover, one may ask to what extent one can call "private" the government-oriented corporations (e.g., for armaments) whose long-term capital is supplied by governmental agencies, whose prices are determined by negotiation and not on the open market, and whose specific standards of negotiation and execution are set by the government.[13] Indeed, as other observers have remarked, in practice the borderline between public and private corporations is not as tight as it seems when one considers as public only those enterprises that are both owned and controlled by the government. Effectively, "the degree of [both] public control and public financing can vary from zero to one hundred percent." In this sense some enterprises may be said to be more public than others, while yet others are in fact only nominally public and have "all the essentials of private organizations."[14]

The question of the nature and extent of governmental controls and constraints is of particular importance with regard to the functioning of both the public and the quasi-public enterprise. It involves the most critical aspects of the problem of "balancing commercial and managerial autonomy against the minimum of supervision demanded by the public character and purpose of government enterprise." The interaction between two types of controls – a priori controls, which embody the power of the state to determine certain actions of the enterprises as a condition of their legality, and a posteriori controls, which embody the power of the state to annul or correct certain transactions – may at times become hopelessly intertwined.[15] A government may rely on the control rights provided for in a company's statute or, in the case of mixed companies, in the companies' articles of association. But the government may also require that while the managers of a public corporation – when the government has itself appointed them – should conduct the business in question in conformity with standard commercial principles, they should also obtain the consent of their superior authority before engaging in certain courses of action (e.g., borrowing). The diversity of the control arrangements may in some situations be due to the occasional and at times accidental participation of a government in private industry, and in other situations to the particular circumstances that made the government intervention in the affairs of an industry appear necessary and desirable.[16]

In France, for instance, after World War II, private corporations, notwithstanding their legal autonomy, had to operate within the framework of national economic plans. Hence they were not always free to attack directly the problems of price fixing, investment choices, employment policies, and wages and salaries. All these matters had to depend on the centralized planning decisions. At the time, the possibility was also envisaged of establishing a "central holding company" that would administer the entire public share ownership and control in all public enterprises. Eventually the government decided to establish "holdings" only in certain sectors.[17] Indeed, in any country sharp discrepancies are bound to arise in many situations between the declared principles of a government corporation operating as an autonomous unit on behalf of but not in the government, and the decisions concerning the detailed operations of that corporation arising from considerations extraneous to government agencies.[18] Governments must continually attempt to strike a balance between excessively intensive controls and the absence of controls, for the latter might be interpreted either as a lack of government responsibility or as an absence of government involvement.

Public enterprises have maintained a presence in certain sectors or branches not only because they have served as convenient government instruments for coping with a variety of problems, but also because they have served political interests, client groups, and even entire constituencies, as well as certain private businesses that have requested the government to continue to operate in such sectors. This has been the case both in the United States and elsewhere with regard to defense contracts, bases, shipyards, and similar facilities, as well as in various commercial-type operations. Government promotion of certain businesses, particularly in energy, transport, communications, and waterworks, have at times spurred beneficial expansions of private investments. In numerous cases public enterprises have reduced risks, increased profit opportunities, and generated jobs, notably in such fields as construction, engineering, and general development.[19]

Certain analysts assert that the differences between a public and a private corporation are in fact unmistakable structural differences easily perceptible if one focuses on such questions as their multiple objectives (in lieu of a paramount role for profit), the gamut of particular incentives shaping the activities of their managers, and the special features of the frameworks within which these activities must be discharged. Critics of such analyses, however, point out not only, as we already noted, that the frontiers between the two kinds of enterprises are in fact hard to draw, but also that both kinds of companies have many decisive features in common.

In connection with the first school of thought, it may be interesting to recall that it was a resolute partisan of the public enterprise, the leader of the British Labour party, Herbert Morrisson, who asserted in 1933 that a clear difference must necessarily exist between the two types of companies. According to Morrisson, "The public corporation must not be a capitalist business. It must have a different atmosphere at its board table from that of a shareholders' meeting; the board and its officers must regard themselves as the high custodians of the public interest."[20] Now, precisely what Morrisson saw as the hallmark of the public corporations – a noncapitalist business committed to the public interest – is what the critics of such corporations view as the cause of their costly "inherent" failures. As a rule, noted the famous opponent of public enterprises Ludwig von Mises, the public authorities indeed do not want to operate their enterprises "from the viewpoint of the attainment of the greatest possible profit. They consider the accomplishment of other tasks more important." And, added von Mises, "Whatever these other goals may be, the result of such a policy always amounts to subsidizing some people to the burden of others."[21] Other analysts also assert that while in the private sector there is one overriding concern, namely profits, in the public sector there may be a multiplicity of objectives, both economic and noneconomic. The consequences of this multiplicity are manysided. Vito Tanzi and Robert H. Floyd, for instance, affirm that many of the difficulties that are likely to arise with the public enterprises are due to the "ill-specified and often conflicting objectives" assigned to these enterprises by the public officials. Evidently, the trade-offs between these ill-defined objectives will be poorly assessed; at least, without a properly quantified base no appropriate determination of pricing policies and financial targets is possible.[22] Referring to France, Warren C. Baum noted that in the absence of any legislative clue as to how a public enterprise should be run "in the public interest," government officials were trying to make public enterprises' decisions in the context of the general objectives of the national plan on output, modernization of production, and other goals – a task obviously not readily achievable.[23] Yet another commentator has pointed out that the root of the difficulties with multiple objectives lay in the fact that the latter simultaneously involve the public firm, the government, and the public (which the government supposedly represents), each one with its own versions of its own interests.[24]

With regard to the incentives that shape the behavior of public enterprise managers, many analysts emphasize that one must take into account the interplay between this multiplicity of objectives and the special features of the framework within which these companies operate and that affect their pricing, investment, and manpower policies. Generally, public enterprises operate under less stringent financial requirements than those prevailing for privately owned ones. This is notably the case with respect to tax burdens, access to low-cost finances, advances of capital funds, subsidies, and so on. Subsidies do not necessarily correspond to clear economic principles: often their amounts are negotiated among the interested parties and contribute to the relaxation of pressures for efficiency that dominate in the private companies. Indeed, nationalized or joint public–private companies – often consisting of sick industries scheduled to be reorganized and modernized or of centralized monopolies (e.g., utility monopolies) – tend to absorb large amounts of capital and yield only minor social gains. Yet at the same time such companies may be in the process of contraction or expansion – often concealed or illegal – via the liquidation or acquisition of certain facilities at home or abroad, so that, in certain countries, the state's control over the scope of their operations may be quite precarious. Unmenaced by bankruptcy, in no danger of takeover by competitors, and exempt from accountability for market performance (relative to the provision of goods and services at low prices and in greater volume), the managers of public companies do not function under the incentive systems necessary to achieve the operating performance of the private companies. On the other hand, the constraints under which they must operate also hamper their performance: public corporations cannot easily resort to shifts in capacity, lower-cost locations, reductions in the size of management, dismissals or displacements of workers, or all-out drives for productivity increases. They must usually aim to ensure certain levels of employment and keep up the scheduled services for certain constituencies. Considering the problem of objectives and the special framework in which the public companies operate, the boards and the managers of these organizations cannot be driven by concerns for high efficiency, cost containment, and increases in productivity, but rather by preoccupations with their own interests as worked out in terms of constituencies such as groups of employees, classes of customers, categories of suppliers of capital goods, and circles of influential politicians.[25] In the opinion of some analysts, the impact of both multiple objectives and the pervasiveness (or stringency) of certain government controls on performance can be appreciably reduced if various controls are minimized, if the government agrees to reimburse the costs incurred by the enterprises for the noncommercial activities imposed on them, and if mutually agreed upon financial objectives between the government and the enterprises are concluded (concerning, for instance, the rates of return on capital that the enterprises seek to achieve over a period of time).[26]

The contentions that the public enterprises must act differently than the private ones – that their performance is "inherently" inefficient because of the indicated multiple objectives, government controls, wrong incentives, and peculiar operating frameworks – are contested by a number of interesting contributions to the debate. To start with, these commentators point out that the state must assume the provision of certain goods and services desired by the public – items for which the public is willing to pay, at least up to a point, and that the private economy may be unable or unwilling to provide. Further, they take issue with the idea that there are different ways of structuring the activities of public and private enterprises in regard to their decision-making processes – as we saw both Herbert Morrisson and Ludwig von Mises assert from two opposing angles. Implicitly responding to the theory of the distinction between the two types of enterprise, David E. Sappington and Joseph E. Stiglitz draw an interesting rapprochement between their hierarchical structures. According to them, in both types there is substantial delegation of responsibility: in both, the hierarchy of authority terminates with the managers who make the day-to-day decisions. Neither government nor the shareholders directly control the activities of the enterprises that in principle are under their command. The only pertinent differences in this respect are that government retains some authority to intervene directly and implement certain policy changes in the case of the public enterprises, while special rights are offered only under certain conditions to the creditors or other major financial interests in the case of private enterprises.[27] On the other hand, as some other analysts point out, through taxes and subsidies, employment, wages, location, and other policies, government is able to affect private enterprises much as it would if it controlled these enterprises directly. As Carl Shapiro and Robert Willig put it, with "carefully crafted taxes, subsidies, and regulatory oversight" privately owned corporations may not be easily distinguishable, at least in some respects, from publicly owned ones. Superficially, there might seem to be an unbridgeable difference between the public enterprises, directed to serve entirely public aims, and the private enterprises, entirely profit oriented. But in cases where there is no market failure, profit maximization coincides with public aims. And even when there is a discrepancy between public aims and profit maximization, the private enterprises can, because of various forms of regulation, be made to "better serve public goals."[28]

Enterprises may be made public for a variety of reasons, for instance, as a result of imminent bankruptcies and the danger that their closing would affect certain sectors, branches, or communities. Put differently, some of these enterprises are "nationalized" precisely because they are running at a loss and not because they are seen as inherently "government enterprises."[29] As Lord Kaldor noted, "Bankruptcies caused by recession simply increase the size of the public sectors, just as, if you look at Mussolini's Italy, which was all against public enterprises, you see that they ended up with almost the whole of industry being owned by the state."[30] In this connection, it is interesting to point out that the modern public corporations, as Sam Peltzman remarked, have been usually concentrated in a handful of industries, notably transport (mainly rail and air), utilities (mainly electricity, water, and gas), and communications (mainly telephone and post). Beyond this "core," they have been involved – though only in a limited number of countries – in steel mills, auto plants, banks, and the like. So as far as genuine industries are concerned, the domain that has particularly attracted state intervention has been characterized by a combination of economies of density and scale. Without state intervention, Peltzman further notes, it is reasonable to assume either that these industries – which are not "examples of laissez-faire" – would be organized monopolistically or that their resources would have been wasted in rivalry. With or without state intervention, they would sell the same kind of service, but at vastly different prices.[31]

With regard to the performance of public enterprises, Lord Kaldor has remarked that there were no "general rules" and that achievements varied according to "country, period, and the particular criteria chosen." In certain countries, nationalized industries brought "enormous benefits" to the economy as a whole; they were "complementary to, rather than competitive with, the private sector" and, through their own expansion, provided the basis for a large expansion of manufacturing industry in general. In other cases, added Kaldor, they have been the only alternative to foreign-owned and/or -controlled private companies. Futher, one should not lose sight of the fact that only "in well-defined circumstances" are markets efficient. The notion of welfare economics – that is, of an efficient allocation of resources generated by the hypothetical case of a perfectly competitive market – posits that both the amount of labor available for employment and the amount and size of funds available for investment "are to be taken as given," and that the profit resulting from any particular investment provides "a measure of the net addition to the national output which can be attributed to that investment.'' However, concludes Kaldor, there are a number of powerful reasons for rejecting such postulates.[32]

Concurring up to a point with Kaldor, but for somewhat different reasons, Joseph Stiglitz also recalls that the traditional exposition of the ''fundamental theorem of Welfare Economics'' provides a set of conditions under which the market economy leads to a Pareto-efficient allocation of resources (i.e., when some individuals cannot be made better off without making at least one individual worse off). The traditional analysis then identifies the exceptional instances in which markets do not work perfectly, that is, the so-called market failures, which potentially provide scope for government activity. But while the traditional literature views market failures as exceptions to the rule, in Stiglitz's (and Greenwald's) view, whenever information is imperfect and/or markets are incomplete – that is, ''essentially always'' – the market ''is not constrained Pareto efficient.'' The term *constrained* is used here to point out that when ascertaining whether there is some governmental policy that could constitute a Pareto improvement, one should not forget that the government also is subject to the same kind of informational and/or incomplete market constraints that face the private sector. In short, while the traditional literature views market failures as exceptions to the rule that markets lead to efficient allocation, in Stiglitz's view, only under exceptional circumstances are markets fully efficient. It follows that if markets are almost never efficient, then there is a vast potential role for the government.[33]

The critics of the performance of the public enterprises, as well as the critics of these critics, in fact develop their arguments within two different theoretical contexts. The first group reject the notion that the state can play any useful role with regard to efficiency or monopoly. They posit that only market mechanisms lead to efficient resource use and that private enterprises conform to the disciplines and incentives of the market. According to them, as we saw above, public enterprises, because of their multiple constraints, objectives, and requirements, are inherently inefficient. It follows then that the creation of a public enterprise ''results in even greater resource misallocation than do the market failures it aims to correct.''[34]

The critics of these critics retort in essence, as noted above, that markets are not as efficient as their most resolute partisans assume, that market mechanisms cannot at all times perform as desired all economic functions (e.g., with regard to high employment and high growth rates), and that the differences between public and private companies are not as sharp as some people contend. Deep down, as we shall see again later, the subject of contention is the question of what is and what should be the scope of government responsibilities, rather than the narrower question whether certain goods and services are better provided by public or private enterprises. Remaining for the moment at the level of this narrower issue, Stiglitz, as I recalled above, asserted that there was a potential for government intervention because markets are only exceptionally efficient. But then Stiglitz – rightly, I believe – adopts what he calls an "eclectic" position. On the one hand, he does note that government interventions are "not perfect" and that waste and incompetence may almost surely arise when these interventions occur. On the other hand, human errors do arise also in the private sector as they do in the public one. Rejecting the contention that government interventions are at all times "inherently" wasteful, Stiglitz finally concludes that there are stronger incentives "to avoid mistakes" in the private sector than there are in the public one.[35]

This eclectic position seems to me the most reasonable one, since it leaves the door open for evaluations and decisions case by case for any and all potential government interventions and since it recognizes the evident fact that inefficiency and mistakes may exist in the private sector just as in the public one (though to a lesser extent overall in the former than in the latter). Thus, the idea that all that is needed in order to achieve efficiency is to move any and all enterprises from the public to the private sector may not turn out to be less compelling than some of its most resolute advocates usually assert. It does not follow, either, that all drives toward privatization always have the same faithful constituencies – as I point out in the next section.

3.3. Privatization's Objectives

In its many forms and guises, privatization primarily reflects the key political objective of downsizing the state. Yet other considerations and criteria may be called forth in order to stress the necessity of privatization: for instance, the preoccupation with increasing efficiency discussed in the preceding section. Are all the potential objectives – political, fiscal, industrial/commercial, or of a general economic nature – convergent or antipodal? To what extent does the diversity of the nature and scope of public corporations affect the patterns and extent of their privatization? Do certain conditions favor resistance to policies of privatization that may endanger their being carried out?

A government's efforts to shed certain state assets (i.e., the exact opposite of nationalizations), along with other forms of transferring the provision of certain public goods and services to the private sector, is a many-faceted process affecting various groups in the society in different ways. Privatization involves a wide variety of measures, including the disposition through sales, leases, or outright liquidation of state-owned assets (including land, infrastructure, and publicly owned enterprises); the replacement through contracting out ("outsourcing") of state-produced services by private services (either for the public at large or for the state organization itself); the complete abandonment of state services, so-called load shedding (which may or may not be replaced by goods and services provided privately); public–private partnerships in investments and management in "exclusive" domains of the public sector; and government distributions of purchasing power to eligible consumers (via vouchers) for designated goods and services.

I return in detail to all these issues in Chapter 5. For the moment, let me recall the caustic remarks of William T. Gormley, who says that privatization conjures up to its supporters "visions of a lean, streamlined public sector more reliant on the private marketplace for the delivery of public services," while to its critics it conjures up "visions of a beleaguered government bureaucracy ceding responsibility for vital public services to unreliable entrepreneurs." To other observers, adds Gormley, "privatization inspires neither rapture nor alarm but rather cautious interest."[36] Actually, I would say that in many cases this may be ascertained with the help of the old legal Roman precept: *Cui prodest*? – that is, "Whom does it benefit?" (a particular change of ownership). The *cui prodest* precept explains the apparent paradox that in practice we may see the most decisive partisans of privatization being opposed to or keeping quiet about certain evidently profitable state divestitures, while we may witness the most resolute advocates of state takeovers tacitly approving certain denationalizations.

For any government, the objective of an imminent privatization may vary. Sometimes it is the liquidation of one or more unprofitable enterprises whose losses are no longer considered to outweigh their usefulness. Less drastic immediate objectives may be the streamlining of certain public businesses by modifying of their statutory sphere of operations, achieving accountability within the public sector, and perhaps also modernizing and diversifying public enterprises' production. These, too, may at times prepare for eventual government withdrawal from direct involvement in the production of goods and services. Governments may tend to view privatization as an appropriate way to unload the financial burdens of subsidizing, servicing, and managing enterprises whose administration they have inherited or had to assume in different economic circumstances; to reduce public demands on the private credit markets; or to raise cash for the Treasury, both for immediate spending projects and for reducing the national debt. Last but not least, privatization may also be a handy way of dismantling the opposition's strongholds, reshaping industrial relations, building new political bastions, and cementing new alliances.

How does the structural diversity of public companies combine with the diversity of the goals of privatization within the diverse constraints (and distortions) prevailing in various economies? Clearly the ensuing combinations yield different patterns of privatization. Consider briefly the main aspects of these patterns in the countries of our interest.

The modern drive to privatize started in Great Britain, with the apparently well-defined political-ideological objective of dismantling Labour's allegedly "collectivist" nationalized industrial base. Privatization yielded some unexpected results, not only in Britain but also abroad, where, by the mid-1980s, some sixty countries had become involved in broadly similar efforts. Privatization drives took place not only in the industrial countries (e.g., in France, Sweden, Japan, and Canada), but also in Third World countries from South America to Africa to Asia. The money involved in the sale of the enterprises reached in the hundreds of billions of dollars, affecting stock market activities in some countries at levels never reached previously. (The privatization of Japan's telecommunications system, for instance, at the time represented more than one-tenth of Tokyo's stock market transactions.)

In Great Britain itself, while the Thatcher government had not been successful in cutting government spending – one of its basic objectives – it had been very successful in promoting privatization not only as its "major political commitment," but also as the foundation of its industrial policy and as a key instrument of its fiscal policy. In its first five years it was able to raise some £5 billion total by selling parts of its state-owned enterprises, and year after year British financial proceeds from such sales increased appreciably. By 1987–1988 the total per year increased to £5 billion. And all in all, by 1994–1995, the government had privatized almost fifty major businesses since 1979, with total net proceeds exceeding some £60 billion. (The privatization proceeds for 1995–1996 and 1996–1997 were projected to reach £3 billion.) As this expansion took place it involved a mixture of aims, including, besides the often stated objective of improving the economy's efficiency, the goals of reducing public sector borrowing requirements (PSBR), easing public sector pay obligations, widening public share ownership (in keeping the government directly or indirectly as a major shareholder), encouraging employee share ownership, and also reaching various political targets. In the process, the government privatized firms in the competitive sector as well as monopolies and even major strategic industries, leaving no industrial sector untouched. (In practice, the only condition required for a state firm to become a candidate for privatization was salability.) In addition, 1 million British council homes were transferred to private ownership. The overall results have been acclaimed in many quarters as an economic and political success. But the critics have pointed out that a correct answer to the question of success would hinge on the importance one attaches to the various objectives of privatization. With regard to what some critics had alleged to be the main criterion of the process – namely the impact of the program on the economic efficiency of the industries concerned – opinions remain seriously divided, as we shall see further on.[37]

Following the British example, France carried out a policy of privatization first under the Chirac government, from 1986 to 1988 – a policy continued, up to a point, under the following socialist government as well – and then relaunched it, more decisively, under Chirac's presidency of the Republic, from 1995 on. The French conservative program aimed from its inception not only to restrict the role of the state, but also to shift the interests and attention of business from the Ministry of Finance to the stock market and to transform France into a country of shareholders. From 1986 on, the policy of privatization aimed to dismantle not only the socialist nationalizations of 1981–1982, but also in certain ways the de Gaulle nationalizations of 1945–1946. The 1986 program put up for privatization 66 industrial and financial assets, including the television company TF-1. With their subsidiaries, these accounted for a total of 1,454 firms with 755,000 employees and an overall value of over U.S. $60 billion. Unlike Great Britain, the more traditionally "statist" France confined industrial privatization to the competitive sector, leaving untouched monopoly utilities and enterprises in the most heavily regulated markets. Also in contrast to Great Britain, the proceeds were not supposed to lighten the public sector's borrowing requirements or to pave the way for cuts in taxation, but rather to help reduce long-term government debt. Under the socialists, a partial privatization, envisaged quite reluctantly, was meant to increase government's limited capability to inject the needed capital into the surviving state-owned industries. Under the Chirac presidency, the privatization drive was relaunched somewhat more vigorously with the goals of raising cash, popularizing the French stock market, and appealing to foreign investors while maintaining control in the hands of a core shareholder group made up of French companies or institutional investors. France's policy has succeeded in increasing the number of small French investors – to some 7 million by mid-1994 – but the latter's notable lack of familiarity with "the stock market game" is a risk that may cause them deep disappointments if privatized stocks fall below their original price. On the other hand, foreign investors have not responded as hoped. One reason is that vast opportunities for investment have been opening on the global market through privatizations in many other countries; the other is that French privatizations have acquired in the meantime a rather bad name. This shaky reputation has been due largely to the poor performance of the big privatized firms BNP, Rhône-Poulenc, Elf-Aquitaine, and UAP Insurance. The prospects for the privatization list look poor in the late 1990s because, as a foreign observer puts it, most of the companies for sale "look pretty sickly now" and because the giants in the noncompetitive sector are likely to remain "off limits for at least several more years."[38]

In the late 1950s, the Federal Republic of Germany (FRG) had already seemed prepared to proceed to some significant transfers of public properties to the private sector. It did privatize the mining and steel works of Prussia (PREUSSAG) and, in part, some holdings of VEBA (which under Prussian tutelage had unified 14 big corporations with shares in 70 companies) and of Volkswagen (VW). But the FRG did not engage more decisively on this path until the early 1980s, when the federal government announced a privatization program with the asserted aim of reducing its participation in business and privatizing those public assets whose transfer would not infringe "the public interest." Even at this time, the scope of privatization remained actually quite limited. The FRG reduced anew its holdings in VEBA, the united group VIAG (active in electricity, gas, aluminum, and chemicals), VW, and some 50 smaller companies. It also partially privatized the Deutsche Bank and other financial institutions, but the federal holdings in this sector remained enormous. Initially, many other companies, including the airline Lufthansa, the steel and shipbuilding company Salzgitter, and the coal company Saarbergwerke, all beset by various structural crises, were earmarked for transfer to the private sector. In the end, however, out of a total of 958 enterprises in which the federal government held an interest, final privatization proposals were confined to a small number of firms only. The *Länder* (states) and municipalities have shown even greater reluctance to proceed to privatization. The consensus at the *Länder* level is still that assets should not be privatized if they appear useful for regional industrial policies. The *Länder* governments prefer to support the policies of the big companies and to subsidize the research and technology programs of the smaller firms. Not one of the *Länder* followed the federal example in establishing a privatization program. Instead, they contracted out various public services, differing from state to state but involving notably education, health, transport, housing, and sanitation. One must, of course, take into consideration the fact that the public sector has had a very diverse origin in the FRG, that it is spread between the federal government, the states, and the municipalities, and that before the FRG's unification with East Germany the public sector had not been placed in the service of a national policy, as in the cases of Great Britain and France. Only after the collapse of the so-called Democratic Republic of Germany (GDR) was the unified FRG confronted by a massive problem of denationalization. On the eve of unification, the East German public sector was composed of 126 national *Kombinate* (vertically integrated groups of enterprises comprising 3,300 enterprises), each with an average workforce of 24,000. In addition, the public sector counted 95 regional multiunit *Kombinate* (each employing 2,000 workers), some 4,000 agricultural cooperatives, and over 1 million hectares of land usable for agriculture and forestry. The state trustee agency Treuhandanstalt (THA), set up in June 1990 and entrusted with the management and privatization of this enormous empire, transferred to private ownership a very large part of the companies it had on its books before closing its operations in 1994.[39] (I return to some of the issues in Chapter 6.)

Given the different historical characteristics of its public sectors, its different economic and political climates, and its different constraints, the pattern of privatization in the United States has tended to differ significantly from those that crystallized in Western Europe. Privatization here has taken some curious turns, which, however, when observed at close range, are less disconcerting than they first seem. Consider to start with the important question of federally owned lands. Adam Smith once remarked that lands for the purpose of pleasure and magnificence – parks, gardens, public walks – "ought to belong to the crown" (i.e., to the state). But, Smith added, many other tracts of land belonging to the crown if sold "would produce a very large sum of money which, if applied to the payment of public debts, would deliver from mortgage a much greater revenue than any which those lands have ever afforded to the crown."[40] This would seem to be pertinent to the United States, where in the early 1990s the federal government owned 28.68 percent of the nation's total land area (namely, 649.3 million acres out of a total of 2,271 million). The federal government owns in particular much of the western lands (close to 47 percent of the combined states of Montana, Idaho, Wyoming, Colorado, New Mexico, Arizona, Utah, and Nevada).[41] That area's economic mainstays, ranching, logging, and mining, depend heavily on federal resource policies. Water on the federal lands is usually not owned by the federal government, but federal irrigation projects involving reservoirs to store runoff and canals to channel it enable individuals to make profitable use of land. The 27,000 ranchers whose livestock are grazing on some 270 million acres of federal land are federally licensed and heavily subsidized, since grazing fees substantially understate the market value of the privilege. The federal grazing managment and licensing programs have been in the red since World War II; the current deficit is estimated to be on the order of $200 million per year. With regard to logging, the United States extends much help to private companies by building roads and growing trees for plywood, lumber, and other wood products. Furthermore, The United States sells its timber at a loss and invests in reforestation at a negative rate of return; in fact, the U.S. Forest Service continues to run a negative cash flow of about $1 billion a year. Concerning mining, the vast federal energy leases contributed in the 1990s up to 17 percent of the domestic crude oil production, 31 percent of the national gas, and 26 percent of the coal. Selling much of the highly subsidized leased assets would seem compelling. Indeed, as Scott Lehman puts it in his book *Privatizing Public Lands*, "What could be more unproductive than valuable real estate that soaks up billions of dollars in administrative costs?"[42]

In his message for fiscal year 1983, President Reagan endorsed the goal of privatizing federal landholdings, stating that "we will move systematically to reduce the vast holdings of surplus land and real property," since some of this property "is not in use and would be of greater value to society if transferred to the private sector." By the following year, the Reagan administration had again stressed its interest in privatizing certain lands in endorsing the recommendations of the Presidential Commission on Indian Reservation Economies on possible leases of tribally held assets. Yet nothing concrete followed with regard to privatization. (It should not be forgotten that while in some respects the Reagan administration inclined toward greater freedom for private initiative "to develop state-owned lands," the previous Carter administration had explicitly endorsed an opposite idea, namely that of more regulations in order to forestall private misuses of state-owned lands.)

The Clinton administration proposed that the federal land policy be reformed – namely that fees for grazing, timber, forage, water, minerals, and recreation be increased and that restrictions be placed on grazing and logging on the public lands to protect against overgrazed grasslands and polluted streams. A serious battle on these issues ensued in Congress. Senator Pete Domenici of New Mexico (where federal lands constitute close to 34 percent of the state) sponsored a bill (S. 852, "to provide for uniform management of livestock grazing on federal land and for other purposes"), aiming to set a fee for grazing on public lands equaling about one-fourth of the rate charged by private landowners; freeing the ranchers from various restrictions, regulations, and liabilities concerning the use of public lands; and preventing everyone except ranchers and adjacent property owners from having any significant say on how these public lands should be managed (apparently the cattlemen want open range). By that time the administration already offered to grant interest groups more input in lands policy and had also thrown in the towel over the proposed increase of grazing fees.[43]

Despite the official federal loss of interest in privatization, the question of public ownership of land remains very much open. A so-called Individual Rights Foundation of Los Angeles has joined with the ranchers, loggers, and public officials of a New Mexico county to fight the government's efforts to curb environmental damage by restricting grazing on public lands. The centerpiece of this effort is a lawsuit arguing that "the government had no authority to own and manage the public domain in New Mexico and that the control of the land should pass to the state, and ultimately to the county" involved in the lawsuit. According to legal authorities, the alleged constitutional theory underlying the suit "has no basis in law."[44] Yet what is to be noted are the incessant efforts of some ranchers to obtain by circuitous methods formal property rights on lands of the public domain – lands they have been using while refusing to pay grazing fees, relying in illegal fencing and

on patrolling by well-organized grazing associations. In direct opposition to
the devious claims of the Individual Rights Foundation, a number of analysts
continue to stress the necessity for the federal government to proceed toward
the methodical sale of public lands. As Scott Lehman, for instance, notes,
such a sale "may come to seem a relatively painless way to reduce the
deficit." The value of the United States' nonreproducible capital, that is, land
and mineral rights, was officially said to be on the order of $226 billion and
$351 billion, respectively (in 1994 dollars). After years of enormous deficits,
these relative values seem small in relation to the national debt. But we are
still talking about a lot of money.[45] Other analysts rightly stress that the
transfer of land to private ownership could increase the productivity, employment, and economic activity of these lands and, in addition, would create
a tax base for states and locales, diminishing their dependence on funds from
Washington.[46]

In practice, U.S. privatization policies have not at all turned in this direction. They have also avoided proposals like the one made in the mid-1960s
by Senator Daniel P. Moynihan of New York, concerning the federal government's gigantic lending programs. Hundreds of federal loans benefit ex-
porters, utilities, farmers, and students and add up to hundreds of billions of
dollars. Senator Moynihan proposed that the government should sell off its
loan portfolio to help reduce the national debt – a sale that, he said, would
save taxpayers $200 billion over a period of seven years.[47] The proposal was
rejected as unhelpful, except for the student loans (in the process of being
reconsidered in connection with welfare). Rather, privatization efforts have
centered on administrative contracting out (namely, outsourcing) for a variety
of goods and services. In the early 1990s, the U.S. federal government spent
$210 billion on such outsourcing. In the case of certain agencies, notably the
Department of Energy, the Environmental Protection Agency, and NASA,
contractors perform most of the work. Besides the Department of Defense,
with its reliance on the private production of defense equipment, most of the
federal agencies that are responsible for the supporting infrastructure (high-
way, tunnels, bridges, rail systems, airports, water supply systems, etc.) have
established programs for extensive private support in building, financing, and
operating that infrastructure. At the state, city, and county levels, contracting
out has been more pervasive. At the state level, in addition to infrastructure,
it has involved data processing, health services, correction, education, and
welfare.[48]

Contracting out is viewed as appropriate not only by the federal government, but also by states and local counties for reducing costs, decreasing
superfluous public employment, and forging useful connections between the
public and the private sectors. In theory, contracting out and delegating the
execution of government programs may lead, if one is to believe certain

authors, to the tendency of the federal government to become primarily a policy formulator and overseer of its outsourcing activities. At all levels it may, in certain conditions, lead to the establishment of broad, useful relations between government agencies and private providers of increasingly specialized business services involving data processing, engineering, managerial, legal, and financial services. Yet one should not forget that while outside contracting may increase government flexibility with regard to the choice among alternative suppliers, it may also have certain negative impacts both on its agencies and on these suppliers. Once a supplier is chosen, decisions may become irreversible for many years. Contractors may not only furnish the goods and services contracted for, but may also suggest and influence the decisions on what ought to be bought and on how to assess what has been bought. Surrendering sovereignty to contractors may undermine the accountability of governments; close surveillance of the private firms is required in order to avoid waste and corruption. The suppliers themselves may also suffer: companies serving the specialized government market may develop capabilities different from those required for successful operation in traditional commercial markets. Only the careful balancing of the yields of contracting out with the cost of managing, enforcing, and monitoring the process can guarantee that private production will indeed be more rewarding and less costly than production by a public entity.[49]

3.4. Reshuffling Welfare

The industrialized developed countries are increasingly preoccupied by broadening demographic changes, mutations in labor market participation, and the persistence of long-term unemployment and large poverty pockets, as well as by the relation of these transformations to the expanding volume and scope of income transfers. All these countries are confronted by the problems raised by an aging population, that is, life span increases; intergenerational shifts; marked increases in single-parent families and the proportion of children born out of wedlock; growing pressures with regard to labor market participation – gender-specific, educational, technological; increases in the needs for pensions, income support, and various forms of assistance, including unemployment compensation; and, last but not least, rising health care costs.

In all the countries under consideration, any attempt at coping with these problems brings forth the following questions with regard to each program separately and for all of them jointly: (1) How can the further growth of the given program(s) be limited? (2) How can the methods of financing these program(s) be changed so as to lower the state's contribution? (3) How can eligibility to the level and scope of the benefits provided be reduced? (4)

How can the structure of the program(s) be altered so as to be open to various alternatives, including privatization? All the reform trials of the indicated programs, which have gained in intensity since the late 1970s and early 1980s on, have moved more or less decisively along some or all of the possible paths indicated. The variations in extents and results have been due to historicopolitical circumstances, unforeseen changes, and the resistances and constraints built within each country's specific socioeconomic framework and tradition.

Consider first the evolution in Great Britain. Since the late 1970s, attempts at serious reform were guided there by the Conservatives' oppositions to Labour's philosophy of "cradle to grave" provision of security by the state and by their own emphases on privatization and people's capacity to provide for themselves. Legislative acts have been adopted almost annually since then concerning social security, the country's most important vehicle for the distribution and redistribution of resources, accounting by far for "the single largest proportion of public expenditure." The changes enacted have affected policies, regulations, and administration with the object of reducing expenditures. But three major unfavorable demographic trends have driven continued growth in overall spending: steady increases in the number of retirement pensioners, the number of divorces and therefore of children in need, and the number of sick and disabled people. Under these conditions, to reduce expenditures, the government would have had to substantially cut virtually all benefits – but it declined to take this road. It chose instead selective cuts, notably in housing benefits (to offset increases in income support and family credit), in the benefits available to the unemployed and the young, and in increments to pensions (by indexing the latter to price changes rather than wage changes). Further, various paths to privatization were opened in the system. First, employers were given the right to pay sickness benefits and maternity allowances themselves, in exchange for full compensation via a reduction in their national insurance contributions. Second, employers were given the right to contract out the state setup concerning personal pensions. The State Earnings Related Pension Scheme (SERPS) gave all the employees a chance to enter an earnings-related pension program; then, employers were given the right to set up private pension schemes, provided that the latter matched the state-sponsored one. By the mid-1980s, about half of the workforce was in SERPS and half participated in the private schemes. Overall, under the indicated reforms, the unemployed and certain families with children lost ground, many of the sick and disabled remained "at the boundaries of poverty," and a number of pensioners felt detached from the living standards of the working population, whether they participated or not in the privatization schemes. With regard to the other key element of the welfare state, the National Health Service (NHS), no substantial changes were envisaged. Toward the end of the Thatcher years, a White Paper included proposals for creating an internal health market, but the principles that had guided the NHS in the past were reaffirmed as applicable into the next century, including keeping the system "open to all regardless of income, and financed mainly out of taxation." Potential for real change is present, but the political costs still seem to be too high to allow a decisive shift toward a more regulated health care market.[50]

In France – the next country on our list – welfare reforms would have to tackle seriously the familiar problems of effectiveness, financing, benefits, and structure. But, as some French analysts have put it, while the French system of social protection is certainly in crisis, nobody is politically ready to focus fully on its ills and propose "lasting solutions." To start with, the French welfare system remains popular, is highly complex, and presents appreciable built-in resistance to deep changes. Efforts to reform often face the danger of social unrest. In addition, in order to be effective, decisions have to be reached in some 540 institutions, and a consensus must be achieved between the representatives of the state, employers, and employees. The French social security system, as I have already indicated, provides pensions, unemployment compensation, and family allowances, as well as national health care. It is the key part of the system of social protection, which includes pensions and other benefits provided by the "local" governments (i.e., by *départements* [roughly counties] and municipalities). Certain efforts have been made, particularly from the early 1990s on, to somewhat reduce the levels of pensions, unemployment compensation, and family allocations, but they have led to violent demonstrations; thus far, overall expenditures have continued to increase in relation to the growth of the GNP. The aging of the population continually pushes increases in the volume of pensions. While persons sixty-five years and over represented 9.6 percent of the population in 1931 and 12.8 percent in 1985, their share in the total population may near 20 percent by the year 2000. In addition, the ratio of retirees to the young, active population is increasing, due to a decreasing mortality rate. A 1993 reform relates the amount of pensions to a new "social contribution" basis, namely to the twenty-five best-paid years rather than to the ten best-paid, and brings the retirement age back to sixty (instead of fifty-nine, as had been decided in 1982). Increases in unemployment have also led to increases in the total volume of social spending, but unemployment compensation was somewhat reduced in 1992–1993 in order to generate higher incentives for job hunting. At the same time, the crucial allocations for children and families were also reduced for all wage earners. Finally, various measures transferred the responsibility for pensions, unemployment compensation, and family allocations to counties and municipalities, thus increasing, with as yet uncharted consequences, the variations of allocations among areas.

The French National Health System is still one of the most liberal (and most complicated) in Europe. Payments to providers involve a system composed of a statutory health insurance fund, mutual insurance companies (*mutuelles*), and supplementary insurance from private institutions. Costs remain high in relation to those in the other European countries, but the price levels for health services are relatively lower than in the OECD as a whole. The government has made various attempts to restrain the overall income of doctors and has put a cap on the budgets of both private and public hospitals, among which patients may freely choose. According to a UN study, health services for virtually the whole population and the still generous welfare benefits "have certainly made poverty a rare phenomenon in France."[51]

The German welfare system, to which I turn now, distinguishes sharply between social security and social assistance – as I pointed out in Chapter 1. The former, predicated on the respect of status differentials and on family priorities, constitutes a "legitimate" system of social insurance, while the latter is designed only as a "safety net" for those not qualified to join the former. The treaty of unification of 1990, which sanctioned the absorption of Eastern Germany, also extended to it the FRG's welfare legislation. The emphasis of the social security system on status involves the direct linkage between the size of the contributions to social security (up to 25 percent of salaries over and above taxes on income) and the size of benefits. As in the United States, this linkage results in a differentiated level of income support in unemployment and retirement, similar to the one prevailing at work. This close correlation between contributions and benefits strengthens the perception that contributions are not a tax but an insurance premium and gives cohesion to a large social opposition to the change of the system.

Like all the advanced industrial states, Germany has an aging population: its "dependency ratio" of retirees to those of working age is projected to rise sharply after the year 2000. Under the impact of demographic and technological changes, health care expenditures (for the Statutory Health Insurance system, which insures 90 percent of the population), as well as those for pensions, have tended to rise faster than the GNP. A basic health care reform focusing on cost control mechanisms took place in 1988. Cutbacks in social security have remained limited: a cutback occurring in 1982 concerned only unemployment rates (whose basis shifted from full work income, including overtime and bonuses, to basic work income only). In Germany, social security has not attracted the same hostility as social assistance, which has never acquired the legitimacy of the former. This hostility sharply increased in the 1980s in the presence of rising unemployment among already resident "guest workers," notably from Yugoslavia and Turkey, and under the pressure of large immigrations from Eastern Europe. To cope with these changes, many permanent work permits have been downgraded to temporary status, and increased federal funds have been made available to the *Länder* for work creation projects to employ social assistance claimants at a salary equivalent to about 60 percent of the average individual income. Wider problems of welfare restructuring are under discussion, but some of them are viewed essentially as matters of debate for the next century.[52]

Quite different is the situation in the United States, where the entire Roosevelt and Johnson legacies in all matters related to social insurance are in debate. The immediate focus from the early 1990s on seemed to be on certain aspects of "welfare" in the narrow sense of social assistance to the poor – but heated discussions began rapidly to involve also Social Security and the health programs (Medicare and Medicaid) enacted by the Johnson administration in 1965. The Republican Contract with America laid down before the 1994 elections the policy principles for the projected Republican majority in the 104th Congress. As in Germany, the Contract continued to make the traditional distinction between social security and social assistance ("welfare"). Concerning the former, it even called for "equity" for senior citizens, an equity involving notably an increase in the Social Security threshold for the retirees who would continue to work and a reduction in the Social Security tax. Concerning welfare, however, and in particular Aid to Families with Dependent Children (AFDC), the Contract – reminiscent of Reagan policies – set as its goal the reform of the system so as to "reduce government dependency, attack illegitimacy, require welfare recipients to work, and cut welfare spending."[53] Yet when the Republicans did secure their majority in the 104th Congress, the House Republican leaders simultaneously raised decisive issues relating to the immediate reform of the entire health program as well, that is, to Medicare, which provides health insurance for recipients of Social Security, and to Medicaid, which provides grants to the states for part of medical assistance to various groups of the poor.

Let us rapidly consider the main issues in these debates. Certain critics have reasserted that by now Social Security itself is an obsolete "entitlement" program that has gotten too big and too costly, has been adding to the country's debt burden, and has been predicated on "an unacceptable generational inequity." Let me start by pointing out that the program is indeed an "entitlement": this is simply a term used in government parlance to designate a program for which Congress has set eligibility criteria, which, when met, automatically "entitles" its appropriately designated recipients to its benefits. There are some 400 federal entitlement programs that entitle the proper recipients to their respective benefits. Social Security and Medicare are entitlement programs to which their beneficiaries are contributing or have contributed through taxes on their incomes. It is a retirement income scheme for former workers and employees, but not only that. It is also an insurance system that protects workers and their families well before they reach age sixty-five. It is, in fact, equivalent to a $300,000 disability policy or a $200,000 insurance policy for everyone who is paying into it. In addition, it is an antipoverty program. In the early 1990s, it lifted the incomes of 9.6 million Americans over age sixty-five above the poverty threshold. Thanks to the financial aid it provides, it makes it possible for many parents to avoid moving in with their children and becoming a burden on them.

The payroll taxes paid in the Social Security trust funds (the OASDI insurance fund) may be legally used only for paying benefits due and for covering administrative costs. The surplus revenue must be invested in special-issue government securities; the government must repay this loan with interest, which in turn bolsters the funds. In 1994, income exceeded outgo by over $58 billion, thus reducing the reported federal deficit from $260 billion to $202 billion. Since 1937, when Social Security started collecting payroll taxes, $4.3 trillion have been paid into OASDI trust funds, of which $3.9 trillion have been paid out in benefits and administrative costs. This left a surplus of about $436.4 billion by the end of 1994, which was lent to the government. In order to meet the increased costs of the large number of baby boomers who will begin to retire about 2020, responsible administrators of the system have suggested that it would be appropriate to invest some of the system's savings into higher-return private investments rather than putting everything into government bonds.[54] Less sanguine advisers suggest that what should be done quickly – even though Social Security will stay solvent until 2030 – is to change the benefit formula so as to curb the cost of living adjustment (COLA), tie retirement benefits more closely to a worker's payroll contribution, raise the retirement age, and, eventually, break the common retirement pool by allowing workers to opt out of the Social Security system, giving up the claims on some or all future benefits in exchange for a reduction in payroll taxes today.[55] The debate continues.

President Clinton's own proposals for a comprehensive national health care system, made soon after the beginning of his first administration, did not receive a legislative sanction. As was the case before that failed initiative, close to three-quarters of the U.S. population continue to rely on private health insurance, provided by some 1,000 private companies. Those under age sixty-five and their dependents obtain private health insurance either through direct purchase or through their employers. Medicare, the national health insurance program for the aged and the disabled administered by the federal government, is still the single largest health insurer in the country, covering (in the mid-1990s) 13 percent of the population, including virtually all those sixty-five years of age or older (31 million people), as well as certain persons with disabilities (3 million people). It should be noted that while Medicare covered less than half of the total medical care expenses of the elderly in the early 1990s, its own expenses were increasing faster than its revenues (namely, taxes paid by all employed individuals plus premiums and deductibles); in the mid-1990s it was projected to remain solvent only until the year 2002. As proposed by the Republicans, the main lines along which a series of reforms of Medicare should take place over the next years should include sharp increases in premiums, deductibles, and copayments, the eventual use of flat benefits (i.e., vouchers) for most beneficiaries, annual limits on the growth of the program, and reductions of payments to doctors, hospitals, and other suppliers of goods and services (e.g., reductions of the amounts allowed to hospitals, notably for new construction, purchases of new equipment, medical training, and costs of treating indigent patients). Eventually, in this case also, the beneficiaries would be called upon to choose between Medicare and various private health plans offered essentially by HMOs and structured to keep costs down. The government may still continue to be the insurer, reimbursing doctors and hospitals for services provided for the beneficiaries who would choose to stay in the Medicare program (and pay high premiums); for those choosing a private health program, the government would pay a fixed amount to the plan chosen by each beneficiary (i.e., the equivalent of a beneficiary's voucher). Reformed Medicare would, in the long run, resemble in various respects the Federal Employees Health Benefits Program (offered to some 9 million employees, retirees, and dependents). In that plan, however, the government contribution is not a flat dollar amount but equals a certain percentage of the average premiums for the six biggest health plans. Critics of the indicated Medicare reforms assert that besides downsizing the federal government, they involve in practice a direct attack on the intricate set of cross-subsidies built into the prevailing health system, as well as a method of fiscal coercion in favor of poorer health care plans, relying on eventually depreciating vouchers and prohibitive increases in premiums, deductibles, and copayments.[56]

The fundamental Republican goal of downsizing the government via the restructuring of the federal antipoverty program – as conceived during the Roosevelt and the Johnson administrations – has aimed to reduce or simply end the government guarantee of assistance to people in need. It has focused both on Medicaid, the second component of the federal health program covering notably children and the aged poor, and on the AFDC programs providing benefits for single-parent families. In the early 1990s, Medicaid embraced preventive, acute, and long-term care services for 25 million people, or 10 percent of the population, financed jointly by federal and state governments (the former matching the state Medicaid outlays at rates varying by state personal income levels). Eligible for Medicaid have been persons with low incomes, as well as those who are aged, blind, disabled, pregnant, or the parent of a dependent child. (Childless, nondisabled adults under age sixty-five, no matter how poor, have not been included in the program.) The vast number of the uninsured have received fewer services than the insured, from a variety of sources, the amount and scope of which have varied by community. Federal, state, and local governments have supported public health clinics and hospitals with the primary mission of providing care to the indigent. The Republicans have aimed to eliminate most federal standards and to hand over Medicaid to the states with a block-grant program, empowering the states to decide who gets covered and who does not. The effect of deep cuts in health care and the prospect of the end of the fees for whatever the doctor orders will profoundly affect not only Medicare and Medicaid but also private insurance costs and programs, as well as the number of the uninsured, for years to come.

The Congress's 1996 landmark votes concerning the AFDC program and the program's redefinition as a kind of temporary assistance have asserted in fact the will of the Congress to "end welfare as we know it." The objectives achieved in this regard have been: the transfer of a vast new authority to the states; the requirement that states make 50 percent of aid recipients work by the year 2000; and the abolition of the federal guarantee of assistance and its replacement by block grants to the states (similar to Medicare block grants). The states now have the option to prohibit (under certain conditions) aid to children born out of wedlock to mothers under age eighteen, and to deny additional aid to mothers after a maximum of five years on welfare. An array of antipoverty programs will eventually be replaced with limited-sum payments to the states. Whether or not all this results from the pursuit of budget cuts in order to achieve a problematic budget balance in the early years of the twenty-first century is not of great import to our study. What is critically significant is that, in the process, the federal government is being markedly downsized. Senator Daniel Patrick Moynihan has called this process a "devolution," that is, a transfer from the federal government to the states, a change that he perceptively defines as "a stage in the long alternating history of federalism." In addition, the effects of increasing deep cuts in Medicare, Medicaid, and the restructured AFDC are bound to have eventual wide repercussions on the entire medical system – on the growth of HMOs, the number of doctors working in managed care organizations (and their personal income levels), the growth of alternative private health organizations created by the doctors themselves, the programs offered and their costs, the number of the uninsured, and the availability of public and private hospitals and other health facilities.[57]

3.5. Concluding Comments

An ideological and political upheaval, which began under Thatcher and Reagan at the beginning of the 1980s, spread and increasingly legitimized the ideas that the state (or the federal government in the United States) had become too big and too intrusive in the economy and was spending too much and crowding out private investments and initiative, hampering private savings, and distorting personal incentives. The new ideas included, in addition, the belief that the welfare state was rewarding dependency rather than encouraging work, breeding illegitimacy and destructive behavior rather than requiring welfare recipients to assume responsibility for their own decisions, and providing handouts instead of extending a helping hand to the neediest. As I indicated above, the latter set of ideas also gained increasing acceptance, notably in the United States. The common goals of conservative reformers, in Great Britain, in the United States, and increasingly in other Western countries, has been to redefine the scope of the state, to dislodge it from preponderant positions, and to confine it to clearly circumscribed boundaries. The primary tools for reaching these goals have been crucial privatizations in Great Britain and the dismantlement of the welfare system in the United States. In practice, of course, both instruments have been put to wide use by these and other countries, though in different degrees and combinations.

Privatization – or "denationalization," as the process is sometimes called – clearly involves the sale of public assets, the shift from publicly to privately produced goods and services, and the disengagement of government from different responsibilities. But as we saw in practice (and as we shall see anew further on), the frontiers between public and private sectors are not always either easy to define or clearcut in all cases. Indeed, states are providers and purchasers, entrepreneurs and trustees, regulators and umpires in many industrial, financial, or commercial ventures in which complex interpenetrations occur between the public and the private sectors, taking many forms in the process. Some of these intermixtures are rooted in mutual interdependencies, for example, in the production of defense equipment and in telecommunications. Moreover, not all downsizing is welcome, even to customary proponents of smaller government. Some decisive shifts toward the private sector may call forth extensive resistance from unexpected quarters. Such opposition is often of sufficient strength to derail any serious attempts at privatization, even of such appropriate assets as state-owned lands (no matter how extensive the latter may be). Notwithstanding the complexity of the subject, many discussions on privatization tend to represent only restatements of the traditional debates about the merits of market versus nonmarket methods of resource allocation. Unfortunately, even the theoretical literature tends to deal in terms of ideal confrontations between perfectly competitive markets versus the complete state provision of goods and services, without much regard either to the enormous diversity of public versus private structures involved or to their complex interweavings.[58]

For the welfare state also, there are no precise boundary determinations.

However, it is possible to identify its main programs. As I have indicated, these consist, on the one hand, of Social Security and health care – primarily for the aged and the disabled – and, on the other hand, of social assistance, providing income and all or certain forms of health care for the needy, along with certain benefits in kind, various educational subsidies for the young, and aid to families and needy children. Not surprisingly, given the difficulty of measuring outputs and benefits in the social sciences – namely, cost per unit of output and yield per unit of results – relatively few studies have attempted to detail the relative efficiency of the public versus the private provision of certain social services, income supplements, educational subsidies, and so on. Many of the ideas about the dismantlement of welfare are often simple re-takes of nineteenth-century ideas and values aimed at replacing the state income redistribution with all-encompassing private charity activities, if possible and feasible, and, if not, with widely decentralized and dissimilar regional and municipal initiatives and decisions.

Economists, rather than politicians, have suggested that the provision of benefits to the aged, the sick, and the unemployed makes it unnecessary for people to save against these eventualities, and accordingly leads to lower efforts to both work and save. But in fact, economics does not provide an unambiguous prediction concerning the impact of Social Security and associated welfare expenditures on saving level. Actually, as we have seen, in the United States, Social Security trust funds are invested in the federal general fund debt. The substantial accumulation of Social Security reserves will increase aggregate savings only if this accumulation reduces the unified budget surplus. But so will any other method of increasing the unified budget surplus, so that there is no special economic reason to use the Social Security trust fund for this purpose.[59]

The idea that there are actually no valid reasons for high-income persons to receive any Social Security benefits has often been advanced in the United States. However, if the receipt of Social Security benefits were to be income tested – as is the case for social assistance recipients – high-income earners would necessarily pressure for the right to quit the system long before retirement. Then the remaining Social Security system, with its income-tested pensioners would become a quite unstable low-income structure superimposed on the even lower means-tested social assistance structure.

The health care systems accompanying these two structures vary enormously among the industrial countries in terms of individual copayments, deductibles, coverage, hospital charges, and physicians' fees. The problems involved are handled essentially within two basic frameworks. The first consists of a national health organization that equilibrates the higher and the lower costs of health care of demographically distinct parts of the population within a single national insurance scheme. The second – in the United States, for instance – tends toward an increasingly wide variety of health insurance schemes involving a fixed state provision (a voucher) per qualified beneficiary along with continuous changes to (and pressures on) these beneficiaries' co-payments and deductibles, as well as to hospital charges and doctors' fees. Both systems reflect divergent social and political conditions rather than comparative economic evaluations.[60]

In many respects the Thatcher–Reagan upheaval and the assumptions and orientations reaffirmed in the Contract with America seem anchored in ideas and values typical of the nineteenth century rather than the twentieth, namely the belief in a smoothly working market without interferences, the existence of limited governments with devotion to well-balanced budgets, and a socially healthy environment with high family cohesion and generous care for the elderly and the needy. With regard to policy, all this suggests the need to replace expanding governments and their macro-demand-centered strategies with small governments, decentralized micro-supply-oriented regimes, smoothly running markets, institutional competition, and fully efficient private enterprises.

Many legitimate doubts may arise with regard to the claims about small, parsimonious governments and traditional respect for balanced budgets, sparing taxation, and the absence of efforts to redistribute income and exercise control over the allocation of output – the whole of it embedded in an ideal social framework with strong values and lasting compassion for the unfortunate. But all this seems certainly realistic and desirable to certain politicians. Yet one may ask, to start with, if government spending, parsimony, and balanced budgets are really what it takes to have a healthy and growing economy, why are the developed Western economies with the highest ratios of public expenditures to GNP precisely the fastest-growing economies? A balanced budget, or a reduction of a budget deficit, is supposedly necessary to increase the real and financial resources available for private investment. But is it really so certain that such a reduction will necessarily generate the additional investment? Some economists (e.g., Robert Eisner) have pointed out that in the United States such deficits have been associated with actual increases in both consumption and investment and have not been detrimental to private investment. True, the Keynesian strategy, which implied an increase in government spending and a decrease in its revenues in a recession – and contrariwise the avoidance of deficits in "normal" times – has fallen into disuse. Its eclipse has left room for unrealistic fears that rising ratios of debt to GNP will mortgage "the future of our children," as if what we are really bequeathing are just deficits and not the physical and human capital financed by these "deficits."[61]

The social framework has changed in developed economies long since the alleged "good old times." As Richard A. Musgrave once noted, "We do not have an idyllic society of small rural communities: we have not only large government but also large corporations, modern industry, banking, etc. Because of this integration, common policies and business cycles affect all of us but their regional impacts differ. It is only fair, therefore, that the consequences of joint policies be borne jointly."[62] In the developed Western societies, maintaining support for cost-effective social insurance and for reasonable antipoverty programs seems to me necessary, among other reasons, for social stability, even though the political environment for such support has drastically changed. The governments have played significant roles in the redistribution of income toward the lower strata of income receivers, and I do not think that this role can seriously be easily abandoned.

Downsizing the public sector can in certain conditions be a very valuable public instrument of management, be it through various forms of privatization, through reducing employment via contracting out, through decentralization and shifting power to regions (states) and municipalities, or through dismantling certain services. But it would be erroneous to view them as always necessarily superior to direct employment by government. If, for instance, contracting out were always superior to direct employment, large corporations would cease to exist: there would be only contractors and no employers. I also tend to doubt that all public programs are by definition "useless," while private uses of funds are in all circumstances productive. Rather, alternative uses of funds and resources should be weighed against each other at the margin – instead of arbitrarily deciding in one direction only.

4   Restructuring the State's Foundations

4.1. The Breakdown of the Soviet System

The Soviet system's protracted economic slowdown and growing "malaise," treated at the beginning of Mikhail Gorbachev's perestroika as correctable deficiencies, started from the late 1980s to be viewed increasingly as incurable diseases of the all-embracing party-state order. In the ensuing uncharted, chaotic processes of disintegration of the Soviet system, begun in the early 1990s, the decaying USSR was sucked into the whirlpools of its dislocated state machine and dissolving multinational empire. At the time, no compelling, conclusive analysis could be effectively carried out with regard to the policy choices between a so-called shock therapy – involving a simultaneous resort to rapid price liberalization, economic stabilization, and privatization – and a gradualistic process involving various preliminary combinations of legislative and restructuring measures. The passage from the decomposing centralized administration to a new economic order indeed proved largely uncontrollable and treacherous. The rapidly sinking central power was leaving behind it resilient centers of power in key positions in industry, banking, and the agricultural collectives, letting them expand their connections with the "shadow economy." Conflicts between various still functioning government organs and their contradictory legislative decisions, and a crisscrossing of more or less spontaneously emerging trade and commercial relations, made the entire socioeconomic organism drift aimlessly.

Before presenting some of the important highlights of 1990 and 1991 – the last years of the dislocating Soviet party-state – let me recall briefly the predicaments of the Soviet economy at the end of the 1980s. According to the 1990 disclosures of N. Fiodorov, chairman of the Committee of the Supreme Soviet of the USSR, dealing with that country's "unproductive losses" in the late 1980s, half of the industrial output and 20 to 40 percent of the agricultural output had been considered "lost," along with similar percentages in construction, transport, trade, and so on, amounting to a total of close to 40 percent of the national product. The causes of this disastrous balance sheet, according to Fiodorov, were the growth through the years of two tendencies flourishing within a widespread system that concealed unproductive expenditures: a tendency to shift some of these expenditures onto the people's living standards, and a tendency of the managerial apparatus to appropriate part of the national income illegally and use it for deals in the "shadow economy."[1]

Another Soviet observer noted at the beginning of the 1990s that for the second time in a century, Russia was experiencing the tragedy and turmoils attendant on the collapse of state centralism. The debacle of the Communist Party – its downfall at the center of power, its splintering and crude internecine conflicts – left behind it a paralyzed, increasingly ineffective and fragmented administration, an unmanageable economy, widespread poverty, semistarvation, and uncontrollable interindustry and interethnic conflicts.[2] Soviet leaders and managers sought relief with increasing urgency: But how could this turmoil be overcome – or, at least, how could one move faster through it?

While a consensus of sorts was emerging as to the need of moving toward a different system of economic management, crucial differences of opinion remained as to the specific ways of coming out of the chaos and the means and pace needed to transit toward that new system. Eventually, these differences coalesced around three basic strategies. The first, embodied in the so-called Ryzhkov Plan, a product of archetypal technocrats, was outlined in December 1989 and finalized in May 1990 in Ryzhkov's "Economic Report to the Supreme Soviet." The second one, the so-called Shatalin Plan (also known as the "500 Days Plan"), was elaborated by an eleven-man liberal group formed by a joint decision of Mikhail Gorbachev and Boris Yeltsin; it was contained in a document released in August 1990 and officially entitled "Transition to the Market Economy." The third one, the Gorbachev Plan, a long, clumsy, and at times inconsistent amalgamation of the preceding two strategies was released in October 1990, embodied in an official document entitled "Basic Guidelines for the Stabilization of the National Economy and the Transition to a Market Economy." Let us briefly consider the key elements of the proposed strategies, the stages envisioned in the transition to a new economic model, and the reactions that they brought about in the prevailing hard times.

The Ryzhkov Plan set as its goal a regulated market economy. The prerequisites for this were stated to be real independence for enterprises to act as free goods producers, a mechanism for price formation sensitive to supply and demand, a competitive rather than a monopolized structure of production, a balanced financial situation, a firm monetary system, and reliable legal backup. But in order to avoid destroying the existing framework of economic links, as well as to protect the population from negative consequences, the government's "proposed variant of transition" would begin with a prepara tory stage in which the necessary legislative acts would first be adopted and put into force. Price, tax, and credit reforms would follow, opening the way to reductions in administrative restrictions and to various restructurings that would finally (by 1995) ensure the promotion of market mechanisms and a "more rational structure of economic links"[3] (Table 4.1). Soon, however, the rapidly worsening situation and the sharpening conflicts inside and outside the collapsing state administration brought the other proposals to the fore. In June 1990, the academician Abel Aganbeghian criticized the Ryzhkov proposal as lacking any "specific measures" for replacing the old management structure and for normalizing the consumer market and living conditions. A new working group including Ryzhkov met in August to reformulate the program so as to include, notably, the option of a onetime price increase, along with the determination of an adequate system of pay. This "democratization of price formation" was supposed, however, to let the center retain control over a "narrow range of prices." Eventually some of these ideas found their way into the Gorbachev Plan, which I examine further below.

In the meantime, while Ryzhkov was still elaborating his first plan, academician Stanislav S. Shatalin was contending that while the directive political center was trying to take leave from the plan-and-command system, it was failing to "fill the vacuum" with appropriate market methods of management. Yet, while stressing that the market was the only way out of the impasse, Shatalin was critical of the shock therapy applied in Poland under Western influence by Polish Deputy Premier Leszek Balcerowicz from January 1990 on. Instead of immediate price liberalization, as then practiced in Poland, Shatalin underlined the necessity for the Soviet Union of minimizing the cost of the transition and of getting by without a "price shock."[4] A few months later, however, the reform plan elaborated by the working group led by Shatalin noted first of all that the USSR's turmoil was due to "a general crisis of the socioeconomic system as well as of the national-state system and ideology." Discarding the perestroika methods as irrelevant and harmful, the group affirmed that the necessary passage to a market economy required, among other measures, the creation of a new Economic Union that would halt the breakdown of interrepublic economic ties. Each republic would be free to choose its own plan of economic reform independently but on the basis of common principles. In addition, each of these plans would have to be coordinated with the general transition plan. Reform would proceed in the following directions: first, the denationalization of certain assets, followed by limits on the distribution of products manufactured for state orders and by demonopolization; second, the removal of state control over certain price areas; third, implementation of a strict monetary, credit, and financial policy and the creation of a strong system of social support for the population; fourth, the beginning of an economic upswing under the newly evolving

Table 4.1. *Comparative Tabulation of the Three Major Soviet Plans of Transition*

Ryzhkov Plan	Shatalin Plan	Gorbachev Plan
Preparatory stage (up to end of 1990) Shaping the legal foundations of the market economy	**First 100 days (Oct. 1, 1990, to beginning 1991)** Denationalizing the economy: transfer to the population of housing and land assets; reorganization of large state enterprises into stock associations; privatization of small enterprises; granting of centralized emergency powers in the realm of monetary and financial policy	**Stage I** Financial and monetary improvement: reduction of the state budget deficit; suppression of the emission of money; restructuring of the banking system; regulation of enterprises' finances; privatization of property and implementation of land reform
	Days 100–250 Liberalization of prices: removal of state price controls over certain areas of output for production, for technical use, and for consumption and services; restraint of inflationary processes by financial and credit policies and reduction to zero of the budget deficit; cancellation of subsidies and grants	**Stage II** Gradual transition to market prices: liberalization of prices for a broad range of production and of technical outputs, as well as of consumer goods; retention of fixed state prices for one-third of all goods; broadening of denationalization; privatization of small enterprises; development of a market infrastructure
Middle stage (1991–1992) Reform of prices: introduction of a system of social support and of taxation; credit reform; development of diverse forms of ownership; improvement in the structure of production	**Days 250–400** Market stabilization: prevailing of supply and demand prices and of a balanced budget opening the way to the convertibility of the ruble, the broadening of competition and of market relations – without a major restructuring of production	**Stage III** Broadening of the sphere of market relations via the housing market, wage restructuring, changes in taxes, and expansion of the infrastructure, along with adoption of various assistance programs
Last stage (1993–1995) Reductions of administrative restrictions: intensification of competition; active antimonopoly policy; vigorous financial and credit policy – all allowing the "market mechanism to gather speed"	**Days 400–500** Beginning of the upswing: privatization – by the 500th day, no less than 70% of the industrial enterprises are changed from state enterprises into joint-stock companies, sold, or converted to lease holdings; conditions then exist for the full functioning of market mechanisms of self-regulation	**Stage IV** Accelerated formation of self-regulatory mechanisms: demonopolization, denationalization, and privatization; predominance of processes governed by supply and demand, which creates the preconditions for solving the key problems of the transition to a market economy

market conditions. For each of these crucial "directions" the appropriate backup with a legal foundation would have to be promptly provided, and the entire proposal would be carried out in 500 days, divided into four progressive stages (see Table 4.1).[5] The coincidental election of Boris N. Yeltsin to the position of chairman of the Supreme Soviet of Russia hastened the process of disintegration of the USSR. Yeltsin rapidly adopted the Shatalin Plan as his program of economic reform and by August 15, 1990, this plan, rebaptized as the Yeltsin Plan (as the *Literaturnaia gazeta* then put it), was set to open "500 days of hope and risk for Russia."[6] Yeltsin announced that the plan would indeed be implemented by Russia starting on November 1, 1990, notwithstanding the "objective obstacles" that had prevented its implementation as a USSR program.[7] Concomitantly, Russia's Council of Ministers suspended the application on its territory of various resolutions of the USSR Council of Ministers.

In the meantime, Gorbachev, who was still at the head of the USSR, released his "Basic Guidelines" for the stabilization of the economy and transition to a sui generis market economy, in October. As the official text itself indicated, the document was prepared on the basis of the "program elaborated by the working group of M. S. Gorbachev and B. N. Yeltsin" (i.e., the Shatalin group) and by the government on the basis of the "proposals made at the sessions of the Supreme Soviet." Acknowledging certain evident features of the Soviet Union's disintegration, the text specified that henceforth the sovereign republics were free to carry out legislative regulations concerning the disposal, use, and possession of "all the national wealth located on their territory" and that they could resolve the questions relating to "prices, incomes, and the social protection of the population." However, a concerted financial and currency policy would still aim at strengthening the ruble "as the only means of payment on the territory of the Union." After defining the specific spheres left to the Soviet Union's activity besides the improvement of finances and money supply (namely, defense, communications and transportation, energy, and research), the guidelines asserted that the "most urgent" tasks facing the country were stabilization and the development of a "full-fledged" market. These tasks were to be achieved in four stages: first, the establishment of financial and monetary stability; second, a gradual transition to a flexible system of price formation; third, on broadening of market relations; and fourth, restructuring, via the formation of self-regulatory mechanisms "squeezing out" the command structure organs of the administrative system (see Table 4.1).[8]

Before going further, let me note that the three indicated strategies proceeded in different directions starting from three different initial approaches to the transition to the market, namely (a) the legal framework (Ryzhkov), (b) denationalizations (Shatalin), and (c) financial and monetary stabilization

(Gorbachev). Each of the programmers was aware of the difficult tasks the transformation of the economy would require, but differed on the necessary steps to be taken, the pace of implementing the measures envisaged, the appropriate coordination among the tasks viewed as imperative along the way, and the actual scope and impact of each program.

In the meantime, the processes of disintegration were continuing in numerous directions. In February 1991 Yeltsin openly attacked Gorbachev and demanded his resignation because, according to him, what the president of the USSR wanted was not to do any essential restructuring but "to preserve the system, preserve rigid centralization of power, and not give independence to the republics, especially not to Russia."[9] As 1991 continued to unfold, recriminations, reconciliations, and then new breakups and reciprocal denunciations further destabilized the Union and exacerbated the innumerable tensions and divergent orientations among the republics. While Russia pretended to follow the Shatalin Plan, V. S. Pavlov, the prime minister of the USSR, launched – allegedly for the benefit of the Union as a whole – a vaguely revised version of Gorbachev's "Basic Guidelines." Pavlov's report to the Supreme Soviet of the USSR proposed a combination of the usual administrative methods with the use of so-called market tools (namely, a monetary reform) in order to "guarantee" changes with respect to ownership transfers, bank credits, and price controls.[10] But Pavlov's monetary reform was extremely unpopular and led to all kinds of conflicts, strikes, and strife among the nationalities. By April 24, 1991, Gorbachev and Yeltsin, along with the leaders of eight other republics, signed a joint statement for the "restoration of the constitutional order" via the adoption of a new treaty of union and a new constitution. That same day, the Central Committee of the Communist Party was debating in plenary session how to extricate the economy from its crisis and whether or not to accept Gorbachev's offer to resign as the party's secretary general. The Central Committee finally decided to keep him at his post "in the highest interests of the country." Yet soon afterward, particularly from the beginning of June 1991 on, the internecine conflicts deepened further. Soon Boris Yeltsin was elected to the newly created post of first president of the RSFSR (Russian Soviet Federal Socialist Republic), defeating his main rival, Nikolai Ryzhkov. By July 20, 1991, Yeltsin had signed a decree banning all party units from agencies and state administrations in the RSFSR and its republics and from all state organizations, institutions, concerns, and enterprises. The drive to dismantle the party-state apparatus of power on the territory of the RSFSR opened the door wide to the splintering of the party throughout the collapsing Union.[11]

In August 1991, the party technocrats aimed to reassert the power of the old system and their own USSR-wide control through a putsch. They set up an "emergency" committee under the Supreme Soviet's leadership, confined

Gorbachev under house arrest, and expected the army to join them. The coup failed: the effective chiefs of the army did not side with the conspiracy. Gorbachev was reinstated in his old (and henceforth totally ineffective) "leadership" position at the head of the Soviet Union. This unsuccessful attempt to shape the course of history discredited the dogmatists, deepened national and regional conflicts, and sharply increased the political, social, and economic power of Russia's new leaders. By October, as the republics were still negotiating among themselves, Yeltsin affirmed his decision to form a proreform cabinet and push resolutely for economic reform in Russia, so as to obtain "real results" by the autumn of 1992.[12] Finally, on December 8, 1991, the republics that were signatories of the so-called Minsk Accord – Russia, Belarus, and the Ukraine – proclaimed the Soviet Union dissolved. On December 25, 1991, Gorbachev finally resigned as president of the USSR, since, as he put it, "a policy line aimed at dismembering the country and disuniting the states has prevailed."

As noted earlier, the bankrupt Soviet regime left behind various centers of power in the disjointed state apparatus, at the heads of ministries, industries, mines, banks, trade, transports, and agricultural collectives. It is these fiefdoms that singly or in various forms of association still attempt to harness in their own favor the contradictory processes of change. In Section, 4.2, I sketch the interplay of the factors that are shaping the ongoing conflicting transformation processes. In Section 4.3, I indicate the characteristic features of the "capitalism of the officialdom" – the so-called nomenklatura capitalism – that has been surging forward from the first phase of the "destatization" (or privatization) of Russia. In Section 4.4, I focus on the spread of poverty after the collapse of the old system and on the new forms and extent of social assistance. I present my concluding remarks in Section 4.5.

4.2. Characteristics of the Transformation Process

In a study entitled *The Economy of the USSR: Summary and Recommendations*, released by the IMF, the World Bank, and the OECD in 1990, the international organizations pertinently recognized that two basic approaches were crystallizing with respect to the processes of transformation of the USSR's economy. In the conservative scenario, reform was to start with some tightening of fiscal policy, while structural reforms would proceed slowly: prices were to be adjusted but remain largely under administrative control, with only gradual macrostabilization. By contrast, the radical approach aimed simultaneously at macrostabilization, liberalization of most prices, and the start of the privatization of small-scale enterprises.[13]

Various Western advisers of some East European economies and of Russia pressed strongly in favor of the second approach. Let me recall briefly their main theses. Jeffrey Sachs, of Harvard, stated in January 1991 that there should be "four simultaneous parts to a program of rapid market transformation. First, let prices find market-clearing levels. Second, set the private sector free by removing bureaucratic restrictions. Third, bring the state sector under control, by privatization. Fourth, maintain overall macro-stability through restrictive credit and balanced budgets." Sachs put special emphasis on the need to take all four steps simultaneously, asserting that "reform is a seamless web. Piecemeal changes cannot work."[14] A supporting group of MIT and Harvard professors, headed by Olivier Blanchard, likewise argued that the East European countries "now have little choice but to move on all fronts at once – or not move at all." In a direct answer to any and all "gradualists," Blanchard and his group added: "Stabilization cannot wait, nor can price liberalization": step-by-step price liberalization, of the sort envisioned in the now defunct five-hundred-day program, "triggers purchases in anticipation of price increases." Comparing the drive of Eastern Europe toward the market with measures that had been needed to stabilize Latin American countries, the group asserted that the task of propelling a former communist economy toward the market and that of repairing the damage to an existing market economy were not "so different as to require a drastically different approach," and then added that "most of the logic behind the stabilization package applies to Eastern Europe as well."[15] In another paper, one member of the group, Rudiger Dornbusch, proposed the following accelerating sequence for the former communist countries: "Day 1: Establish rules of the game and of an economic model; Day 2: Create institutions, the fiscal, legal, pensions, and social safety net systems; Day 3: Implement macro balancing; Day 4: Move ahead with privatization; Day 5: Introduce trade liberalization and convertibility; Day 6: Integrate into the world economy via trade not aid; Day 7: Revamp domestic finance." All this followed by the advice: "Do not sacrifice priorities in trying to 'manage' a soft landing."[16]

Let us see now how and why the actual measures taken by the Russian leaders fluctuated between the "conservative" and the "radical" approaches, keeping in mind the special characteristics of the Soviet legacy: the closed nature of the economy, its particularly biased price structures, its distorted exposures to market pressures, the disintegrating links between its fiefdoms and its former republics, the general lack of experience with private ownership, and the inertia, open opposition, or hidden resistance to change characterizing various parts of its population.

On December 25, 1991 – the day of the official final collapse of the USSR – Russia's President Boris Yeltsin signed a decree he had promised two months earlier concerning price liberalization. The decree specified that as of January 2, 1992, a changeover was to be carried out in the main "to the use of free (market) prices and rates, formed under the influence of supply and demand. In addition, the use of state-regulated prices (rates) was "to be established by enterprises and organizations regardless of their form of ownership, only for a limited range of production and technical output and for basic consumer goods and services." Essentially, prices for bread, milk, sugar, vodka, medicine, fuel, electricity, rents, and fares were to continue to be regulated but could rise three to five times in amount. At the same time, however, the executive powers of the republics within the RSFSR – its territories, provinces, autonomous formations, and cities and local authorities – were authorized to change the list of consumer goods and services to which state-regulated prices and rates would be applied.[17] This shock therapy was launched on the date scheduled by a team of liberal economists led by the new Yeltsin-appointed premier, Yegor Gaidar. This price liberalization was supposed to lead to the standard results obtained elsewhere in market economies. Liberalization was to be followed by short-term hyperinflation, succeeded by a production upswing accompanied by moderate increases in prices. This is certainly part of what Yeltsin had had in mind on October 28, 1991, in offering his "pledge" about the eventual results of a "one-time changeover to market prices" – a "forced" measure, but certainly, a "necessary" one. As he put it, repeating the mantras of Gaidar and Sachs: "For approximately six months things will be worse for everyone, but then prices will fall, the consumer market will be filled with goods, and by the autumn of 1992 there will be economic stabilization."[18]

But soon after the reform was launched, the difficulty of its application in the country's widely diverse regions became obvious. As Gaidar himself would note, "The level of the ability of the government to govern is critically low. There is no control over what happens in the outer regions." Gaidar added that the main problem was "how not to collapse after we have been compelled to unfreeze prices and set new regulatory mechanisms in motion. The core of all this is the budget. If the budget survives after prices are unfrozen . . . there will be confidence after the initial jump in prices."[19] But in fact the government was increasingly losing its controls over the financial, monetary, and credit flows. Moreover, as Yeltsin stated publicly, the unfreezing of prices had not provided the hoped-for incentives for increased production. Quite the opposite. "The monopolists are ready to curtail production, shift to expensive outputs and even shut down production facilities. The customer remains quite defenseless." Yeltsin was adding that a series of adjustments – curbed monopolism, tightened credit and monetary policy, beginning privatization, adjusted taxes, and stepped-up social guarantees for the population – would effectively support the reform and extricate Russia from crisis.[20] But by May 1992, Grigori Yavlinski, the liberal rival of Yegor Gaidar, could readily chastise the government for failing to produce a deficit-free budget, miscalculating the decentralization of price controls, overestimating income from taxes and Western aid, and misunderstanding the actual impacts of high inflation on such decisive matters as the standard of living, production slumps, and the management of the economy.[21] In addition, following old, worn-out patterns of behavior, a large number of enterprises had been continuing to get raw materials and components from the suppliers on credit. The industries had thus been accumulating such enormous debts to the banks that the government had passed the point when it could have declared the enterprises bankrupt and solved the problem that way. By the beginning of July, the Gaidar government and the Central Bank had no other solution than to proclaim in a joint resolution that all mutual debts were to be frozen and that a new agency was henceforth to manage them. The latter divided all these obligations into three categories: obligations to the other republics of the Commonwealth of Independent States (CIS), obligations to one's own state; and debts to other enterprises. The first group was to be left "as is" until the CIS financial interrelations could be clarified; the second and the third were to be checked against one another and canceled whenever possible, while the government would extend certain credits if and when needed. By transferring the debts to the agency, all the enterprises were to begin "a new life": only current payments would remain on their books. However, as we shall see below, the industrialists would both continue to ask for massive state credits and, in their absence, continue to accumulate new trade debts.

In midsummer 1992, celebrating the first anniversary of the failed 1991 communist putsch, Gaidar asserted with feigned optimism that the government was mastering the levers of economic management, was overcoming the crisis of legitimacy caused by the collapse of Union structures, and was emerging as an "influential arbiter" in the affairs of the former Soviet republics. Actually, by that time the Russian government was under heightened pressure for the executives of the country's major industries (using parliamentary factions, leagues, and unions of industrialists) for massive state credits and for changes in the pace and direction of economic reform. In addition, the acting chairman of the Central Bank (a bank subordinated by law to the Supreme Soviet, not to the government) was strongly denouncing the strict monetary policy "conducted in Russia with the support of the IMF," affirming that the reform plan could actually "destroy Russia's economy."[22]

By the autumn of 1992 it became increasingly evident that the reform had run into an impasse. Already (in July) Yeltsin had contended that Russia "was not satisfied with the IMF position and could not work in accordance with its standard program." He had then appointed representatives of the old military-industrial complex to various posts, including that of deputy prime minister, announcing in November that the time had come to "support production" – namely, fuel, energy, food, transportation, utilities – and that massive credits on the order of 1.5 trillion rubles had been directed to industry. Yeltsin then added the crucial remark that "there is not one example of market relations introduced by decree or by popular vote." What was actually needed, he said, was to create "the necessary legal basis . . . for changing the stereotypes in the public mind. Whoever counts on a superfast, all-at-once, administrative-command changeover to the market . . . arrogantly ignores the natural laws inherent in the process of development of market relations." After Yeltin's open critique of the "shock therapy," Western advice, and Gaidar's policy, Yavlinski could readily assert that since May of 1992 the Gaidar government had become "merely a government bearing Gaidar's name" and that the opposition had indeed managed to place its people in high positions of command.[23] In mid-December 1992, Gaidar was finally replaced by Viktor S. Chernomyrdin, a former energy and gas branch-minister who had turned into the head of a giant petroleum and gas complex, a fact that made some people assert that the entire country was becoming "a single petroleum and gas complex."

Defending his just-ended regime and assessing the new government's prospects, Gaidar stated candidly that "today's economy is in disastrous shape, in something like primordial chaos, but it can recover." He then added that it would have been impossible to have asserted different priorities (like the ones in the 500 Day Program), but what was now necessary was "putting the brakes on hyperinflation" while adjusting the course of economic policy: the reforms must "from now on rest on a broad social base." After all kinds of fluctuations, by midsummer 1993 the Council of Ministers had adopted a resolution asserting that a strict monetary and credit policy had to be followed, but the Supreme Soviet adopted a budget with an unprecedented deficit. As one of the regime's management experts noted, Russia was "holding down inflation with one hand while supporting production with the other." The economy, he added, was in a seesaw, and the primary task was to prevent it from "swinging too violently." The government was, in fact, subsidizing not only Russia's faltering production but also that of the other republics, with which in some respects it was still forming a single, loose economic complex.[24] This ambivalent anti-inflation policy was to continue for years to come, even though the political scene was to undergo violent, critical changes.

As the conflict over the budget increased, Yeltsin decided by mid-September 1993 to call back Gaidar and appoint him as first deputy prime minister. Gaidar openly asserted that the government – to which he henceforth belonged – had in fact two policies: one, to "try to please everyone," and the other, to aim at limiting budget expenditures and creating a market economy. This duality corresponded, according to Gaidar, to an array of social forces and to a divided society. As Gaidar pointed out, the Supreme

Soviet's policy of "extensive financial handouts" was forcing the government to forgo a number of important programs and was prompting local authorities to reduce their payments to the federal budget.[25] To pull the country out of the impasse, Yeltsin's decree no. 1400 dissolved the Supreme Soviet on September 21, 1993. At the beginning of October, the ensuing open conflict between the executive and the legislative branches turned violent. A bloody military attack by the army finally closed the Supreme Soviet, accused of "insurrection," and placed its leaders, Rutskoi and Khasbulatov, in the famous Lefortovo Prison. The period of "dual power" was officially declared over. By mid-December 1993, on the basis of elections and various appointments, a new parliament came into being: the State Duma (with 450 members) and the Council of the Federation (with 178 members, 2 for each of Russia's eighty-nine regions). But the "lyrical fantasies" – as a Russian newspaper put it – of a "pocket parliament that would follow the 'shock-reform' line in unison with the President" turned out to be indeed only wishful thinking. The elections brought forth a deeply divided and basically antagonistic Duma, with a large number of seats for the revived Communist Party and its affiliates and with numerous other seats for a boisterous ultra-nationalist party, leaving only some 100 seats in the hands of the divided liberal proreform organizations. The heterogeneous opposition, united by a hostile attitude toward Yeltsin's government and the reforms, once again left the country condemned to instability and unending political confrontations. These deep divisions, were to be reconfirmed two years later, by the mid-December 1995 elections, with only a different balance of seats between the communists and their affiliates and the ultranationalists (in favor of the communists).

As the keen observer Yevgeni Yasin noted at the beginning of 1994, the political system that would have made it possible to carry through the reform had not come into being. The Russian Federation remained plagued by a dual impulse that it could not fully reconcile: to pursue financial toughness against inflation or to step back from reform, refloating production and accepting a continuing rise in inflation.[26] By mid-January 1994 Gaidar had resigned, refusing to be a "fireman for hopeless situations," while Chernomyrdin had consolidated his hold on power, winning virtual independence from Yeltsin. An *Izvestiia* reporter commented that "Gaidar's departure brings to a close the romantic period of market economy reform, when a young group of scholars tried to carry out an economic revolution without having enough political support or a solid social base."[27] Actually, the "romantic" commitment had ended much earlier. Almost from the beginning, Gaidar's group had in fact had to provide state subsidies for the coal-mining and other industries, increase pensions and salaries for employees in the state sector, and take various other decisions clearly not backed up by budget revenues. Be that as it may, Chernomyrdin fell prey to the same contradictory impulse. Consolidating his power, he asserted that "the period of market romanticism is now over" – but as an adroit politician, he also added that "it should not be replaced by a fetish of boosting production." Chernomyrdin thus became prone to attacks both from the proreform people (monetarists) and from the antireformers (so-called nonmonetarists). The former claimed that Chernomyrdin's cabinet consisted of "people of the old system who do not understand a market economy or the monetarist approach," while the antireformers – among them a number of quarreling academicians from the perestroika era – affirmed essentially that an open retreat from the anti-inflationary policy was imperative, that "the naive faith that depersonalized monetarism can automatically restore the economy" was a fallacy, and that state economic regulation had to be restored.[28] Even the liberal Grigori Yavlinski astutely recommended abandoning a policy based on "oversimplified liberalism," which allegedly led to the "gradual erosion of the processing industry," and replacing it with a policy predicated not on market forces but on a series of government programs "to develop the processing industries on a new base."[29]

With Russia's economic and financial experts divided as to how to cope with inflation versus slump, Jeffrey Sachs, the eager and consistent adviser of shock therapy, suggested that the country's torments could be ended if only it would discard the idea that "continued small steps taken internally and internationally can resolve Russia's financial problems." Actually, stated Sachs, inflation reduction, the budget deficit, and debt service relief could be taken care of if Russia would finance its deficits by issuing bonds rather than more money, with the Western powers jointly purchasing the Russian government bonds. This solution, which John Williamson rightly defined as "big bang supported by big bucks from abroad," did not gain strong acceptance anywhere.[30] In practice, in 1994, 72 percent of the state budget had to be covered by credits from the Central Bank, that is, by printing money that had nothing behind it.

By mid-1995, according to Anatoli Chubais, then first deputy prime minister, the situation was improving markedly: the Russian economy was showing "incipient strength," the decline in production was decreasing, financial recovery was "in sight," and 1996 would be the first year without any fall in production.[31] Yet, notwithstanding this optimistic balance sheet, one should recall that while the enterprises' old debts had been "frozen" (as I mentioned, in July 1992), since then new enterprises' debts had continued to grow in the form of trade credits. According to data furnished by the Russian Federal Administration on Bankruptcy, at the beginning of 1995 the ratio of bank loans to de facto trade credits ranged from 7 to 90 percent. The authorities carefully avoided letting large enterprises go bankrupt because of the eventual social consequences. Open "orchestrators" of nonpayments were at work among the executives of debtor enterprises. In addition, the judges were, as usual, handling economic disputes through "amicable agreement" rather than through a declaration of bankruptcy.[32]

I examine in some detail the basic questions concerning privatization – the third problem in the debate after price liberalization and stabilization – in Chapter 6. For now, let me indicate briefly how the critical issues of rapid and extensive ownership changeover, the distribution of ownership claims, and the eventual methods of management and control of the ensuing structure of ownership were tackled in Russia. Before sketching the Russian approaches let me first recall succinctly the Western advice given by the usual Harvard–MIT economists. Olivier Blanchard and others indicated in 1991 that the most appropriate solution for the efficient management of the state's enterprises would be to have all their shares given to holding companies. The latter would be empowered to restructure, divest, and sell the firms in question, with the proceeds distributed to shareholders. For political and other reasons, some shares would be left with the government (as a source of revenue), some would go to pension funds, and some – as ownership claims to their own firms – would be given to the workers.[33] For his part, Jeffrey Sachs noted on the basis of Poland's debates and experiences in 1990 that the most appropriate role of corporate governance could be given to privatized former state banks, licensed management groups, or licensed investment trusts. After the distribution of shares to the entire population, the shareholders would be assigned randomly to appropriately licensed investment trusts. The latter, however, would not be allowed to have controlling interests in enterprises that could block the development of capital markets for the enterprises.[34]

Privatization in Russia proceeded along different lines. As I indicate in detail in Chapter 6, a number of legal measures – taken before the Supreme Soviet's important law of July 3, 1991, mandating privatization – played a significant role in these processes. Among them were measures reorganizing the state enterprises' industrial associations and cooperatives, leasing state enterprises, and commercializing state enterprises, all enacted under perestroika in the late 1980s. After the collapse of the Soviet Union, Boris Yeltsin also issued certain decrees and guidelines concerning privatization. Subsequently (in June 1992) the Supreme Soviet enacted the State Program for Privatization of State and Municipal Enterprises, which together with a voucher program announced in August 1992 shaped the basic lines of the first phase of the ownership changeover in the Russian Federation. The voucher program gave each citizen a direct 10,000-ruble subsidy to purchase privatized assets, which "insiders" – workers and managers in a particular concern – could use to purchase the shares of their own enterprises at a nominal price. At the end of this process, on July 1, 1994, around 14,000 medium-size and large state enterprises had been privatized. The distribution of shares, reflecting the pattern of the new ownership, was as follows: the combined shares of workers' collectives and managers accounted for 65 percent; those of "outsiders" – that is, owners of investment funds, both domestic and foreign, usually associated with the new management – 28 percent; and 7 percent remained in the hands of the state. The process consolidated the positions of the top managers – the "second fiddles" of the old regime in which the party's top leaders were the so-called masters of life – and also opened the door to foreign investors, whom the Russians subsequently accused of having obtained "controlling blocks of shares for a song." As the head of the State Duma's Committee on Privatization, Sergei Burkov, put it, revisions of the privatization outcomes were necessary, notably in the crucial military-industrial complex and in nonferrous metallurgy.[35]

The Russian privatization program was set to go through two stages. The first, the voucher (or "check") privatization begun in 1992, integrated, as we saw, voucher distribution with favorable arrangements for insiders. The second, the auction (or "money") privatization, was designed to carry the process to its conclusion – only 49 percent of state ownership had changed hands in the first stage – and significantly increase both the enterprises' efficiency and the state's fiscal resources. The fiscal budget receipts had been rather small (and getting smaller) during the first stage, from 1992 through 1994, and all kinds of new mechanisms were proposed for increasing the receipts and dividing them among the center, the regions, and the enterprises. Meantime, under a deal known as "loans for shares," a number of Russian private banks – among them a consortium led by the biggest among them, the Oneskim Bank – started in 1995 to lend money to the state in return for the right to manage blocks of its shares and to organize auctions for their sale in favor of the state; this would also avoid throwing a large amount of securities on the market and bringing about a drop in their price. Eventually, foreign investors were barred from bidding on the most valuable assets, notably in the oil conglomerates, shipping, and metals, and some of the banks assigned to organize the auctions ended up winning them at only a fraction over the minimum bid. The scheme, publicly defended by friends in high places, cast a shadow on the top administrators of privatization and on the banks and strengthened both resistance against privatizations and clamors for renationalization. The state looked like an insolvent institution that could not sell its properties but was ready to mortgage them in order to cover the budget deficit.[36]

With regard to the crucial agricultural sector, the privatization measures were even less substantial for a number of reasons that I examine later. For now let me note only that numerous issues have still to be resolved concerning (1) the demonopolization of this and ancillary sectors involving distribution and marketing, (2) the completion of land privatization legislation, (3) the improvement of agricultural credit markets, and (4) the strengthening of various agricultural institutions. In 1995, out of 25,000 agricultural enterprises, about one-third still kept the old status of collective and state farms, while the rest had changed into new business forms. Besides the some 286,000 peasant farms (or "peasant agricultural enterprises") that have come into being, a number of agricultural associations, cooperatives, and companies have been created but have not been given the right to buy and sell land. The state still hampers private land use, an unrestricted land market, and credit operations using plots of land and other immovable property as collateral. As the Russians put it, "Russian land ownership is an endless story."[37]

What kind of system has been finally emerging through all these changes? And what are its future prospects? I turn to these issues in the following section.

4.3. Nomenklatura Capitalism

As already noted, the chaotic processes of political and socioeconomic transformation that preceded and followed the Soviet collapse and disintegration have left behind fiefdoms run by the old class of high officials (nomenklatura). They have also generated various clans of rich "New Russians" and widespread groups of black marketeers. All these groups do not coincide, but intersect in a variety of ways. "Voucher privatization," combined with various associated measures, got in Russia the name of *prikhvatizatsia* – a blend of the terms *privatizatsia* and *khvatat'* (i.e., "privatization" and "to grab"), hence "grabitization."[38] As Yegor Gaidar noted in the mid-1990s, in this version of capitalism "state and private property have been divided, but at the same time they are inseparably fused." Indeed, the system has offered unlimited ways of redistributing money for the benefit of "friendly" private companies and firms: the shifting of money from the state to the private sector has been its hallmark. In fact, any commercial, industrial, or financial group that reaches a certain size must try by all means to provide itself with its own "political superstructure," since in Russia any big business can exist only if it keeps close ties with the state.[39] The banks have also been involved in interconnecting old and new businesses. The old enterprise directors who have become the new heads of the privatized companies have been getting special export and import privileges – export entitlements for metals, oil, timber, and natural gas; import advantages for cigarettes, alcohol, video recorders, and other goods much in demand – all with the help of the new banks.[40] The core of the enterprises remaining in the hands of the state are large and particularly low-performing, requiring government support for eventual downsizing, production shifts, and asset liquidation.

The intimate relations between Yeltsin's top employees, including former KGB personnel, and "private business" leaders could be illustrated with many examples. Many high governmental positions have been handed over to leaders of the former Soviet hierarchy. For instance, the position of prime minister has been entrusted to the former head of both the state and the then privatized natural gas monopoly Gazprom, Viktor Chernomyrdin. Subsequently, however, Yeltsin carefully counterbalanced the power of the "nomenklatura premier" by appointing the "privatizer" Anatoli B. Chubais as chief of staff and titular "first assistant to the president."

These processes have posed excruciating dilemmas for reformers at every step of the way. Most of the reformers are former communists who have junked their ideological luggage and who have decided to help the state "leap out of the Eastern paradigm into the paradigm of Western society," to use Gaidar's expression. However, they have often been driven to compromise with the former elites in the hope that the old nomenklaturists will integrate peacefully and loyally into the new system. This explains in part the contradictory nature of certain reforms, the advances and retreats, certain weaknesses and mistakes, all aiming at avoiding a real civil war inspired or controlled by a cornered nomenklatura. But the capitalism that has been emerging under the impact of these measures and adjustments has been, again according to Gaidar, "repulsive, ghastly, thievish, and socially unjust" – creating a kind of unstable, divided, self-destructing society akin in some respects to the hopeless Weimar republic. In the absence of an appropriate legal framework, an adequate monitoring of the movement of capital, and the skills and patterns of behavior nurtured by market conditions for large strata of Russian society, the problem of widespread criminalization has become increasingly worrisome. In the pursuit of rapid control or acquisition of profitable spheres of activity and command over government administrations, criminal elements have stepped up economic crimes and corruption, have organized and armed themselves, have drawn parts of the state apparatus into their orbit, and have penetrated its multiple structures. Flaws in banking legislation and the failure of financial organizations to adapt to market realities have created appropriate conditions for using the banks to launder money and have turned certain of these institutions into overtly crime-ridden channels, notwithstanding official anticrime decrees. According to official data for the mid-1990s, the several thousand criminal gangs operating in the country – usually organized on the basis of nationality – have united into 150 associations and divided the country into spheres of influence. Besides the usual business of robberies, hostage taking, rape, and murder, gangs are running banking operations, exporting petroleum and metals, and conducting various forms of trade, naturally controlling the gambling business, but also trafficking in narcotics and, with army help, weapons of all kinds. By some accounts, a significant amount of corporate "voting" shares have moved into criminal hands through exacting "tribute" from commercial structures: the mafia groups can thus have representatives on a company's board or in its directors' council.[41]

According to some Western views (those of Jeffrey Sachs, for instance), among the causes of Russia's corruption, pride of place is held by (a) the Central Committee of the former Communist Party, "the breeding ground of today's leadership," (b) the type of early reform, which provided "unparalleled opportunities for theft by officials," particularly with regard to natural resources, and (c) the West's "missed chances" to provide financial backing to the young reformers, which forced Yeltsin to "compromise with the corrupt old guard."[42] Sachs is, I believe, partly right in stating that much of the ("second fiddle") Russian leadership became the breeding ground for the illegal transactions widespread in post-Soviet conditions, notably in the key sectors of natural resources. It is also true, up to a point, that Yeltsin felt compelled to compromise with parts of the nomenklatura because he wanted to avoid civil tensions rather than because of the lack of sufficient funds from the West.

But certain Russian sources present more cogent reasons for the country's corruption and criminalization. For instance, according to Andrei Neschadin of the Russian Union of Industrialists and Entrepreneurs, the assertions that the criminal structures came from the communist past "is both true and false." Focusing on the possible impact on the present of the former Soviet shadow economy, Neschadin notes that what represented a shadow economy according to Soviet norms had ceased to be illegal under the legislation changes of 1990–1991. During the latter turbulent period, a variety of options arose for accumulating capital through arbitrage thanks to the discrepancies between world and domestic prices, between state prices and the free prices of commodities and raw materials, and between wages in the cooperatives, private enterprises, and state enterprises. Gaidar's legislation concerning registration, taxation, credits, and the conduct of small business stymied the development of the latter and made it easy for bureaucratic corruption and racketeering to flourish. A new shadow economy thus arose that could not apply to courts for arbitration, conclude legal contracts, or legally demand that debts be paid back. Thus, the entire services sphere sank into the shadows, dragging along with it large as well as small firms and corporations. In addition, as a Russian sociologist pointed out, political shakeups in the state's coercive structures have led to the dismissal of employees from the Internal Affairs Ministry, the army and intelligence administration, and the KGB, some of whom have then participated in the creation of legal or illegal private, coercive, or commercially "protective" structures, and some of whom have emerged also as "protective armies" for politicians or big businessmen. In 1996 Yeltsin himself had to get rid of the chiefs of his personal security guard, namely two well-known, offensive black marketeers, the ex-KGB generals Alexander K. Korzhakov and Mikhail B. Barsukov.[43]

The enactment of criminal justice legislation establishing an effective system of commercial and criminal laws would help rid business of organized crime and corruption and would, of course, facilitate the transition to broader market-based relations. But this still proves a slow and difficult process. According to Michael Gray (director of a criminal division of the U.S. Department of Justice), Russian lawmakers do not as yet seem ready to agree on the scope of substantive legislation against crime. A draft penal code passed by the Duma, overriding a negative vote of the Federal Council (Russia's "upper chamber"), was vetoed by President Yeltsin, who stressed the need for the prior development of a criminal procedure code. Lack of consensus is also delaying a proposed law on money laundering. On top of all this, the judiciary is still without the necessary independence to enforce laws without fear of retaliation.[44]

Broadly defined, what kind of socioeconomic structure has emerged from the chaos following the Soviet collapse? The vast income differences now prevailing in Russia can be easily ascertained with the help of some official indicators. According to official sources, the average monthly wage from January to June 1994 was 160,000 rubles – eleven times the established minimum wage set for various accounting purposes. At this time, 79 percent of the population (i.e., 117 million people) had an average monthly income below the 160,000-ruble benchmark, while 21 percent (i.e., 31 million) had an average monthly income above it. Now, over 47 percent of the population (i.e., over 69 million) got less than one-half of even this low level (i.e., 80,000 rubles). On the other hand, a monthly income of roughly the double of 160,000 (namely, above 300,000 rubles) was received by only 5.3 percent of the population (i.e., 7.8 million), while the highest level of 400,000 rubles monthly and above went to only 2.4 percent of the population (i.e., 3.5 million people).[45]

Who are now Russia's new millionaires? According to a recent sociological study, they are not predominantly the old establishment: the top representatives of the former policy-making nomenklatura still possess wealth, but not capital. They still own fashionable apartments and dachas, as well as valuable art, book, and weapon collections. But among the wealthiest people in the capital, only 12 percent had had a successful career in the Communist Party, the Young Communist League, and/or the KGB. These nomenklatura capitalists include Mikhail and Raisa Gorbachev, Ruslan Khasbulatov, and Nikolai Ryzhkov, as well as reform leaders Anatoli Chubais and Yegor Gaidar and Premier Viktor Chernomyrdin. The other Moscow millionaires have grown rich by engaging in legal or illegal trade, producing consumer goods, banking activity, raw material exchanges, and publishing.[46]

The system now taking shape in Russia orients itself toward building interconnected, bureaucratically organized and directed markets, rather than fostering competition and demonopolization. It tends to fit logically in the traditional framework of centralized Eastern despotism, rather than in Gaidar's hoped-for democratic Western market-directed paradigm. The anarchic processes that started to unfold in the twilight of perestroika and have grown ever since are likely to roll on for years to come.

In many respects these developments recall to mind another "time of troubles" that deeply marked Russian history. In the early years of the seventeenth century, grievous misfortunes afflicted Russia after the death of Ivan IV (Ivan the Terrible) and the extinction with him of the line of Ivan Kalita. Ivan IV's demise brought on the breakup of his despotic centralized state and deepening conflicts between what remained of his special governmental/military police apparatus, the *oprichnina*, and the citizenry at large, the *zemschina*. The period in question, designated in Russian history as the "confused time" (*smutnoe vremia*), extended over some fifteen years, from 1598 to 1613, until the election of Michael Romanov as czar or later, when order and stability finally took hold. It was a period of troubles filled with the intrigues of a new regime in the making – a succession of pretenders to the throne, foreign interventions, social anarchy, relentless violence, unsown fields, pillaged estates, and brutal impoverishment. The old term *smutnoe vremia* well fits these years following the collapse of the dictatorial Soviet state and empire, with its conflicts and intrigues; its nascent system opposing the remnants of the old Soviet state apparatus, the nomenklatura, even as surviving nomenklatura members adjust their hold on power to new conditions and the slow coalescence of new forces; its secret and open pillage of the centralized state's legacies; and its wasted fields, massive impoverishment, and dark horizons.

4.4. Poverty and the Safety Net

Summarizing in the mid-1990s the main social characteristics, particularly with regard to poverty, of the changes undergone by the Russian Federation since the beginning of the postcommunist transformations, the World Bank noted: "Many households have been seriously affected by inflation-induced erosion of real transfers (especially minimum pensions and unemployment benefits), the decline in wage-earning opportunities, and a distinct widening of income distribution. The incidence of poverty has increased significantly since the onset of transition. Moreover, regional variation in poverty and unemployment is widening."[47]

The basic developmental trends clearly sketch a pattern of decline through the years of the "voucher privatization" phase. According to official data, wages and pensions, along with industrial output and the GDP, declined drastically, while inflation remained at very high levels. Against this background it can be easily perceived why the per capita income and real wages, consumption, and welfare benefits have fallen, resulting in a high share of the population living in poverty. I referred in the preceding section to the remarkable width of the new pattern of income distribution, using as point of reference the January to June 1994 average monthly wage level. Additional aspects of income distribution with regard to poverty levels can be obtained from other official data. At the end of the first privatization drive in 1994, on the basis of the 1991 level equaling 100, wages stood at 34 percent and pensions at 22 percent of their previous levels. Official data for August 1994 indicate that at that time the minimum monthly living standard was set at 68,000 rubles, while the minimum pension level was set at 21,850 rubles, leaving half of the pensioners far below the poverty line. It should be added that since January 1, 1992, the date of price liberalization, such a large part of the population had fallen below the minimum consumption level that it was stated that minimum consumption had become "irrelevant" for policy and that, accordingly, no data needed to be computed in this regard. According to a law adopted by the Duma in May 1995, as of January 1, 1996, all social payments were to be calculated on the basis of the amount defined as the minimum living standard, determined individually for each region on the basis of the cost of a "basket" of nineteen food products. Taking the August 1994 minimum monthly living standard of 68,000 rubles as poverty's division line, we find that 33 to 40 percent of the population (i.e., roughly 50 to 59 million people) would fall below that benchmark. At the nonofficial standard proposed by the Russian Center for Public Opinion (VICOM) of 194,000 rubles, poverty would include around 85 percent of the population (i.e., some 125 million people out of the total 148 million). Whatever benchmark one chooses, these standards compare only to those typical for underdeveloped countries.[48]

The related questions of wage-earning opportunities, wage dispersal, and unemployment benefits further underline the deterioration in living standards. Again according to official data sources, total employment had fallen between 1990 and 1994 by 6.5 million, with heavy losses in job opportunities in industry and construction. Now, it is in the latter branches that average wages

Table 4.2. *Russian Federation: Employment by Sector, 1990 and 1995 (Millions)*

| | Russian Federation | | Comparison: Russian Federation and United States in 1993[a] | |
	1990	1995	Russian Federation	United States
Total employment	75.2	68.7	100.0	100.0
Agriculture and forestry	9.7	9.7	13.9	2.6
Industry	22.8	18.1	26.6	17.4
Construction	9.0	6.6	10.0	6.1
Trade and catering	5.9	8.1	10.9	23.2
Transportation and communication	6.0	5.1	7.6	7.1
General administration and defense	1.8	3.9	4.8	11.5
Education and culture	7.2	8.4	9.4	8.0
Health and social services	4.2	4.3	5.9	8.9
Other	9.6	4.5	10.9	15.2

[a]Numbers are percentages.

Sources: International Bank for Reconstruction and Development, Studies of Economies in Transformation, Paper No. 19, *Statistical Handbook, 1995: States of the Former USSR*, Washington, D.C., World Bank, Dec. 1995, p. 493; *Rossiia, 1995*, p. 177.

are the highest, while the lowest-paid workers have continued to be concentrated in agriculture, health care, education, and culture, where wages have ranged from 29 to 49 percent below the average. As Table 4.2 shows, by comparison with the overall U.S. employment structure, the Russian Federation displayed a far higher concentration in agriculture, industry, and construction, about an equivalent share in transportation, and far lower shares in trade, state administration, and the military.

The unemployment data and the question of unemployment benefits raise some interesting issues. According to *Rossiia, 1995*, in December 1994 the active population of the Russian Federation was estimated to have reached 74.9 million, yielding in relation to a total of 69.6 million employed a potential of 5.3 million unemployed (7.1 percent of the active population). For 1995, the respective data for the total active population was estimated to have reached 75.2 million, with the total employed shrinking to 67.8 million, leaving a potential of 7.3 million unemployed (9.7 percent of the active population). The official data on the employed population involve some caveats. Enterprises have strong incentives to report a larger workforce than they employ effectively, in order to strengthen their access to credits and subsidies. In 1993 and 1994, for instance, only 40 percent of the workforce was paid fully and on time; in 1994, some 20 million workers and employees worked part time, were given unwanted vacations, and/or had unpaid wages and salaries. Further, wide variations in unemployment were registered among the country's basic economic regions. Typically, the poorest regions have a relatively higher percentage of rural residents, a substantial portion of whose real income and consumption is connected with private auxiliary farming. Hence, officially, the status of being unemployed, and therefore of having access to unemployment benefits, is extended only to a small number of the actual unemployed.

Real pensions have been terribly eroded by inflation and various kinds of official regulations and limitations. The financing structure for the pension fund has changed noticeably since 1992. At the time most people lived mainly on their wages and salaries, and the wage fund, from which pension insurance contributions were deducted, made up 80 to 90 percent of this income. By the end of 1994, that percentage decreased to 46.6 percent; in the second quarter of 1995, it dropped to 37 percent. Then the pension structure was set to provide from 50 to 70 percent of the amount defined as the minimum living standard. Thus, by official standards, a minimum of 10 million pensioners (out of some 37 million) received less than the minimum subsistence income set for pensioners.[49]

Nominally, shrinking benefits from extrabudgetary funds covering unemployment insurance, pensions, family benefits, and overall assistance, as well as various consumer subsidies, still continue to form Russia's social safety net. Yet about one-fifth of the poor have not received any kind of public assistance during the years under review. Moreover, significant cuts in social investments have accelerated the physical deterioration of public housing, neighborhood facilities, and water and sewage systems, as well as hospitals and medical systems in general. As we learned earlier, under Gorbachev the hospitals were already old and run down, life expectancy was plunging, and infant mortality was increasing alarmingly. The latter two harmful tendencies – in the past statistically counterbalanced by immigration from the other independent states of the former empire – will continue to affect the population of the Russian Federation for a long time. The shrinkage and deterioration of the safety net have not been due to an ad hoc policy objective; rather, the conclusive processes of sociopolitical and economic transformation have pushed unrelentingly toward the decline and the debasement of welfare.

4.5. Concluding Comments

To what extent did Russia's application of only part of the Western advice promoting shock therapy help or hinder its eventual transition to a new economic order? Would the situation have been different if Russia had simultaneously and immediately applied all Western advice – on price liberalization, financial stabilization, privatization, and a sound safety net? Would the latter solution have yielded faster and better results? Or could other specific policies more easily and perhaps more successfully been applied in the conditions prevailing in the Soviet Union after its collapse?

As I have already indicated, the extensive price and foreign exchange liberalization of January 1992 did not stimulate producers to produce, eliminate goods shortages, or expand competition in all directions through invigorated and unhampered market relations. Financial stabilization, budget balancing, and money and credit controls proved unattainable in the conditions of the disintegrating old structure with its dangerous social instability and the weaknesses of the new central and regional powers emerging on the former system's ruins. In addition, in a country where the old nomenklatura fiefdoms were grabbing new powers, where controls over the legal or illegal deals of firms, banks, and financial flows were illusory, where Russia's frontiers were open to its former republics to all kinds of traffic, no stability was in sight. Voucher privatization did occur, though not rapidly, only because it emphasized granting privileges to managers and workers' collectives without leading to demonopolization, efficiency, and expanded competition. Institutional chaos, ambiguous ownership rights, and spontaneous creation of small-scale private firms mixed in an inextricable private sector tangle, leaving in the hands of the state principally those enterprises that were commercially unattractive without extensive reorganizations, subsidies, and/or cheap liquidation. It should not be forgotten in this connection that in the late 1980s only 16 percent of the Russian industrial complexes were stated to have reached world standards, while 56 percent required technical modifications and 28 percent required replacements. How could anyone believe that such an industrial establishment could readily compete and be easily integrated into global market relations? The absence of a powerful center of decision and control in the crumbling old social and economic order, the declines in GDP and in key outputs, and the rapidly rising inflation and unemployment all rendered unworkable the naive idea of a miraculous "jump" out of Russia from the Eastern paradigm into the Western one. As the Polish economist Zbigniew Hockuba remarked (with reference to Poland), there is no continuity between a collapsing social system and a new social order that is in progress of establishing itself and/or is spontaneously emerging; there is a chaos born out of the transformation, a chaos of replacements, adjustments, and mutations among dissimilar institutions, regulations, and patterns of behavior.[50]

As late as June 1992, the Russian government, with Yeltsin presiding, defined what it appeared to believe was the sequence of stages Russia would follow in its transition to the market. The first stage would be completed when the production slump ended, the budget deficit did not exceed 3 to 5 percent of GDP, and inflation did not exceed 3 to 5 percent per month. The second stage, devoted to the restoration of the national economy, would be considered completed when the precrisis level of the GDP was attained and the state's share of production amounted to 40 percent or less. Finally, the third stage, marking the economy's upswing and setting the goal of reconstruction, would be considered complete when economic growth attained 3 to 4 percent per year. When the program was presented to the Supreme Soviet on July 1, 1992, it was asserted that the first stage would be completed in 1993, the second in 1994, and the third in 1995 or early in 1996.[51] Yeltsin's three-stage program, like the multistage programs drawn before the collapse of the USSR (namely, by Ryzhkov, Shatalin, and Gorbachev), all assumed predictable transitions rather than chaotic transformations. Events proved them wrong. As it turned out, by 1995 the Russian GDP had fallen to less than 50 percent of its 1989 level, declining in relation to each preceding year by 2 percent in 1990, 13 percent in 1991, 19 percent in 1992, 12 percent in 1993, 15 percent in 1994, and 3 percent in 1995.

In many discussions about the turbulent transformations of Russia it is asserted that China has succeeded where Gorbachev and Yeltsin have failed. Commentators point out that, from 1978 on, the Chinese reforms have been kept firmly under central control while achieving the crucial purposes of decollectivizing agriculture, shrinking the state sector in industry and services, expanding complex nonstate sectors, increasing the country's participation in world trade, and yielding very high rates of economic growth. The contrast between what appears at first blush as the smooth economic transformation of China against Russia's chaotic metamorphoses is attributed to a variety of different causes by the analysts of the two developments and deserves a lengthy analysis. Let me point out only some of the basic responses to these issues concerning the implied strategies of transformation.

Jeffrey Sachs and Wing Thye Woo, in a paper entitled "Understanding the Reform Experiences of China, Eastern Europe, and Russia," assert that what was felicitous in the case of China's reforms was neither experimentation nor gradualism but rather China's economic structure. According to them, China's problem is the classic one for a less developed country. The problem for such a labor-surplus economy is moving the surplus from low-productivity agriculture to high-productivity industry. In contrast, the problem of the more developed East European countries was the pruning of inefficient industries in order to create new, efficient ones. China's strategy has accordingly involved a two-track approach. The first goal was to facilitate the flow of peasant-workers into "a new labor-intensive, export-oriented sector that is largely outside state control"; the second, "to keep most of the state-enterprise workers in their privileged positions." By contrast, in Russia and Eastern Europe, the objective of "shrinking a long-standing state sector" in order to create a new sector turned out to be a much more difficult and risky process than that of drawing on agricultural surplus labor.[52] Sachs and Woo's thesis raises a number of issues, both theoretical and factual. The model they use with regard to China is the familiar model of Arthur W. Lewis on surplus labor and on its contribution to development. According to this model, agricultural surplus labor – from which agriculture does not derive production use – is channeled into nascent industries, to the mutual benefit of both sectors. The critics of this model have long pointed out, inter alia, that it underestimates the impact on a poor economy of a rapidly growing population, that is, its effects on agricultural surplus, wage rates, employment opportunities, and so on. Further, if industrial development involves a more intensive use of capital than labor, then the flow of labor from agriculture will simply contribute to an increase in unemployment. Indeed there are plenty of displaced, unemployed ex-agricultural workers clogging China's towns and cities. And, these places would be further swamped by the countryside's surplus labor, without the strict controls on movement imposed by the authorities. Further, in China, the nonstate sector consists not of a new "labor-intensive export-oriented sector," but rather of a complex mixture of labor- or capital-intensive enterprises, including township, village, and individual businesses, as well as various foreign enterprises (to a large extent Taiwanese) and joint ventures (involving state companies). China's growth since 1979 was initially fueled by agriculture and then by the nonstate sector. The state-owned enterprises, while performing poorly, still accounted in mid-1995 for 46 percent of the industrial output and were responsible for half of China's exports and for most urban employment and wages. The state enterprises are still responsible for most large-scale activities that are attractive to foreign investors.[53]

Joseph S. Berliner advances entirely different reasons for the Russian–Chinese contrast. According to Berliner, Gorbachev had actually adopted the Chinese model – or tried to – when he launched perestroika. The model in question provided for the introduction of a sector of independent enterprises operating outside the state plan with the support of the vast, decollectivized agricultural sector. Unlike the situation in China, however, in Russia the urban economy dominates agriculture and agriculture had not been decollectivized. Consequently, the agricultural sector could not play the leading role in the expansion of industry that it successfully played in China. Instead of the remarkable improvement that took place in China, Russia's economic conditions deteriorated rapidly. After the collapse of the Soviet state, Russia abandoned the Chinese model and adopted a set of policies that ruled out the possibility of returning to that model.[54] While he is on the right track, I believe Berliner overlooks the fact that both post-1978 China and Gorbachev's post-1985 Russia followed the same model – namely that of Soviet Russia under the NEP (1921 to 1928). The NEP created the original of this mixed two-track economy, with the commanding heights of the economy in the hands of the party-state on the one hand and, on the other hand, a market-oriented economy with relatively free small industry and service sectors and a noncollectivized agriculture. The NEP was destroyed by Stalin's regime, which discarded Nikolai Bukharin's advocacy of a free and profitable agriculture in favor of Trotsky's emphasis on heavy industry. Berliner is, however, right in drawing attention to the role of decollectivized agriculture in the case of China and implicitly, in the case of Russia, to the bad consequences of both Gorbachev's and Yeltsin's inability to resolve the land ownership question in their country.

Yegor Gaidar has offered a different and intriguing interpretation of the China–Russia contrast with respect to reforms and their results. To the question of why Russia could not and did not use the gradualist economic reform strategy of China, relying on a two-sector system of management combining state discipline with the "consistent development of entrepreneurship," Gaidar answers that Russia is not China simply because the latter has retained a powerful structure of authoritarian management, is not a federal state, and has no separation of powers. For Russia to be able to follow China it would have been necessary to work out a different political strategy than the one chosen by the Supreme Soviet in 1990 when it adopted its decision on Russia's sovereignty, that is, when it accepted the dismantling of the Soviet Union. Gaidar then goes on to attribute China's success to its "cruel suppression" of attempts by the opposition to "destabilize the situation" and to the state apparatus maintaining its grip over a united country. In other words, gradualism with regard to reform in the former USSR would have been possible only in a dictatorial state that inter alia, would have kept in check any efforts at federalization and power decentralization. Once the center lost its power, instability became unavoidable under the impact of a multiplicity of factors.[55]

I believe that Gaidar's suggestions, with respect to both gradualism and China's reform, can be elaborated in many ways. First, gradualism can take many forms, as one can see when recalling Ryzhkov's, Shatalin's, or Gorbachev's programs of reform before the collapse of the USSR. Second, after the collapse, the uncharted and unchartable paths of transformation manhandled the recipes of the "shock therapists," namely price liberalization, attempts at financial stabilization, and finally the interplay between voucher privatization, marketization, and economic restructuring in general. Gaidar's thesis suggests also – and I believe rightly – that if and when the Chinese party-state collapses, we will witness there too the chaotic, uncharted, dislocating transformations that we have witnessed and are still witnessing in Russia. One should not overlook the facts that China's average income in the early 1990s was at a level not much higher than India's and Nigeria's and well below even that of Indonesia; further, that nearly a third of its population lives below a poverty line of less than one dollar a day; and, last but not least, that masses of the poor are more heavily concentrated in vast peripheral regions – such as Inner Mongolia, Ningxsia, Gansu, Qinghai, Xinjiang, and Tibet – in which about one-tenth of China's population lives.[56]

I return to Russia's further problems during and after the crucial first phase (1991–1995) in Chapter 6.

Part III

Comparisons Within Broader Frameworks

This part places the various changes undergone in the industrial countries and in the former Soviet Russia with regard to privatization, welfare, and their respective connections to the state's agenda into two broad frameworks: for the West European countries considered, the framework is the group of the most advanced industrial countries, the G7; for the Russian Federation, the framework is Eastern Europe, comprising both Russia and its former East European satellites.

To begin with, I point out in Chapter 5 that the debates on the state's size and functions – which I presented in detail in Part II – are predicated on certain basic theoretical assumptions concerning the factors that determine changes in output and employment and on how these changes affect the state's agenda. In this regard, the opposition between classical economics and Keynesianism (and between their respective current offshoots) reflects vastly different views on "activist" governments and, accordingly, on the types of functions assumed by the state. To illustrate the point I present the U.S. agenda – as embodied in federal budget data – both as it might have been constituted on the basis of the classical theory and as it has actually evolved as a function of sociopolitical pressures, the requirements of economic growth, and the amplitude of technological change. A simple comparison shows that within the classical framework the state agenda would be reduced to two narrow blocks, namely general government and defense, while the modern agenda adds a variety of activities concerning economic development and social protection. Yet the United States is by no means different with respect to size when compared with all the other members of the G7, based on the usual key variables of government employment, magnitude of government outlays, volume of its taxes, dimensions of government-mediated income transfers, structure of its services, and weight of its assets. In fact, the United States is in many respects comparatively smaller. In addition – contrary to the assertions of some critics – the federal government's expenditures have shrunk relative to the growth of the country's GDP. Privatization programs also involve broad redefinitions of the role of the state in its relation to the market. Chapter 5 presents further and in great detail the various procedures in use for carrying out privatization programs, as well as the possible forms the latter may take given the great diversity of public enterprises in origin and position in the economy. The chapter then focuses on the overall consequences of the measures taken in this respect in the West and evaluates the results in terms of the main objectives set – namely the expansion of competition and an increase in the economy's overall efficiency.

Chapter 6 focuses on the ways in which Russia and its former satellites cope with the problems posed by the collapse of the old state structures and the needs of creating a new legal framework, promoting vast privatizations, and reorganizing social protection – all in the context of sagging and unstable economies. I indicate the extensive scope of their legal problems, notably those concerning property, commercial companies, credits, contracts, the forms of privatization processes, the regulation of trade and investments, and the transfer of technologies. I then examine the actual patterns of privatization in the region (including those of East Germany), elaborate on the enormous resources needed for carrying these processes to their expected conclusions, and point out the difficult choices that need to be made – that is, which should take priority, industrial restructuring or privatization? Should there be immediate or delayed application of bankruptcy laws? Attention is also paid to the special problems posed by the needs of the general restructuring of the financial sector. The detailed comparison of the respective paths of economic change shows clear distinctions between the transitional economies of the Russian Federation, Central Europe, and Southern Europe. Evidently the critical first phase of transition, 1990–1995, has deeply affected all these economies, but most of all the "truncated" economies of Russia and Yugoslavia, with important consequences for their structures of production, industrial output, investment, trade, employment, and social protection. The chapter's concluding comments contrast the scope of privatization and various concurrent measures in the West and the East, the first carried out within the framework of well-established institutions and aimed primarily at circumscribing the scope of the state's intrusions in the economy, the second aimed at remodeling the entire state structure and functions so as to make them fit into a new economic environment.

5 Options and Outcomes in the Industrial Economies

5.1. Privatization, Welfare, and the State's Agenda

As I pointed out in Chapter 3, the political and ideological upheaval brought about by Margaret Thatcher in Britain and by Ronald Reagan in the United States in the late 1970s and early 1980s aimed at liquidating the so-called postwar settlement in the first country and the Roosevelt era consensus, in the second – both viewed as embodying the ideas of activist governments preoccupied with full employment and the welfare state. The new leaders intended to redefine the role of the state, reduce its functions, and bring to an end what they perceived as the era of overcentralized, bureaucratic, and interventionist governments. Margaret Thatcher directed her attack in particular against public ownership, that is, against Labour's nationalizations and Labour municipalities' extensive power, ownership, and control. Accordingly, privatization there became a key instrument for remodeling both the state and the power relations in society. In the United States, Reagan's emphases on increased defense spending (because of the Soviet menace), along with large tax cuts, decreased welfare spending, and an eventual balanced budget – the whole denounced as "voodoo economics" by his electoral competitor and eventual partner George Bush – also aimed at redefining the scope of the state. Tax cuts – with taxes viewed as evil – and decreased income transfers became Reagan's instruments for downsizing the state and limiting its functions. The same emphases were repeated by the Republicans during and after their successful parliamentary elections of 1994. Some of their leaders reasserted Reagan's creed that taxes were not only evil but also unnecessary. This reaffirmed plan brought forth, again to no avail, the warning (this time from the distinguished Republican economist Herbert Stein) that "we can't afford voodoo 2" and that taxation was evidently "a legitimate and necessary function of government."[1]

Many of the discussions on the state's size and functions are predicated on basic assumptions concerning the factors that determine changes in output and employment. The classical economic school focused its attention on the distribution among different uses of a given volume of employment and on the conditions that determine their relative rewards. It postulated that involuntary unemployment does not exist in the strict sense, that the real wage is equal to the marginal disutility of the existing employment, and that supply creates its own demand. By contrast, the main critic of the postulates of the classical school, John Maynard Keynes, postulated that in a given situation of techniques, resources, and costs, both money income and real income depend on the volume of employment. Consumption, he added, depends on the level of income, and therefore on that of employment; and the latter's level depends on the amount the community expects to spend on consumption and the amount it will devote to investment – without any absolute reason that their total should equal full employment. On this basis, Keynes asserted that "the central control necessary to ensure full employment, will, of course, involve a large extension of the traditional function of government."[2] The fulcrum used for pulling the economy up to the full employment level was, according to Keynes, aggregate demand and stability among the economy's aggregate flows. By making deliberate choices for the flows it controls – namely the budget – and by acting on aggregate demand the government could affect the overall level (not the composition) of all other flows.

By the turn of the 1980s, the idea of an activist, Keynesian government was called into question and displaced in Britain and, especially, in the United States by new attention to the supply side rather than to aggregate demand; to concerns about the state's "overextended" spending capacity; to advocacy of large tax cuts to stimulate private consumption, investment, and growth; and to proposals for conforming with strict monetary rules, welfare reform, and varied recommendations for privatizing public property and service. Interestingly, at the same time, an offshoot of classical economics started to develop a new macroeconomics based on the new so-called rational expectations school. The theses of the new school were predicated on perfect foresight, infinite time optimization, and universal perfect competition. The school implicitly assumed that the actual economy approximated the infinite-time-discounting, utility-maximizing program of a single representative agent, which it modeled. The only admissible constraints it posited in the economy came from initial resources, the supply of labor, and the technology for producing goods, excluding any coordination failure. Policy proposals arising from the new macroeconomics would necessarily depend on unique equilibria and well-behaved dynamics. Eventually, the critics of the school, notably Frank Hahn and Robert Solow, pointed out – as Keynes had done against the traditional classical school – that in the actual world many equilibria are possible and that policy action can help determine which one the economy will attain. Moreover, they added, in this world imperfect competition and the state of the labor market have direct bearings on policy. When there is imperfect competition, every firm understands what is meant by "lack of demand,'' though there are certain supply policies that may also be relevant. In short, the possibility of multiple steady-state equilibria raises serious doubts as to the coordinating power of markets and leaves open the possibility for government action.[3]

In any case, the actual policies of Thatcher, Reagan, and their followers have clearly continued to reflect the old classical assumptions and conclusions rather than those of the newly evolving macroeconomics. How exactly does the reaffirmation of the classical postulates – notably in the United States by Reagan's followers – raise the question of assessing each item of the state's agenda? In which specific ways does this reaffirmation involve a retreat from the concept of an activist government? What would a full compliance with the classical view mean in terms of the agenda?

Even a cursory view of the U.S. state agenda and the responsibilities of the federal government that it displays shows to what extent their complexity reflects the growth and evolution of a developed economy, immense technological changes, and wide diversification of functions and patterns of employment. Using the data on the U.S. federal budget for 1995 presented in Table 5.1, we see that total federal outlays were distributed among four basic groups: entitlements (accounting for 33.3 percent); sectoral and other growth and development expenditures (23.3 percent); general government spending, including that for all nondefense functions and interest (22.6 percent); and defense spending (20.8 percent). A simple comparison with the 1940 outlays shows how sharply the allocations to these groups may vary: clearly, entitlement, general government spending, and defense expenditures have significantly increased, while sectoral expenditures, particularly on education and training, have sharply diminished.

In the classical view, though the central government could resort to a variety of measures in order to regulate certain economic operations (e.g., interest rate level, banking, and tariffs), the structure of its economic agenda was to consist of two groups: general government operations and defense. According to Adam Smith, the government's agenda should meet ''the expenses necessary for enabling the sovereign to perform his duties,'' those of administering justice, and those of maintaining good roads, communications, institutions for education and religious instruction, and public works ''which are not maintained altogether by contributions of the particular members of the society who are their beneficiaries.''[4] In terms of the 1995 U.S. budget, Smith's budget would involve expenditures for general government operations (including the administration of justice, 4.1 percent), transportation (3.3 percent), education (4.6 percent, for a subtotal of 12.0 percent), plus defense (20.8 percent), giving an overall total of 32.8 percent – that is, less than one-third of the 1995 federal budget. In this theoretical framework, the state's agenda and its spending could be reduced by as much as two-thirds.

Table 5.1. *United States: Percent Composition of Federal Outlays by Function Groups, 1940 and 1995*

	1940	1995
Entitlements		
Income security	16.0	17.5
Social security (on budget)	NA	0.4
Veterans' benefits and services	6.0	3.0
Medicare	NA	12.4
Subtotal	22.0	33.3
Growth and development		
Natural resources and the environment	10.5	1.8
Commerce and housing	5.8	0.5
Transportation	4.1	3.3
Community and regional development	3.0	1.2
General science, space, and technology	0	1.3
Agriculture	3.9	1.1
Energy supply	0.9	0.3
Education and training	20.8	4.6
Health	0.6	9.2
Subtotal	49.6	23.3
General government		
All nondefense	1.4	4.1
Interest	9.5	18.5
Subtotal	10.9	22.6
National defense	17.5	20.8
Total	100.0	100.0

Note: NA denotes "not available."

Sources: Computed from *Budget of the United States Government, Fiscal Year 1992*, Washington, D.C., U.S. GPO, 1991, part 7, pp. 30–41; and *Budget of the United States Government, Fiscal Year 1996: Analytical Perspectives*, Washington, D.C., U.S. GPO, 1995, pp. 69–80.

The focus of the U.S. radical reforms of federal expenditures concerns first of all entitlements – in particular welfare, in the narrow sense of the term. Because of the size, rates of growth, and specialized financing of all these programs, policy reformers frequently try to identify each of these expenditures separately from all other federal taxes and spending. Before World War

I and even after, views concerning welfare still reflected the ideas prevailing in the United States at the turn of the twentieth century. At that time the U.S. approach to welfare was still rooted in the English poor laws: assistance went to those willing to live in the poorhouses or to place their children in institutions, with other families, or as apprentices. The big changes of the 1930s transformed the scope of both social security and social assistance and defined numerous categories of people who, by their age, health, or employment situation, were entitled to specific benefits. In the budgeted entitlements group, Social Security (covering old age, survivors, and disability insurance, which I examined earlier) figures only as a relatively small share – the bulk of Social Security is off-budget; the main budget entry concerns Medicare, a key target of the partisans of downsizing the federal budget. The other entitlements, under the rubric of "income security," cover general retirement and disability insurance (excluding Social Security), particularly federal employee retirement and disability programs, unemployment compensation, and other forms of assistance (housing assistance and food stamps notably). Even a cursory look at the next two groups of expenditures – those concerning growth and development and general government – further illustrates the enormous scope of the U.S. government's presence in the economy and the complicated structure of its responsibilities.[5]

The growth and development group begins with expenditures on natural resources and the environment, involving water resources, land conservation and management, recreational resources, and pollution control and abatement. The next-listed allocations, those for commerce and housing, involve a complex set of mortgage programs and administrations. Transportation at the end of the twentieth century refers, of course, not only to "good roads" but to a highly diversified set of ground, air, and water transport systems, along with miscellaneous associated programs. Community and regional development covers grants for community, local area, and regional growth, plus disaster and relief insurance. General science, space, and technology spending supports science research, aeronautics, space flights, and supporting technological activities. Agriculture is a sector that has called forth long-standing interwoven grants for farm income subsidization and agricultural research, services, and marketing programs. Energy supply, besides the famous TVA, requires a variety of funds for energy research, conservation, preparedness, nuclear programs, policy, and regulation. Education and training, at the elementary levels left mainly to local and state responsibility, have nonetheless involved federal expenditures notably for school improvement, for education of the disadvantaged at the elementary, secondary, and vocational levels, for financial assistance at the higher educational levels, and for all kinds of training programs and social services. Health, in the broader sense of health care services, health research and training, and consumer and occupational health and safety, accounts for a substantial portion of the federal budget and remains, I believe, an important and indispensable element in the support of growth and development.

Expenditures for general government operations, in their modern form, of course, exceed by far the scope of "the expenses necessary for enabling the sovereign to perform his duties." The government's legislative functions, executive direction and management, central fiscal operations, administration of justice, and conduct of international affairs involve an enormous set of activities. (Incidentally, spending for the executive branch's direction and management in the 1995 budget was only one-eighth that of legislative functions.) One of the biggest outlays was for the collection of taxes (which cost more than double that needed for the administration of justice – the latter including all federal law enforcement activities). Along with all the other expenditures, an important budget allocation was for international affairs, which included a variety of critical programs – international humanitarian assistance, security assistance, the conduct of foreign affairs, information and exchange activities, and international financial programs – all corresponding to the crucial position that the United States occupies on the world scene. Clearly, many expenditures for an "activist" government are not due simply to certain aspects of unemployment or welfare: they involve a gamut of complexly interwoven modern activities, far exceeding the limited compass of the classical era.

In the next section, I present comparative trends regarding government size in the Group of Seven (G7) from 1960 to 1993, with attention to employment, outlays, receipts, income transfers, and ownership. In Section 5.3, I examine the restructuring methods and procedures of various types of state enterprises scheduled for privatization with regard in particular to the techniques used, the valuation of the assets transferred, and the nature of the controls retained by the state. In Section 5.4, I discuss the issues related to monitoring and regulating the performance of privatized enterprises. My concluding comments constitute Section 5.5.

5.2. Comparative Government Size in the G7

As mentioned earlier, the key variables used to assess a government's size are usually the extent of its employment, the amplitude of its outlays, the volume of its taxes, the dimensions of the income transfers it mediates, the structure of its services, the weight of its assets, and the compass of its regulations and controls. In the framework of the most highly industrialized countries in the world, the group known as G7, how large are the Western governments on which we have focused our analysis?

As can be seen from Table 5.2, in 1993 the U.S. GDP was equal to roughly

Table 5.2. *Group of Seven: Main Aggregates of the National Accounts Based on PPPs, 1993 (Percentages)*

Main Aggregates	United States	Japan	Germany	France	Italy	United Kingdom	Canada
Government final consumption expenditure	17.1	9.6	19.7	19.3	17.7	22.0	21.7
Private final consumption expenditure	67.7	58.1	58.0	60.9	61.9	64.3	61.1
Increase in stocks	0.2	0.1	-0.2	-1.3	-0.2	-0.1	-0.2
Gross fixed capital formation	16.2	29.8	22.2	18.9	17.1	15.1	18.0
Exports of goods and services	10.3	9.5	21.6	22.6	23.4	25.3	29.5
Less: Imports of goods and services	11.5	7.1	21.3	20.4	19.9	26.6	30.1
Gross domestic product	100.0	100.0	100.0	100.0	100.0	100.0	100.0
Gross domestic product (U.S. = 100)	100.0	40.4	24.0	17.2	16.2	15.7	8.9

Note: Underlying data in $ billions at current prices and current on purchasing parity prices.
Source: Computed from OECD, *Historical Statistics*, 1960–1993, Paris, OECD, 1995, p. 18.

Table 5.3. *Group of Seven: Government Employment as Percentage of Total Employment, 1960, 1980, 1993, and Averages*

Group of Seven	1960	1980	1993	1960–1993	1990–1993
United States[a]	14.7	15.4	14.5	15.6	14.7
Japan	NA	6.7	5.9	NA	5.9
Germany	8.1	14.6	14.9	13.0	14.9
France	NA	20.0	24.6	NA	23.5
Italy	NA	14.5	16.1	NA	15.7
United Kingdom	16.4	21.1	16.9	19.9	18.7
Canada	NA	18.8	21.1	19.7	20.6
Total	11.5	14.4	13.9	13.7	14.1

Note: NA indicates "not available."
[a]Federal, state, and local governments.
Source: OECD, *Historical Statistics, 1960–1989*, Paris, OECD, 1991, p. 42; and OECD, *Historical Statistics, 1960–1993*, Paris, OECD, 1995, p. 44.

two and a half times that of its closest economic competitor, Japan. Furthermore, the total of GDPs of the other five countries equaled 82 percent that of the United States. Remarkably, with the exception of Japan, the share of total U.S. government expenditures (federal, state, and local) in the GDP was the lowest (while the relative share of U.S. private final consumption was the highest).

In terms of employment, as can be seen from Table 5.3, again except for Japan, the U.S. government's share was relatively the lowest in the G7. A comparison between 1980 and 1993 shows that only in the United States and Japan did government's share in total employment decrease. In the case of the United States, this share was equal in 1993 and 1960. An analysis of the U.S. patterns of government employment and payroll from 1960 to 1990 can be undertaken on the basis of the data in Table 5.4. In terms of both total employment and payroll, the U.S. increases were on the order of 108 percent. But in terms of the expenditures of the federal versus the state and local governments, the increases were due to the latter. Indeed, the federal share in total government employment decreased from 27.5 to 16.9 percent, and its share in the total payroll fell from 33.6 to 22.9 percent. Those who advocate the downsizing of the federal government tend to gloss over the significant growth of government at other levels. Incidentally, while local governments' share of total government employment and payroll remained consistently around 50 percent, it is the share of the states that continued to increase during the period considered.

Table 5.4. *United States: Government Employment (Thousands) and Payroll ($ Millions), 1960, 1970, 1980, and 1990*

	1960	1970	1980	1990
Employment				
Total	8,808	13,028	16,213	18,369
Federal (civilian)	2,421	2,881	2,898	3,105
State and local	6,387	10,147	13,315	15,263
Percentage of total	72.5	77.9	82.1	83.1
State	1,527	2,755	3,753	4,503
Local	4,860	7,392	9,562	10,760
Payroll				
Total	3,333	8,334	19,935	39,228
Federal (civilian)	1,118	2,428	5,205	8,999
State and local	2,215	5,906	14,730	30,229
Percentage of total	66.4	70.9	73.9	77.0
State	524	1,612	4,285	9,083
Local	1,691	4,294	10,445	21,146

Sources: U.S. Department of Commerce, Bureau of the Census, *Statistical Abstract of the United States, 1971*, Washington, D.C., GPO, 1971, p. 420, and *Statistical Abstract of the United States, 1993*, Washington, D.C., GPO, 1993, p. 317.

How large was the share of the GDP cleared through the G7 governments – or, to put it differently, how large were the outlays and receipts of these governments? The data presented in Table 5.5 for 1960, 1980, and 1993 show a significant increase in total outlays in relation to total receipts. For the G7 as a whole, between 1990 and 1993 the share of outlays was on average 37.9 percent of the total GDP, and the share of receipts was 36.5 percent – that is, an appreciable share of the GDPs involved were cleared through the government. The highest relative shares of the GDP passing through the hands of the government were accounted for by Germany, France, Italy, the United Kingdom, and Canada – all exceeding 40 percent (except for the United Kingdom, with respect to receipts). The lowest relative share of outlays was that of Japan, followed by that of the United States; the lowest relative share of receipts was that of the United States, slightly surpassed by that of Japan.

The advocates of downsizing do not envisage downsizing in relation to the 1960s, but in relation to far earlier dates, namely before World War II and the Great Depression – that is, in relation to 1929. To illustrate the point,

Table 5.5. *Group of Seven: Governmental Current Outlays and Receipts as Percentages of GDP, 1960, 1980, 1993, and Averages*

Group of Seven	Outlays[a]					Receipts[b]				
	1960	1980	1993	1960–1993	1990–1993	1960	1980	1993	1960–1993	1990–1993
United States	24.8	32.4	35.8	31.0	36.0	26.3	30.8	31.7	29.5	31.9
Japan	13.0	25.0	26.9	20.4	26.1	18.8	27.6	32.9	25.6	33.9
Germany (West)	28.1	42.9	45.5	38.6	44.0	35.0	44.7	45.5	41.7	44.5
France	30.9	42.4	50.9	40.2	48.1	34.9	44.5	47.0	41.9	46.6
Italy	26.2	37.7	52.9	38.2	50.8	28.8	33.0	46.5	34.6	44.0
United Kingdom	29.5	41.5	42.7	37.2	40.6	29.9	39.9	36.8	37.9	38.4
Canada	25.1	37.5	49.0	35.7	47.9	25.7	36.2	43.0	35.3	43.0
Average	25.3	34.3	38.6	32.3	37.9	27.8	33.8	36.4	32.6	36.5

[a]Consumption expenditures, transfer payments, net interest, and subsidies.
[b]Direct and indirect taxes and contributions for social insurance.

Sources: OECD, *Economic Outlook, Historical Statistics, 1960–1989*, Paris, OECD, 1991, pp. 67, 68; OECD, *Historical Statistics, 1960–1993*, Paris, OECD, 1995, pp. 71, 72.

consider the case of the United States. In 1929, outlays and receipts accounted, respectively, for only 3.3 and 3.9 percent of the GDP; in 1960, for 24.8 and 26.3 percent. Clearly great changes occurred between 1929 and 1960. From 1960 to 1993, while the relative shares of outlays and receipts continued to grow, actual government expenditures compared with the size of the GDP decreased. Indeed, real GDP (computed at 1992 prices) increased between 1960 and 1993 from $2,261.7 billion to $6,383.8 billion. Compensation to government employees (federal, state, and local) increased from $429.3 billion to $782.9 billion. Accordingly, the government's share in the GDP fell from close to 19 percent in 1960 to 12 percent in 1993. During the same period, compensation to federal government employees fell even more sharply, namely from 10.4 percent of the 1960 GDP to a low 4.1 percent of the 1993 GDP. Put differently, while the size of the economy almost tripled, the government shrank.

Consider now the question of income transfers and the absolute and relative changes in welfare expenditures. Welfare expenditures (see Table 5.6) have tended to increase appreciably over time in all the G7 countries. They have also increased as a percentage of government expenditures and of GDPs. In relation to the latter in the early 1990s, as Table 5.6 indicates, the average share of welfare as here defined ranged from around 12 percent of GDP in Japan and the United States to nearly 15 percent in the United Kingdom and 23.6 percent in France. Evidently welfare expenditures are bound to remain a key issue in debates on the remodeling of the state.

With regard to government's size, some measurements concerning public ownership are clearly indispensable. As I indicated in Chapter 3, the state sector can encompass holdings that include industries viewed as strategically important for defense (and/or the economy as a whole), banks, utilities (water, electricity, gas, telecommunications), public transportation, and government services, as well as nonreproducible capital, namely land and mineral rights. As far as the main industry blocks are concerned, in the mid-1980s the G7 presented the characteristics displayed in Figure 5.1. High levels of public ownership in the tabulated industries were typical for the European countries, that is, for Germany, France, Italy, and the United Kingdom. In the West European countries on which we have focused, the public enterprises, as I have already noted (see Section 1.1), played significant roles with regard to each country's total employment, national product, and capital formation.

With regard to the European Economic Community's overall public enterprise sector, in the mid-1980s, French and German public ownership played a decisive role: the French public sector accounted for 27.7 percent of total industrial ownership and the German for 23.1 percent, that is, for over 50 percent of the total public enterprises of all twelve EEC countries.[6]

Table 5.6. *Group of Seven: Income Transfers^a as Percentages of GDP, 1960, 1980, 1993, and Averages*

Group of Seven	1960	1980	1993	1960–1993	1990–1993
United States	5.0	10.9	13.2	9.1	12.4
Japan	3.8	10.1	12.1	7.9	11.5
Germany (West)	12.0	16.5	15.8	14.8	15.1
France	13.5	19.2	23.6	18.3	22.3
Italy	9.8	14.1	19.3	14.7	18.8
United Kingdom	6.8	11.7	14.6	10.3	13.3
Canada	7.9	9.9	16.1	9.9	14.9
Total	7.0	12.2	14.7	10.8	14.0

^{a}Social security for sickness, old age, family allowances, etc., and social assistance. *Source:* OECD, *Economic Outlook, Historical Statistics, 1960–1989*, Paris, OECD, 1991, p. 67; and OECD, *Historical Statistics, 1960–1993*, Paris, OECD, 1995, p. 71.

Recall that according to OECD data, U.S. public enterprises' shares in the U.S. gross value added, gross investment, and total employment were quite small (see Chapter 1).

Most observers are willing to accept as appropriate the indicated yardsticks of government's size, namely its final consumption expenditures, employment outlays, receipts, income transfers, and scope of public ownership. These are, in fact, serviceable yardsticks – provided one recognizes that they yield different results depending on whether one focuses on growth in amounts or on falls in relative shares – both of which offer useful insights as long as one understands their limitations. Obviously, proponents of downsizing may take as argument various of the indicated relations, as I pointed out with the help of the U.S. example. If one considers the increasing amounts of GDP cleared through the U.S. government at successive dates, the government appears to have greatly increased its size. Contrariwise, if one looks at the growth of government spending (in real terms) in relation to the growth of the country's economy (as expressed by its GDP), the U.S. government appears to have shrunk.

Consider further some of the theoretical relations of the data presented above with the state's agenda. Specifically, is it true that the larger the government's spending, the smaller the private savings and investments? Recall the data in Tables 5.2 and 5.5 for 1993. With the exception of Japan, the U.S. government's outlays in relation to GDP, as well as its final purchases, were the smallest of those of all the other countries. Yet, except for the United

Group of Seven	Telecommunications	Electricity	Gas	Oil Production	Coal	Railways	Airlines	Automobile Production	Steel	Shipbuilding
United States	○	◑	○	○	○	◑	○	○	○	○
Japan	●	○	○	NA	○	◐	◑	○	○	○
Germany (West)	●	◑	◐	◑	◐	●	●	◑	○	◑
France	●	●	●	NA	●	●	◐	◐	◐	○
Italy	●	◐	●	NA	NA	●	●	◔	◑	◐
United Kingdom	●	●	●	◑	●	●	◐	◐	◐	●
Canada	◑	●	○	○	○	◐	◑	○	○	○

Figure 5.1. Group of Seven: extent of state ownership of industry, 1980. Private sector: ○ More than 75 percent. Public sector: ● More than 75 percent; ◑ 75 percent; ◐ 50 percent; ◔ 25 percent (NA indicates not available). From J. Vickers and V. Wright, *The Politics of Privatisation in Western Europe*, London, Frank Cass, 1989, p. 11, based on the *Economist*.

Kingdom, its gross fixed capital formation was also relatively the smallest, while the highest relative capital formation was registered by Japan – which had even lower relative shares of government outlays and final government purchases than the United States. Obviously, the consequences of downsizing are not predictable on the basis of the indicated zero-sum assumptions.

The partisans of downsizing may attempt to buttress their case by selective reliance on the yardsticks of government size. But in practice, of course, the effectiveness of their attempts will ultimately depend on prevailing socioeconomic pressures, traditions with regard to "statism," and evolving attitudes toward the government in general and toward each of its specific functions and levels (central, regional, local) in particular. No single uniform pattern is predictable in this respect, as no fully identical patterns have evolved historically with respect to the forms and focus of government responsibilities in the broadly market-directed economies.

5.3. Variations in the Disposal of Public Property

Whatever its form, a privatization program involves a broad redefinition of the role of the state and of its relations to the market and the society. Specifically, it aims at shifting the prevailing balance between the public sector and the private economy, by rolling back the state's power and activities via public ownership and public services – but in practice its impact is far more widespread. Recall from Chapter 3 that in the strictest sense of the term, *privatization* concerns the transfer in whole or in part of public ownership to private owners through the sale of state assets (i.e., public enterprises, land, mines, highways, transport facilities) and the contracting out of public services to private providers instead of their direct production by the state. But in the process of shedding publicly produced goods and services, a decisive role is played by the political, economic, and legal contexts that contributed to their creation and functioning and that a program of privatization is bound to recast in many ways.

As I have pointed out on the basis of a variety of examples, public enterprises are extremely diverse in origin and purpose. Some owe their existence only to the pursuit of state revenues (e.g., various monopolies); others owe their formation to the state, or have enjoyed state participation from the start, because at a given historical moment their existence and functioning were viewed as indispensable primarily for military reasons; still other privately created enterprises may have been given state promotion and joint public–private participation in order to ensure their survival, concentration, and modernization within a technologically changing framework. State participation and control in some financial institutions (in all the Western countries, including the United States) have been viewed as instruments for extending state loans (on-budget or off-budget), government-sponsored enterprise loans, and credits aimed at stabilizing farm income and prices – as well as means for extending controls over different types of enterprises in different sectors and regions. The recent broad internationalization of certain enterprises with state participation has brought to the fore new and very specific problems with regard to the strength, extent, and effectiveness of the state's overall controls over their operations. Public services are also becoming increasingly diverse in their ways of contracting out, load shedding, and combining with private partnerships (including sharing in public investment projects). Public offices at various government levels resort to all kinds of contracting-out arrangements involving legal, entrepreneurial, and managerial services, as well as those in engineering, hospital care, electricity, and water supply. The goals of privatization, as mentioned earlier, are in fact multiple. They may include the reduction of public involvement in various types of decision making and the search for improved economic efficiency, as well as budget savings, the canceling and/or gaining of certain political advantages and, with respect to welfare, "a diminished commitment to include the poor in the national household" (as Paul Starr puts it)[7] or an increased commitment to conservative social engineering. More specifically, the targets with respect to welfare are the reduction of benefits, "distributed with little or no consideration of their effects on behavior," particularly with regard to illegitimacy, the breakdown of families, and the "perverse encouragement for idleness and cheating" (as Margaret Thatcher assures us).[8]

When privatization processes are launched – notwithstanding the socioeconomic, political, and technical obstacles that may be erected in their way – they do dilute the strength of the public sector at times quite significantly, well beyond their immediate specific target (say, the transfer to the private sector of the given industrial public enterprises, transport facilities, utilities, public housing, land, and the like, and the modification of the content and extent of social security and social assistance). Like the other methods that I examine further below, contracting out also contributes to this dilution, but in a way that leaves in place the established organizational structures and frameworks. This allows the state to maintain, at least in these fields and at various levels, its capacity to adjust, retrench, suppress, or expand its relations with the private sector as it may see fit. Whatever the specific privatization path chosen, its actual application, and even the mere danger of its application, tends to deeply influence first of all the behavior of the workforce, its sense of security and stability, and, up to a point, its efficiency. Of course, these processes also affect decision makers and private investors in various ways. Besides being acutely aware of the multiple directions in which the state agenda can thus be redefined, decision makers have to understand that, whatever their commitments, they must learn to cope with the inevitable criticisms that such processes are bound to generate. As for investors, they usually recognize that a possibility of expansion has opened for them in fields where tradition, stalemate, and inertia had previously barred their entrance.

Let us consider now exactly how privatization programs are prepared and carried out. What assessments must be made? How are public enterprises earmarked for sale readied for their transfer to the private sector? What valuations are necessary, and how are the prices set? What must be done to ensure that the state retains powers of approval over the decisions of an already fully privatized enterprise? I shall consider the issues involved and their various alternatives as implemented or implementable in any country, at any level of development, and within any established or evolving socioeconomic framework.[9]

The preparatory procedures for planning and managing the processes of privatization usually require enactment of an ad hoc piece of legislation, establishment of a supervisory organism (state constituted or state authorized), and expert analysis of the assets and obligations involved. Usually, the legislative authorization along with mandatory rules specify the basic conditions of the transfer of public enterprises, aiming to achieve their orderly disposition, guarantee a fair process, avoid irregularities, and maximize returns to the state. Concomitantly, an ad hoc government committee or commission – or, in some cases, an investment bank or the appropriate holding company – is empowered to restructure, supervise, or provide for the necessary assessments leading to the transfer or dissolution of the public company. The analysis in question, carried out with the help of expert advisers, concerns the enterprise's capital assets, performance, and debt situation. Specifically, it must evaluate (1) the assets and shares of the company, (2) the privileges guaranteed to it by the state and their impact on performance, (3) financial commitments to suppliers, contractors, customers, and employees (allowances, pensions, etc.), and (4) possible preference rights of its shareholders, managers, and employees requiring that, in case of sale, a given quantity of shares would be offered to them at a predetermined price.

The appropriate restructuring measures involving public companies earmarked for privatization may concern their breakup into various component parts, the redefinition of their legal status, and the creation of new financial frameworks of operation. The resort to fragmentation may be necessary when the state wishes to sell only certain parts of a public company while maintaining its direct control and operation of some of its activities. This may be useful because it allows the state to employ diverse methods in the disposal of the various parts of the fragmented corporation, possibly maximizing the state's returns. Fragmentation may also increase output, since recapitalization often takes place as a monopoly is broken up and as the doors are opened to competition. It may also turn out that the breakup is indispensable because a complex corporation may not be in the aggregate as attractive to potential investors as some of its parts may be. Thus, a breakup may be due to many causes and occur in a variety of ways. The legal restructuring or complete legal transformation of a public company, on the other hand, may involve revision or abolition of the special privileges that had been granted to it, fragmentation of its assets and their allocation to newly established (or to already existing) companies, and the sale of some of its shares so as to secure, say, new and more favorable constituencies. Legal restructuring may in fact range from simple amendments to the company's legal status to various forms of transfer of its assets and liabilities (including pensions and allowances), to changes in its accounting practices and management, and even to advantageous commitments by the government to the purchasers (e.g., with regard to pricing) so that they can operate that business satisfactorily. Financial restructuring, likewise varying from company to company, may relate to asset write-downs (when the assets on the books are overvalued); debt restructuring, including state takeover of part or all of the public company's liabilities and/or conversion of part of that debt into equity (i.e., conversion of the government from creditor to equity holder); the issue of new shares to raise new equity before or at the same time as the sale of a company; and various other measures to which I refer later in discussing problems of valuation and pricing.

The most common methods of privatization include (1) public offerings of shares or direct sale of assets, (2) private sale of shares by competitive bidding or auctions, (3) management/employee buyouts, (4) management contracts and leases, and (5) contracting-out scenarios. Each and/or several of these methods may be implemented partially, gradually, or in various combinations. Let us consider them sequentially, keeping in mind that the choice of any one of the methods may be determined by particular or general objectives pursued by the state at given historical junctures, the financial condition and performance of a given public company or set of companies, the need and ability to mobilize both domestic and foreign investment resources, and generalized popular pressures on the state to abandon a catalytic role in the development of the economy.

The state may sell the public 100 percent or a given block of shares it holds in a public company, or it may offer the public a new issue of shares. When the government sells only a portion of its shares, the result is a joint state–private ownership. The latter approach, involving the sale of a minority or a controlling share to private interests, may aim to turn a company around on its own, or it may represent only an intermediate step toward full privatization intended to attract interesting potential investors. Partial sales may also have the objective of lessening demand on the private capital market. Indeed, when a government is committed to an extensive range of privatizations, it may be necessary to have them spaced over time so that the capital market is not clogged with too many privatization shares. The main advantages of an open, public offering of shares is that it permits widespread shareholding and that with the help of clearly expressed mandatory restrictions and incentives, it may on the one hand eliminate certain types of investors (e.g., nonnationals) while targeting strong national institutional investors on the other. It is certainly not true that the state can sell only profitable enterprises. Money-making operations are generally easier to sell, but state firms that lose money may be bought precisely because people believe that they can turn around these companies with better management and with new investments. It is often said that profitable parts of the state sector should not be sold because "they are sources of future revenue, while loss-making parts cannot be sold." But the argument can be reversed by saying that "profitable parts *can* be sold, while loss-making parts *should* be sold."[10]

In a so-called private sale of shares, the state may sell all or part of its shareholdings in a company or companies to a preidentified single purchaser or group of purchasers. This kind of transaction may be carried out through direct negotiation with the preidentified purchaser or through open competitive bidding with prequalified bidders. Private sales may also be conducted through auction by state organs or, in certain cases, by a financial institution that has purchased the state's shares in part or in toto. The auction sale may hopefully lead to a price in line with the market value of the company or companies' assets. Private sales of shares may be used concomitantly with a public offering of shares or after a public offering. The preidentification of purchasers through direct negotiations or through bidding by preselected bidders may be very useful if the selected party or parties have recognized market access, managerial talent, or other appropriate abilities. On the other hand, preselection of a purchaser or purchasers may lead to collusions and unfavorable postprivatization consequences (e.g., dismantlement and sale of certain company parts) unless mandatory procedures and guidelines prevent such outcomes. As for auction(s) through a financial intermediary, much depends, of course, on the way the intermediary's commission is determined.

Under certain conditions public companies may be sold directly to their respective managerial groups, to the employees, or to both. The terms *management buyout* and *employee buyout* may refer to the acquisition of a controlling share or of an entire company by its management or workforce. Some public sector companies with a discontented and highly organized workforce may hold little attraction for private investors. On the other hand, the same workforce may see in the prospect of its own ownership an opportunity for business success. The leaders chosen for the new employee-owned company may be quite different from its previous leaders. For the state, this kind of sale may seem the appropriate means of disposing of even losing enterprises, which under employee-owners may yield a profit both for them and for the state – though this may not always be the case. The British government under Margaret Thatcher encouraged employees of nationalized companies to purchase stock in these companies as they were privatized, for this purpose offering free shares to employees, free shares in proportion to the shares bought by the employees, or priority for the employees in the shares sold to the public. British privatizations among employees and the public at large were supposed to result in "popular capitalism," to erase the old conflict between "them" and "us," and to bring about a decline in both trade unionism and the socialist opposition party.[11] Incidentally, from the 1950s on, in Tito's socialist Yugoslavia a half-hearted attempt was made to disentangle the state enterprises from the state administration. This resulted in the creation of the so-called system of worker (actually employee) self-management. One should not forget, however, that in that system the employees were not owners: they enjoyed only temporary use conditional on their continuous employment. In addition, that system transferred the management of state enterprises to their respective workforces in name only. Indeed, the control of these enterprises remained in the hands of the managers, who in their turn were controlled by the local state organs. In post-1992 Russia, as I recalled before, manager–employee buyouts accelerated privatizations. There, too, it strengthened control over employees by their former (communist) state managers, but this time independently of state patronage.

Management contracts and leases are arrangements that aim to provide private sector management and technical skills, under contract, for an agreed period and with compensation, without involving an immediate or eventual full ownership. The injection of private management may represent an effective nonsale privatization. The management contractor (or an ad hoc business contractor) is given full management control and is paid by the state for these services – though in some cases the state may also require the contractor to take an equity share participation in order to deepen his or her commitment to the enterprise. The lessee uses the state-owned facilities but takes full control over its operation, hires its personnel, assumes the commercial risks for operating the assets, and makes payments to the state, regardless of the profitability of the operation. There are no standard procedures for leases and duration performance bonds; maintenance arrangements, renewal obligations, and so on may vary from case to case.

I have already alluded to the specific characteristics of contracting out operations. Let me add here only that keeping their financing in the public sector while moving production and services over to the private economy is essentially a method of partial privatization. Even where "it is difficult to have firms in competition, while doing certain tasks, it might be possible to have them compete to do the tasks in the first place'' – to bid against each other for the right to provide the given service for a period of time. Recall that beside contracting out at local levels – particularly with regard to construction, fire protection, transportation, data processing, landfill operations, street maintenance, garbage collection, and so on – traditionally the most important and diverse instances of contracting out have involved defense and durable infrastructure construction for public use (including highways, bridges, tunnels, airports, rail systems, sewers, water supply, and locks and dams).[12] In the process of redefining the responsibilities of the state, the new focus has shifted to proposals for replacing the services of the welfare system's collective provision and finance with privatized systems for health and hospital care, education, and the support of the disabled and economically disadvantaged.

Privatization thus takes many forms, depending on the state's short-term and/or long-term objectives, the market framework, traditions and customs, evolving public opinions, and, last but not least, the extent and effectiveness of various resistances that it may have to overcome, whatever the method chosen for selling public assets or shares. Indeed, certain taxpayers will always view any state divestiture critically. Usually valuation and prices are at the heart of many of the critiques. These are difficult matters even where developed markets exist, and of course they are still more debatable where market operations are vitiated by many uncertainties and corrupting factors.

The price of shares in a public corporation may rapidly rise after its sale, immediately drawing the opposition's accusation that the offering price has been deliberately set at an unacceptably low level. Certainly a low initial price may create a questionable windfall for the investors. But too high a price may hamper the progress of a privatization drive. Indeed, one may point out that if the shares of a public corporation earmarked for privatization start trading at a premium, the expected returns are enticing for investors – an important factor in a general program of privatization. If the offering price of shares falls (or if it turns out to have been too high for the acquired assets or shares), the investors may lose interest in further privatization offers – as indeed happened in the case of France. In 1993 and 1994, after marketing certain crucial financial and industrial public companies (Banque de Paris, Rhône-Poulenc, Elf-Aquitaine, Union d'Assurances de Paris), the barely noticeable rise in the prices of their shares after their sale, along with the poor performance of the privatized companies themselves, hampered the French privatizations that followed, notably those of its metallurgical plants and iron-works.[13] Whatever a specific case may seem to indicate, with respect to valuation and sales, privatization processes involve complex assessments even by highly experienced traders. The state privatization commissioner may set only rough guidelines even when they are supposed to be mandatory. And no matter what the practice and standards for valuation – using book values, assessing net values, relying (up to a point) on market values of diverse securities, taking into account the record of company earnings, trusting flexible cash flow techniques – the results may still be open to criticism. Further complicating these questions is the fact that shares may be offered at a fixed price set before the public offerings, and then scaled down in proportion to the total applications for sale. Or final prices may be based both on tenders made at different prices and on the number of available shares. Whatever the assessment processes and the final sales methods, contentions that the sales price was too low – less legitimate perhaps in a highly advanced market economy, but often quite legitimately so in countries where market relations are coalescing and imperfect – are bound to be a product of all privatizations.

5.4. Aftermath of Privatization

As a doctrine, privatization, as Paul Starr once put it, is promoted as a kind of "cure for all ailments of the body politic." As a strategy, privatization aims, as we have seen, to downsize the government, that is, to cut its taxes and spending, eliminate its deficit, liquidate public ownership, use private organizations to deliver public services, shrink or dispense with public welfare, and restrain government intervention in the economy. What is new with regard to the current privatization drives is how widely and rapidly they have gained acceptance throughout the world. Incidentally, from the early 1980s on, privatization transactions have spread dramatically throughout Europe, Latin America, and the developing countries of the Pacific Rim. Altogether there were about $240 billion worth of privatization deals in the market place in 1994, and that number was scheduled to double in 1995–1997.[14]

What are the actual results of privatization? What, in particular, are the sizes of the financial yields of privatization in the Western countries of our focus – the United Kingdom, France, and Germany – and in the case of the United States, what are the financial dimensions of welfare reform and contracting out at the federal level? What does privatization accomplish with regard to competition and efficiency? How does it affect consumers, employees (in terms of employment, wages, benefits), income and wealth distribution, related firms, and the rest of the economy? What kind of links does the state continue to have with the firms it privatizes? Let us consider these issues in turn.

The actual financial yields of privatization, though significant, have been in fact smaller than one might have assumed at the beginning of these processes in Western Europe. In the United Kingdom, between 1979 and 1994, privatization involved some fifty major businesses, yielding the government the total net proceeds of £60 billion British (roughly U.S. $90 billion at the

1995 rate of exchange). Recall that the early sales involved such entities as British Telecom – the first privatization in a series of utility companies with great market power – British Airport Authority, British Gas, British Airways, Rolls-Royce, and numerous electricity and water authorities, subsequently jointed by British Steel, British Coal, and Northern Ireland Electricity. To be added eventually were British Rail and the UK nuclear power industry. The budget statement for both 1995–1996 and 1996–1997 projected annual privatization proceeds on the order of £3 billion (compared with £6.25 billion for 1994–1995). To place these results in an appropriate framework, let me note that the forecasted budget expenditures for 1994–1995 were set at £284.1 billion and that the public sector borrowing requirement (PSBR; which includes the financial deficit plus net increases in certain assets), was put at £35.6 billion, that is, at the level of 5.3 percent of the British GDP. (This compares with a PSBR of £45.4 billion in 1993–1994, i.e., at a level of 7 percent of GDP.) The British government has been also seeking, through a so-called Private Finance Initiative (PFI) program, to increase private sector participation in the provision of both capital assets and services in areas that had previously been restricted only to the public sector.[15]

In France during the first period of privatization, from 1986 to 1988, transfers to the private sector yielded 70 billion French francs. From 1988 to 1990 official policy aimed at maintaining the status quo ("neither privatization nor nationalization"). Partial privatizations began in 1991. Then a new law (of July 19, 1993) earmarked twenty-one crucial companies in banking and industry for privatization. By 1995, total privatization sales (including those of 1986–1988) had yielded 185 billion French francs (roughly U.S. $37 billion). The latest sales included, as I already indicated, the great companies Rhône-Poulenc, Banque Nationale de Paris, Elf-Acquitaine, and Union des Assurances de Paris, but encountered market resistance in finding major investors for unloading Usinor-Sacilor. The total yield of 185 billion French francs is also rather modest when compared with the total budget expenditures for 1995 of 1,592 billion French francs and to a deficit for that same year of 322 billion French francs (some 4.5 percent of GNP).[16]

In Germany, at the federal level, privatization reduced the state's holdings of companies from 958 in 1982 to 400 by the mid-1990s. After the limited privatization initiated from the 1950s on and again from 1980s on (as indicated in Chapter 3), new privatizations have included such notables as Telekom and Lufthansa and are set to absorb Deutsche Post A.G in 1998. However, action at the important *Länder* and local levels proceeds slowly. As already pointed out, resistance there has been very marked. Yet these lower levels have a much greater potential for privatization, given their large participation in banking, transport, utilities, and housing. In the process of liquidating the all-encompassing public sector in East Germany, some 13,700 enterprises have been sold since 1990 at a total of over $30 billion, with the purchasers assuming the obligation to invest an additional $110 billion in these enterprises. However, the need to support consumption there and to encourage investment has led to the very high level of gross transfer from Western Germany of some 6 percent of its GDP per year, to which should be added debts accumulated in the process of liquidating various public enterprises also taken over by the unified government in 1995.[17] During the rest of the 1990s the policy of market harmonization in the European Union will likewise increase the pressures for both deregulation and various privatizations, notably in telecommunications, banking, energy, and utilities.[18]

Privatization in the United States, as already noted, has involved proposals for the sale of federally owned properties, the contracting out of public services, and the elimination of various positions at the federal level, along with the modification of various aspects of welfare (in particular AFDC [Aid to Families with Dependent Children]). Proposals for the sale of federal properties (excluding land) are often repeated, but without much impact. Contracting out is pursued with much more vigor, but not necessarily with the results usually attributed to it. Under political pressures from many sides, President Clinton has frequently referred to the elimination of close to 200,000 federal positions – about 10 percent of the federal workforce – as an indication that "the era of big government is over" (as he put it in his 1996 State of the Union message). But, while these jobs have vanished on paper and have thus resulted in the "downsizing of government employment," many of the responsibilities involved are now fulfilled by outside contractors, who, incidentally, use some of the laid-off workers to do the same work. The problem in all this is that the shrinking of the federal payroll is more than matched by the increase in federal spending on outside contracting. According to John A. Kostinen, deputy director of management at the Office of Management and Budget, the government spent $103 billion in salary and expenses for its employees in 1995, about $1 billion less than its payroll costs in both 1993 and 1994. On the other hand, the dollar value of federal service contracts with private companies has risen by 3.5 percent per year since 1993, to $114 billion in 1995.[19] As for AFDC, in 1992 its benefits reached 4.8 million families (13.6 million persons), accounting for the relatively small share of 0.9 percent of the federal budget (i.e., $13.6 billion) and for 2 percent of the states' budgets ($11.4 billion). An additional 6 percent of the federal budget was devoted to other income support and related programs such as housing assistance, food and nutrition, and Supplemental Security Income for low-income, aged, and disabled persons. Particular attention has been paid in the case of the AFDC to the serious disincentives it has generated with respect to work and the pattern of behavior of its beneficiaries. Yet contrary to the commonly held view, only a small share of

AFDC recipients have remained on welfare for long periods of time: half of all periods on welfare have lasted two years or less, and only 14 percent have lasted ten years or more.[20]

Did privatization deliver what it was presumed to with regard to the pre-eminent goals of competition and efficiency? Recall, as Lord Kaldor put it, that there are no "general rules" for analyzing the performance of privatized enterprises.[21] No convincing data are available in this respect. Indeed, the criteria for assessing the performance of public versus private enterprises necessarily differ because the activities of such enterprises do not always overlap sufficiently. Further, the empirical evidence that the private enterprise performs better than the public one in comparable industries may be ambiguous because there are insufficient examples of both operating side by side. The privatization process itself brings about complex changes in the property rights, business environment, objectives, incentive structures, and leadership of each firm. Moreover, the nature of each sale may also differ. Certain companies, such as the export-oriented industries (whose standards of performance may be easily derived from international standards), as well as small concerns, are usually good candidates for privatization; assessing the results of their sale may be straightforward and relatively simple. On the other hand, the sale of capital-intensive industries, which require large investments with no guarantee that they will yield a reasonable rate of return (if their prices must be held down in order to satisfy the consumer), may raise a host of problems that need to be carefully weighed if a satisfactory balance is to be finally achieved between the objectives of the government and those of the investors. Also, different privatizations are bound to affect suppliers, consumers, employees, and many other industries in different ways. The passage from public ownership to private ownership may often lead to changes in the ways firms acquire their inputs and sell their outputs, thus affecting on the one hand a variety of suppliers and on the other hand a variety of consumers. And, once privatized, firms may reduce their labor force, reduce wages, and increase prices – that is, significantly change their operational framework.

As already noted, the government itself pursues a set of objectives when it engages in the privatization processes. The use of privatization to increase competition and efficiency may go against its use to increase revenues. Ad hoc policy decisions and procedures must be weighed, and different objectives must be traded off: inevitably, in certain cases competition and efficiency will be subordinated to other goals. Typically, certain monopolies may have to be transferred to the private sector without being broken up, both because splitting them up would diminish their market power and because their managers would resist any dismembering that would diminish managers' privileges. In short, inevitable changes in the firms' operational environments, variations in financial and economic conditions at the moment of sale, and conflicting sets of government objectives and policies render most comparisons of the performance of an enterprise before and after privatization of rather limited value.

The role of the government after privatization is also not as simple and transparent as one might assume. Of course, in principle privatization aims to free enterprises from government ownership and control in order to increase their efficiency. Indeed, in some cases, the government does remove itself up to a point from the operation of the privatized firms. But more often than not, the government decides to continue to play a role – for instance, that of a critical shareholder – while in other cases it vests new and extensive controlling powers over the privatized enterprises in the hands of regulatory authorities. Furthermore, shares are not always placed competitively through the financial markets. As part of underlying arrangements, a substantial number of shares may be kept by the state or placed in the hands of certain groups of investors. As we already know, the government may reserve "golden shares" for itself or may select a "hard core" (*noyaux durs*) of investors to whom it allocates a proportion of the capital, with restrictions placed on its disposal over a number of years. Again, privatization, just like its opposite, nationalization, allows the state bureaucracies and the party in power to transfer wealth and award patronage to their supporters. In all the Western countries considered, in particular under both Thatcher's and Chirac's privatizations, reliable political friends were placed at the head of privatized public enterprises.[22] On the other hand, change-resistant employees of public enterprises may also be encouraged to acquire stock in these companies as they are privatized. Methods include offering free shares to the employees or giving the latter priority in the allocation of shares sold to the public. This much-advertised way of promoting "popular capitalism" does not, however, necessarily lead to "shareholder democracy," since people are attracted to this kind of transaction mostly in order to make a quick profit. In any case, ill-informed and largely uninterested small shareholders have few effective powers.[23] In sum, privatization does not necessarily herald a more market-oriented economy, but only a differently structured economy.

Everywhere in Western Europe the state has continued to intervene in the economy – at times openly and massively, at times discretely yet effectively – by regulating the terms and the environment of public and private enterprises. Subjected to sagaciously crafted taxes, subsidies, and regulatory oversight, private enterprises may find themselves in some respects enclosed in a framework not too different from that of public enterprises. As Vickers and Wright have remarked, throughout the world "the state continues to be provider, regulator, entrepreneur, purchaser and umpire in industrial affairs"[24] – of course, in varying degrees in each country and in each of these activities.

5.5. Concluding Comments

Privatization – like its opposite, nationalization – is an instrument for redefining the scope and functions of the state. It aims not only at changing certain property rights and shifting the boundary between the public and the private sectors, but also at downsizing the state and recasting its agenda. Certainly, the latter cannot be simplified to the point where it would match the agenda of Adam Smith's time. But, as we saw, it can be redefined in many respects (with or without the illusion of perfect foresight and rational expectations), notably vis-à-vis executive direction and management, central fiscal operations, education, and income transfers (particularly to certain welfare programs).

Among the G7, the United States is by far the biggest in terms of GDP. Yet, as we have seen with regard to the state's shares concerning outlays, receipts, and employment, the U.S. federal government has consistently been relatively among the smallest. Paradoxically, however, it is in the United States that the clamor against "big government" has been the loudest since the early 1980s. But the ideas and the actions they command depend of course on many factors – political, social, economic – whose complex interactions are variable and whose weight changes from period to period.

While state ownership in industry has consistently involved basically the same type of industries, privatization's chief targets have not necessarily been the same in all these countries. In the United Kingdom the emphasis has been on utilities (plus some industries); in France the emphasis has been on banks and insurance companies (along with a limited number of key industries); in Germany (West) the emphasis has been on industries (banks remaining largely in the hands of the *Länder*, which also control regional industries). Whatever the emphasis, the transfer to the private sector has in most cases involved complex restructuring measures and a variety of forms of liquidation (through the sale of the whole state property via public shares, or a proportion of the whole, the sale of parts to private buyers, or the sale of parts or whole to the workforce and managers). With regard to services through various forms of contracting out, privatization has also involved load shedding and diverse public–private "creative partnerships."

As we have seen, public ownership has not been established to serve a unique state objective, nor is its liquidation meant to serve a single objective, notwithstanding the usual emphasis on that of increased efficiency. In trying to assess the results of privatization in relation to the goals pursued, one is confronted by many imponderables. Certainly some specific results can be obtained with regard to the financial yields of privatization. But no such results can be obtained with regard to the dominant goals of competition and efficiency. Again, insurmountable problems are faced in any attempt to weigh one against the other objective – in part because not all of these objectives are quantifiable and in part because they are mixed in variable proportions from case to case. Further, notwithstanding privatization's clear goals concerning government size, outlays, receipts, employment, and income transfers, all cannot be combined in a single indicator reflecting the government's range, functions, and success at its downsizing. The most that can be said with certainty is that the privatization drives begun in the Western world in the late 1970s and early 1980s undoubtedly constitute the most wide-ranging effort since the 1930s to redefine the state.

6 Options and Outcomes in the Transitional Economies

6.1. An Evolving Legal Framework

The Soviet Union disintegrated as a political and legal entity in 1991. Following the Accords on the Commonwealth, signed in Minsk and Alma Ata on December 8 and 21 of that year, the USSR was replaced by a fifteen-member Commonwealth of Independent States (CIS). In all the states of the new commonwealth, the Soviet All-Union legislation was discarded and its legal effects suspended except for certain laws and regulations that did not conflict directly with the new republican laws. Thus, every CIS republic started to develop its own distinct legal system.

The need for the sovereign Russian Federation to fill the virtual void of civil and commercial legislation to govern expanding market relations brought about an extensive production of new laws. But many of these laws were inconsistent and ambiguous, rendering the legal situation often confusing. Theory and practice of Russian law were also often at odds with each other, and thus the entire legal system remained in a state of flux – a situation likely to continue for many years to come. Uncertainties as to the government's capacity to continue reforms, as well as the struggles between the center, the republics of the former USSR, and the "autonomous" republics within the Russian Federation, further complicated the state of affairs. The Russian Constitution of December 1993, despite declaring all subjects equal, granted to autonomous republics the right to pass their own constitutions. The center–periphery conflicts over the ultimate redistribution of powers in the Russian Federation extended to the fifty-seven Russian regional *oblasts* and *krais*, which aimed to have the same status as the republics. The privatization programs conducted at the provincial level placed formerly centrally controlled state funds under the control of republics or regions. This put important resources in the hands of regional leaders and contributed to significant variations in the speed and extent of privatization among the regions.[1]

The abandonment of ministerial controls and of the state monopoly over investment, production, and distribution, along with the myriad privatization processes, the commercialization of state enterprises, and the expansion of markets, changed in various ways the business procedures and the inherited patterns of civil and commercial relations. Yet, until the legal and regulatory system stabilizes and a fully consistent and workable structure for commerce and trade coalesces, Russia will continue to remain a source of serious commercial uncertainties.[2] The revolution of 1991 has not been carried out to its necessary ends with respect to the quashing of certain Soviet structures and institutions. State-owned industrial, commercial, and financial entities continue to play crucial roles in the economy, even though they have acquired independence in their business decisions and even though they act in certain respects as independent private entities. Privatized companies in the hands of midlevel colleagues of the former nomenklatura continue to join forces to combat federal decisions that they consider unwelcome. But the federal government and the entire state structure at all its levels continue to exercise a substantive degree of direct regulation and control over private business activities. Russia and the other CIS republics have announced that they will abide by the international treaties and agreements previously signed and ratified by the Soviet Union, provided that they are not inconsistent with the new national laws. In practice, however, many of these treaties are either ignored or negotiated anew.[3]

After abandoning the principles of the Soviet property rights model, the Russian Parliament adopted and the government enacted a number of laws that guarantee the sanctity of individual, cooperative, and corporate private property rights. But some provisions of the old Soviet Civil Code (partially amended) are still in force. Now the Russian property law rests on three foundations: the Fundamentals of Civil Legislation (which revised in 1991 the USSR Fundamentals of Civil Legislation), (2) the enactment of the first half of the Civil Code, titled the Right of Ownership and of Ownership Rights, and (3) the Law on Privatization adopted in 1991, which established the basic framework for transferring the state and municipal properties to the private sector. Legal experts point out that both the revised Fundamentals and the revised Civil Code are grounded in Western concepts and that the conflicts between the two involve mainly issues of terminology and interpretation. As for the Law on Privatization (and its associated programs of 1992 and 1994), its focus is on the transformation of the economy's structure so as to open the way to a viable market economy.[4]

As in the case of the Russian Federation, in the entire ex-communist area in the CIS, as well as in Central and Southern Europe, legislative models of Western origin are playing useful theoretical and practical roles. Both the recent attention paid to these models and their adoption in various ways (often with substantial changes) have certainly shattered the legal homogeneity that seemed to prevail with regard to fundamentals in the area as a whole until 1989. Yet one should not overlook the fact that modern Western influences had started to seep into Eastern Europe already from the 1940s on, first in Yugoslavia, and then from 1953 on, under diverse forms, in most of the countries of the area. Indeed, all kinds of centrifugal and national tendencies played there, openly or covertly, against the normative Soviet political and legal precepts. These forces also worked against the integrated models of planning and management that had emerged in the USSR under Stalin in the 1930s. Each specific Soviet precept – concerning (1) the interlocking of political and economic leadership under the control of the Communist Party hierarchy, (2) the integration of the economy's sectors into a single state-owned complex, and (3) the centralized, directive planning and management of the short- and long-run goals of the economy as a whole – came under increasing criticism, debate, rectifications, and/or regulation. Little by little, the postulates, component parts, arrangements, and underlying assumptions of the Soviet model became targets of wide-ranging, probing, and often devastating critiques, conducted from the standpoint of so-called market socialism as opposed to the autocratic and autarkic Soviet system. As an outgrowth of the crises and upheavals that have shaken Eastern Europe since the 1950s, variously defined alternatives to the Soviet-type organization and management were proposed, and in some cases actually implemented there,[5] while the Soviet leadership itself did not depart from the basic underlying concepts of its social, political, and economic model until the mid-1980s. Gorbachev's perestroika was prefigured in many respects – and deeply influenced – by the normative proposals and practical experiments carried out in Yugoslavia after 1946, in Hungary during and after the 1960s, and in Poland after the early 1980s. All these changes inserted themselves in various ways into the ideas that had been debated in Russia itself in the NEP period of the early 1920s but that became increasingly unusable in Russia as its political and economic structures began to crumble, from the second half of the 1980s on.

During the "socialist" phase of research and debate on the appropriate ways of modifying the Soviet model and of coping with its consequences, the influences of Western legal concepts and Western civil law were hidden and necessarily limited. In the postsocialist phase from the early 1990s on, the situation has changed significantly. At least some of the liberal intellectuals in this region have acquired an extraordinary legislative optimism – and exceptional confidence in the capacity of law to play a decisive role in "social engineering." The new legal codes, in particular the laws on privatization, have been proclaimed by them to be the birth certificates of the new market relations system. Various institutions created during the socialist era for helping the Soviet legislator have readjusted themselves to "help" the postsocialist legislator. For instance, the famous Russian Scientific Institute for Soviet Legislation now pursues its activities under a new capitalist name –

and this is not at all an isolated case either in the CIS or in Central and Southern Europe.

Actually, the legal domains that still require complex and judicious intervention concern particular legislation with respect to (1) property rights, credit titles, pledges, nominal contracts, bankruptcy, competition, taxes, rights of the consumers, and protection of the environment, (2) the forms and conduct of privatization processes and the regulation of restitution to owners expropriated before and after World War II, (3) the framework of operation of banks, insurance companies, and the stock market, and (4) foreign trade, foreign investment and its fiscal management, tariffs, and the regulation of technology transfer. Various measures concerning some of these issues have been adopted at a time when readjustments to the old dogmas were still imperative or when immediate decisions had to be taken in order to obtain admission to various international institutions, such as GATT (General Agreement on Tariffs and Trade).[6] But in these unsettled societies, each and every one of the legislative interventions runs the danger of mobilizing against them all kinds of collusive resistance. Consider, for instance, the complex issues called forth in the case of Russia by the time of the second stage of privatization, the so-called money stage in which state property was transferred to the private sector. This stage, as I previously indicated, concerns the use of state-owned blocks of shares, either for sale to private investors or as collateral for bank credits to the government. From the second half of 1994 on, a conflict arose between the legislative and the executive branches as to the legality, extent, and control of the operations involved. In the meantime, broad opposition coalesced against the entire operation, first of all in the military–industrial complex and more broadly among the directors of the state enterprises, who opposed the entrance of foreign investors into their domains. Resistance grew for several notable reasons: certain managers wanted to acquire blocks of federally owned shares in order to become independent of the state, bankers had a stake in gaining full control over the privatization operations and were also interested in an unstable exchange rate for the ruble, and importers preferred a low ruble exchange rate. For these and other reasons as well, Yeltsin was eventually forced to pull some 3,000 "strategically important" enterprises out of the privatization process, including 400 major firms in the defense industry and other attractive companies in the fuel and power complex, the chemical industry, and the transportation sector. These measures have not, however, put an end to the deep issues involved, which will continue to plague the legislative and executive branches for years to come with regard to the forms, range, functions and controls of the money stage – including whether or not the government returns to the banks the shares pledged for credits or the funds already acquired for them (and spent).

Notwithstanding all these obstacles, the new phase of codifying the Civil Law continues to unfold in the East European region, as well as in the CIS. The first states to adopt new legal codes – with different degrees of actual bearing on the complex issues at hand – were Albania, Bulgaria, and the Czech Republic. In these as well as in the other postsocialist countries, the main efforts have been channeled toward eliminating the quantitative and qualitative limits to the access and exercise of property rights (still particularly unsettled with regard to land). Various international or European organizations have helped and are continuing to give advice on framing new laws or amending existing ones. The International Monetary Fund helped particularly in the formulation of banking laws and the elaboration of fiscal measures relating to the protection of foreign investments. However, adopting these and related judicial measures does not necessarily signify that they have been coherently integrated into the evolving judicial systems of these countries.[7]

It would, I believe, be erroneous to assume that under the impact of Western judicial models and economic advice (with regard, for instance, to ownership and the reallocation of property rights), the postsocialist countries will henceforth rely consistently on both normative legal solutions and economic rationality. The changes achieved through massive privatization have affected, of course, not only the redistribution of wealth, but also the complex and diverse needs of restructuring; of readjusting to enormous shifts in prices, costs, demands, and outputs; of searching for development and capital; of finding ways to safeguard employment; and so on. In this period of transition from the old system's methods of command and control to the still irregular spread of the new one's methods, it is not at all certain which particular changing framework will finally provide a basis for price liberalization, attempts at stabilization, restructuring, and massive privatization.[8] I return to these and related issues in the next sections.

6.2. Patterns of Privatization

There is only one former centrally planned economy where the breakdown of large state-owned conglomerates and their restructuring and transformation into viable capitalist firms has been carried out fully, effectively, and at a rapid pace. The liquidation of the communist economic heritage in East Germany and the latter's readjustment to market-driven relations illustrate the enormous resources needed to carry such a process to a successful conclusion. It also shows, in contrast, why privatization in Russia and its other former Central and Southern European satellites has often been faltering, contradictory, and, at times, unpredictable.

Treuhandanstalt (henceforth, THA), which, as I mentioned previously, received from the West German government the tasks of restructuring and privatizing the state proprieties of the annexed East Germany, was created in 1990. This institution, the largest holding company in the world at the time, completed the main privatization processes in the retail sector in 1992 and in most of the industrial sector in 1994. The viability of the privatized firms was a key consideration, leading to a primary focus on buyers that could take a long-term view with respect to investment, restructuring, and the integration of these firms into a competitive framework. THA thus secured new investments totaling DM (deutsche marks) 207 billion and obtained as proceeds of privatization about DM 65 billion. Before privatizing itself out of business, it disposed of 14,600 former socialist enterprises, part enterprises, and mining rights, of which 860 were purchased by foreign investors and about 2,700 were management buyouts. After THA succeeded in liquidating the East German dinosaurs, by the end of 1994, 470,000 small and medium-sized enterprises were operating in the area. In appraising THA's success, one should not, however, lose sight of the enormous sums of money needed to secure it. The Bonn government transferred more than DM 150 billion annually (financial gross transfers) during the five years of THA's life, and further transfers will have to continue for years to come (to a variety of newly established agencies responsible for the remaining firms that THA did not manage to sell). THA's operations alone required DM 275 billion net from the German taxpayers – a drain on West German resources not anticipated at the time of German unification.[9] This balance sheet clearly suggests why privatization – and the restructuring of enterprises that it entails – has had to lurch through various stages in the other countries of the area, why most of the dinosaurs bequeathed by the communist regimes are still functioning just as inefficiently as before, why privatization processes have generated various alternative arrangements, and why, last but not least, the influx of foreign capital has been reluctant and, overall, limited. (In fact, large parts of the region have remained virtually untouched by foreign direct investment linked to Western European firms.)

Two basic approaches were possible in countries with large privatization programs: mass privatization, that is, the grouping of firms to be privatized using some standard system of procedure for their privatization; and case-by-case privatization. The mass privatization approach was used in Russia (as I indicated in Chapter 4) and under certain conditions was also applied in its former Central and Southern European satellites. Hungary was the first in the area to start privatization in a sui generis case-by-case way. Under its reformed command-and-control system, it approved a so-called enterprise law in 1988 and a transformation law in 1989 that allowed state-owned companies to convert themselves into joint-stock or limited liability companies. Within this legal framework, the companies' managers were allowed to sell either assets or whole companies. In 1990, the government decided to centralize the privatization program and established for this purpose the State Property Agency (SPA), which drew up an ambitious plan aimed at privatizing 40 percent of state assets during the following three years and 80 percent within ten years. In practice, however, the Hungarian privatization eventually slowed down. A switch to a mass privatization program was adopted in 1993, but this program had also slowed down by 1995.

Poland's privatization program was the second one started in the area. A 1989 bill proposed a similar approach to that of Hungary, namely the conversion of nationalized properties, under workers' and management's control, into joint-stock companies to be sold to the public, while reserving a small portion for the employees. Eventually, a more general framework for privatization became law in 1990. But the drive to privatization finally took off only at the end of 1994, when various investment funds were created to which shares of the participating firms were to be allocated.

The Czechoslovak Republic was the next country that started a privatization program.[10] Its privatization process was divided into two phases: the first was to consist of a small-scale program, applied to small shops and catering enterprises, as well as to certain industrial companies (provided the latter could be brought by a single bidder in sales by auction). Under the second phase, started in 1992, each citizen above age eighteen was authorized to obtain a voucher for a nominal fee; these vouchers could be converted into shares via auctions or placed into investment funds. (In the two independent Czech and Slovak republics, the mass privatization drives eventually accelerated, but at different speeds.) Other countries, notably Poland (as indicated) and Romania, opted for state-created investment funds owning all or part of the companies to be privatized.[11]

As can be seen from Table 6.1 concerning Russia and Eastern Europe – with the subaggregates of the Central European Transitional Economies and the Southern European Transitional Economies (CETE and SETE) – the contribution of the private sector to the GDP in 1995 has been estimated to be 70 percent for the Czech Republic and 60 percent for Hungary, Poland, and the Slovak Republic. For Russia, it is assumed to have reached 55 percent, for Bulgaria some 45 percent, and for Romania 40 percent. However, all these figures have to be considered with much caution. As OECD studies have noted, the dividing line between public and private sectors remains uncertain with regard, for instance, to state shareholding. Moreover, in some countries leased state and municipal property is not classified in the private sector. Getting and keeping statistics on the private sector is proving difficult, given the need to update business registers, devise appropriate sampling methods to collect the data, introduce new ways of estimating for nonresponse, and so on.

Table 6.1. *Russia and Eastern Europe: Mass Privatization Programs and Foreign Direct Investment*

Country or Area	Privatization Legislation and Approaches	Restitution Legislation	Private Sector Percentage of GDP, 1944	Cumulative FDI, 1994	
				Millions of Dollars	Percentage of Regional Total
Russian Federation	P act of 1991; MPP 1992 (voucher); second wave 1994	No R act in place	25	2,300	12.2
CETE				15,224	80.8
Czechoslovakia	P act 1991; MPP 1991	R act 1990	—	—	—
Czech Republic	(voucher – two waves)		62	3,542	18.8
Slovak Republic	(voucher – one wave)		58	474	2.5
Hungary	Multitrack; MPP 1993	R act pending	70	6,804	36.1
Poland	P act 1990; multitrack; MPP, 1994	R act pending	48	4,404	23.4
SETE[a]				1,318	7.0
Bulgaria	P act 1992; MPP 1992	R act 1992	23	457	2.4
Romania	P act 1991; MPP 1991	Land (R) act 1991	35	861	4.6

Abbreviations: MPP, mass privatization programs; FDI, foreign direct investment; P, privatization; R, restitution; CETE, Central European Transitional Economies; SETE, South European Transitional Economies.

[a]No data available for Albania and the five former Yugoslav economies.

Sources: René Gatling, *Foreign Investment in Eastern Europe*, London, *The Economist* Intelligence Unit, 1993, pp. 51–76; UN Secretariat of Economic Commission for Europe, *Economic Survey of Europe, 1994–1995*, New York, 1995, p. 83; UN Conference on Trade and Development, *World Investment Report 1995: Transnational Corporations and Competitiveness*, New York, UN, 1995, p. 101; European Bank for Reconstruction and Development (EBRD), *Transition Report, 1995*, London, EBRD, 1995, p. 11.

In addition, formal transfer of ownership does not necessarily mean either that effective corporate guidance has immediately been provided or that the behavior of the privatized enterprise has changed.[12] Both the high and the low figures concerning the contribution of the private sector must be treated with some skepticism – the first because they may overstate "genuine" privatization, the second because they may understate the complex and not yet fully evaluated contribution of small and medium-sized privatized firms. In this regard it is interesting to consider the Russian situation. According to the official Russian data, by the mid-1990s, 51 percent of its enterprises (namely, 119,314) had been privatized, while 11 percent (27,543) had had their shares submitted for sale; the state sector continued to operate the remaining 38 percent (88,926 enterprises). It is still not fully certain whether the contribution of the private sector to the GNP was on the order of 55 percent, though the state still continued to control the largest and the most advanced enterprises, well known for poor performance.[13]

As can also be seen from Table 6.1, by the mid-1990s in all countries considered, cumulative foreign direct investment (FDI) reached a total of $18.8 billion – the rough equivalent of 5 percent of their total GDP. The inflow has tapered off as the pace of reforms has slowed down in some of these countries. Compared with the FDI stock in developing countries, the area's FDI stock was at that time marginal, and the gap between investors' commitments and actual implementation still remained high. In addition, as indicated by the data in the table, the Central European countries that welcomed foreign ivnestors – Hungary, Poland, and the Czech Republic (by order of the magnitude of inflows) – accounted for 78 percent of the total FDI, while Russia along with the Southern European countries considered accounted for less than 20 percent. Clearly, foreign capital tended at the time to shun the countries where privatization programs still favored resident ownership and to prefer the countries with more liberal approaches.[14]

In all of these countries, privatization per se failed to secure broad-based efficiency, either in the privatized sectors or in the remaining state-owned enterprises. The collapse of the old command system, along with the enormous handicaps that arose during the process of transition in the form of rising prices, falling output and wages, and uncertainties with regard to jobs, increased many of the old negative features of the area's managers, trained in the repressive paternalistic traditions of the communist regime, while the new openings of the transition enticed some of them to engage in illicit speculation, theft, and fraud. On the other hand, one must also note that it was not easy for these managers to establish effective controls within workplaces that had never been within their direct domain. Restructuring the entire public sector appeared increasingly necessary throughout the countries of the area in order to modernize and incrcase the efficiency of at least the most crucial state-owned industrial enterprises; to facilitate their adaptation to the changes in costs, prices, and demand; and to make them eventually attractive to investors.

Actually – as the European Commission's UN Secretariat pointed out – in the broad sense of the term, restructuring may be equated with the overall process of adapting firms to a new environment. In this sense, the entire course of transforming the centrally planned economies can be viewed as restructuring, the term encompassing any corporate or state action whereby the old economic framework is altered, including changes in ownership, coordinating systems, and contractual relationships. On the other hand, in the more usual (and more narrow) sense of the term, restructuring involves actions aiming at reordering, displacing, modifying, or removing various physical, organizational, and financial components of an enterprise and its established frame of operation. Physical restructuring may entail the breakup of unwieldy conglomerates, plant closure, removal of equipment, reallocation of productive facilities, modernization and use of new technologies, and recourse to new investments to improve the overall functioning of an enterprise. Organizational restructuring may entail staff reductions, retraining, and development; changes in the output mix; supply changes; and market reorientations; as well as various types of outsourcing and possible combinations with other firms. Financial restructuring may involve adjustments to the loss of government subsidies and government transfer of resources, handling the question of debt accumulation (including interenterprise arrears, tax arrears, and wage arrears), and establishing new financial rules, regulations, and connections. All these processes are difficult to handle, and they are very costly and time consuming. Certain countries – for example, the Czech Republic – gave priority to rapid privatization and planned to limit restructuring to a minimum, while other countries resorted to partial transformations as the processes of privatization started to stumble badly.

A major decision related to these kinds of changes concerns who should be responsible for the transformation measures. The state? And if so, which bodies of the state? The government's organizations representing the state as a shareholder, some of its specific restructuring departments, its financial institutions? Or the state enterprises themselves? These critical questions have often been debated throughout the area and have been handled in a variety of ways. In this regard, the case of Russia is particularly telling. As privatization unfolded there, it was observed that companies that had started to reduce inventories, shed labor, change their output mix, and require prepayment for their products tended to be small or medium-sized enterprises. Less progress took place among the larger enterprises, with the exception of certain high-technology and defense establishments active in both the domestic and foreign markets. (Note that, throughout the area, most large money-losing state enterprises have avoided restructuring because they were allowed to roll over credits from state-owned banks and accumulate tax and social security arrears.) Finally in April 1993, the G7 sponsored a $3 billion Privatization and Restructuring Program (PRP) to support the restructuring of privatized Russian enterprises. The PRP adopted a regional focus and provided foreign assistance in equity investment, technical assistance, and loan guarantees.[15]

Privatization and restructuring require for their successful unfolding a supporting financial sector capable of collecting and channeling savings to their most productive uses and able to manage an effective system of payments. In the specific conditions of the passage from a command-and-control system to market-driven relations, the transformation of the financial sector necessitates the restructuring of bank assets and enterprises' debts, along with radical changes with regard to the incentives available to both bank and enterprise managers. In the early phases of the transition, important changes were made in traditional Soviet banking – as had also been the case in the other transition economies: a two-tier system was established through separating commercial banking from the monetary authority, and efforts were then made to decentralize the financial decisions. Yet the transfer of assets from the old centralized system to the new commercial banks did not always provide them with an adequate capital base, a fact that at times made them unable to handle the actual and potential losses from loans that could not be serviced or repaid. The bad loans included nonperforming assets on banks' balance sheets, mostly in the form of overdue credits extended to enterprises that could not properly adjust to the changes in the macro-environment caused by the transition. The problem of bad loans in fact became a central problem whose implications went far beyond the banking sector alone. Three approaches developed in this respect, in both the former USSR and elsewhere in the region. One solution was simply to write off the old bad loans, putting the burden of the new loans on the banks with the hope that they would eventually grow out of the problem by widening the spread between lending and deposit rates of interest. A second solution was to impose the burden of restructuring on enterprises through enforced bankruptcies of the insolvent debtors. A third option was to get the state directly involved in the process of restructuring. All three solutions were experimented with in the transitional economies.[16] Nonetheless, the banking system is still the Achilles' heel of most of these economies. The payment system is still inefficient, bank portfolios are still unhealthy, and bad debts and interenterprise debts are still accumulating. Commercial banks detached from the old centralized system still play dominant roles in the loan and deposit markets, despite the proliferation of private banks, while a series of bank scandals have shown that regulation and supervision remain inadequate.[17] Paradoxically, the proliferation of commercial banks – for instance, in Russia, where there were 2,350 such banks registered in 1994 – although a necessary condition for market-oriented reforms, has also been one of the causes of the accumulated bad debts. Indeed, as a study of the *Economist*'s Intelligence Unit has pointed out, these banks have channeled, as under the old Soviet system, cheap credit to "their" enterprises (i.e., companies in which they hold shares), and then the banks obtained matching credit from the Russian Central Bank.[18]

A kind of trade-off has developed between the speed and extent of privatization and the adoption of effective bankruptcy procedures. Some countries placed their emphasis on privatization, while others placed their emphasis on enforcing financial discipline on companies not yet privatized. In the Czech Republic, for instance, most of the state-owned enterprises were rapidly privatized, while the government deliberately delayed the implementation of the bankruptcy law until 1993, because of the threat this law represented for them. In the end, the government found itself in the difficult position of having to choose either to liquidate the insolvent companies or to renationalize them through a debt-for-equity swap, preparatory to their eventual reprivatization. In Hungary, the early (1992) bankruptcy law implementation helped lower interenterprise arrears, made insolvency procedures mandatory for debtors, and then stimulated privatization. Yet it should also be noted that Hungary shielded some 100 large money-losing companies from insolvency and transferred them from the privatizing authorities to the entity holding the bad debts, thus making their privatization more difficult. Poland, in a kind of intermediate approach, rapidly adopted a lax bankruptcy law applicable to both private and state enterprises. The law left some crucial state claims, such as tax and social security payments, outside the scope of reorganization.[19] Within the Russian Federation, laws relating to bankruptcy were erratic and contradictory. Russia enacted two important pieces of legislation: one in 1990, before the dissolution of the Soviet Union, and one in 1992. But in practice it delayed their application for a variety of reasons, giving consistent preference to reorganization over liquidation of any insolvent enterprise.[20]

6.3. Comparative Paths of Economic Change

During what might be called Russia's and its former East European satellites' "first critical phase of transition" from their collapsing command-and-control order to a system with increasingly significant private sectors – say from 1990 to 1995 – none of these countries reached their 1989 GDP level. However, after deep drops in income and production, all of them, with the exception of the Russian Federation, started to register increases rather than decreases in their economic growth. How did the transformation processes express themselves in changes in the GDP, the structure of production, gross industrial and agricultural outputs, volume of investment, shifts in employment, patterns of foreign interdependence, and the evolution of relative prices? To which particular factor(s) may these changes be attributed? The detailed tabulations that follow seem to me indispensable for visualizing – as clearly as the available data allow it – not only the broad directions of these developments, but also the essential similarities and differences that arose in these processes among the countries considered.

As can be seen from Figure 6.1, and as detailed in Table 6.2, the fall in the GDP of the Russian Federation and of truncated Yugoslavia were of the same order by the end of the period under review: they hovered at around 50 percent of the 1989 level. One can certainly infer that the dismemberment of these countries' former territorial frameworks markedly affected this decline. In contrast, by 1995, in both the CETE and the SETE groups, all the countries reached 75 to 80 percent of their 1989 levels, with the exception of Poland – which attained 97 percent of its 1989 level. For all the countries considered except the Russian Federation, the period of deep decline – as clearly observable in Table 6.2 – extended over four years (1990–1993), with the troughs in 1991 and 1992. Recovery started in 1994 (slightly earlier for Poland and Romania) and continued, with variations, into 1995. Only Russia still registered a deep decline in 1994 and a smaller one in 1995. At the time of the steepest fall in GDP, in 1992, the per capita incomes in some of these countries dropped below Third World averages. According to UN calculations, in the CETE these levels ranged from a low of $2,085 for Slovakia to a high of $3,378 for Hungary, with Poland (at $2,356) and the Czech Republic ($2,623) in the middle. Within the SETE, the differences were more striking. Per capita income reportedly ranged from $197 for Albania to $3,840 for truncated Yugoslavia. Figures in between included $827 for the Russian Federation, $833 for Romania, and $1,070 for Bulgaria.[21]

We have already examined some of the factors underlying the deep changes in output and employment, including the transformation of ownership relations and the inevitable concomitant disruptions of traditional internal and external links. Other important contributing elements include large shifts in the structures of production, in gross industrial output, and in the volume of investment – all interacting unfavorably with changes in the supply and demand picture and with fluctuations in costs and prices. The shifts in the structure of production can be rapidly perceived by focusing on changes in the sectoral contributions to the GDP – of agriculture, industry, and services – between the crucial 1990 and 1994 dates. Broadly put, the contribution of industry has fallen, that of services has sharply increased, while that of agriculture (except in Russia) has fluctuated up or down within narrow ranges. Briefly, the size of the contribution of industry to the Russian GDP fell by

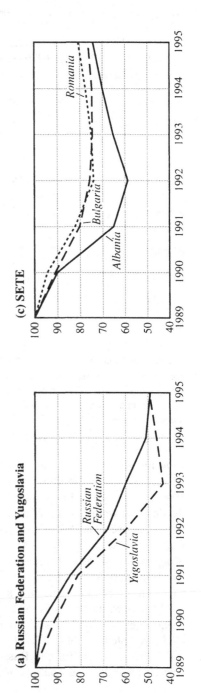

(b) CETE

(c) SETE

Figure 6.1. Russian Federation and Eastern Europe: GDP, 1989–1995 (1989=100). (a) Yugoslavia in the new frontier (would normally be included in SETE); gross material product; (b) Central European Transitional Economies (Czech Republic, Slovak Republic, Hungary, and Poland); (c) South European Transitional Economies (Albania, Bulgaria, and Romania). Based on *Economics of Transition*, Oxford University Press for the European Bank for Reconstruction and Development, Vol. 3, no. 4, 1995, pp. 525–532; and UN Secretariat of Economic Commission of Europe, *Economic Survey of Europe, 1994–1995*, New York, UN, p. 249.

(a) Russian Federation and Yugoslavia

Table 6.2. *Russia and Eastern Europe: Rates of Growth of Real GDP,
Annual Percent Change, 1990–1995*

Country or Area	1990	1991	1992	1993	1994	1995 Proj.	1995 (1989 = 100)
Russian Federation	−2	−13	−19	−12	−15	−3	49
CETE[a]							
Czech Republic	0	−14	−6	−1	3	4	83
Slovakia	0	−15	−7	−4	5	5	82
Hungary	−4	−12	−3	−3	2	2	82
Poland	−12	−8	3	4	5	6	97
SETE[b]							
Albania	−10	−28	−10	11	7	6	74
Bulgaria	−9	−12	−7	−2	1	3	76
Romania	−6	−13	−10	1	3	4	81
Yugoslavia	−8	−11	−26	−27	7	7	49

Note: Rounded figures.
[a]Central European Transitional Economies.
[b]South European Transitional Economies.
Sources: Based on *Economics of Transition*, Oxford University Press for the
European Bank for Reconstruction and Development, Vol. 3, no. 4, 1995, pp.
525–532; and UN Secretariat of Economic Commission of Europe, *Economic
Survey of Europe, 1994–1995*, New York, UN, p. 249.

1994 by 5 points in relation to the respective share it held in 1990. In the
CETE, except for the Czech Republic and Hungary, the drop in relation to
1990 was as high as 19.4 points for Poland and 23 for Slovakia. In the SETE,
the declines were on the order of 16 to 17 percent. By contrast, increases in
the respective contributions of services in all the countries considered, including Russia, ranged from 15 to 22 points. Finally, while the contribution
of agriculture to GDP decreased in Russia by as much as 10 points, in the
CETE the decreases were on the order of 3 to 6 percent, and within the SETE
slight increases were registered in Albania and Romania.[22]

The marked decreases in industry are delineated year by year in Table 6.3.
Clearly, the trends in industrial output parallel the direction of changes in the
GDP presented in Table 6.2. The deepest troughs again center around 1991
and 1992 – except for the Russian Federation and truncated Yugoslavia,
where severe declines continue later on. After the massive falls in industrial

Table 6.3. *Russia and Eastern Europe: Gross Industrial Output, Annual Percent Changes, 1990–1995*

Country or Area	1990	1991	1992	1993	1994	1995 Proj.	1994 (1989 = 100)
Russian Federation	NA	–8.0	–18.0	–14.1	–20.9	–13.0	51
CETE[a]							
Czech Republic	–3.5	–24.4	–7.9	–5.3	2.3	NA	65
Slovak Republic	–4.0	–17.6	–14.1	–10.6	6.4	NA	64
Hungary	–4.5	–19.1	–9.8	3.9	9.1	4.0	79
Poland	–24.2	–11.9	3.9	7.3	13.0	NA	84
SETE[b]							
Albania	–7.5	–41.9	–30.1	2.5	–18.6	2.0	35
Bulgaria	–16.8	–22.2	–15.9	–10.0	2.0	NA	50
Romania	–19.0	–22.8	–21.9	1.3	3.3	NA	52
Yugoslavia	NA	–17.6	–22.4	–37.4	1.2	9.0	35

Note: NA denotes "not available."
[a]Central European Transitional Economies.
[b]South European Transitional Economies.
Sources: UN Dept. of Economic and Social Information and Policy Analysis, *World Economic and Social Survey, 1995*, New York, UN, 1995, p. 306 (for 1990 only); all other, UN Secretariat of Economic Commission of Europe, *Economic Survey of Europe, 1994–1995*, New York, UN, pp. 70 and 250.

output in 1991 – foreshadowed in Poland and in the SETE by sharp drops in 1990 – a slow recovery is clearly under way in most countries (with the exception of Russia and Albania). Yet by 1994, in comparison with 1989, the gross industrial output was on the order of only 65 to 85 percent in the CETE, while lingering in the SETE at between 35 and 50 percent and in Russia at around 50 percent. The fall in industrial output, along with the increases in services indicated before, reflects up to a point both the illogical development of some of the industries concerned (built under the spur of the unbalanced military orientation of these economies) and the new, vigorous contribution of private initiative to the expansion and diversification of much-needed and long-neglected services.

In a period of contractions in the GDP, gross investment in fixed capital also exhibits massive decreases. While again the troughs were in 1991 and 1992, the decreases continued unabated in most countries in 1993, and sharp

Table 6.4. *Russia and Eastern Europe: Gross Investment, Annual Percent Changes, 1990–1995*

Country or Area	1990	1991	1992	1993	1994	1995 Est.
Russian Federation	0.1	−15.5	−40.0	−12.0	−27.0	−11.0
CETE[a]						
Czech Republic	−2.1	−17.7	8.9	−7.7	6.0	NA
Slovak Republic	11.7	−25.2	−15.3	−16.0	−14.3	NA
Hungary	−7.1	−10.4	−2.8	−0.7	35.0	NA
Poland	NA	−4.4	2.3	2.9	8.0	5.0
SETE[b]						
Albania	−14.8	NA	NA	NA	NA	NA
Bulgaria	−18.5	−19.9	−23.2	−29.7	−20.2	NA
Romania	−35.6	−31.6	13.1	2.8	15.6	NA
Yugoslavia	−20.1	−14.0	−29.8	−37.0	NA	NA

Note: NA denotes "not available."
[a]Central European Transitional Economies.
[b]South European Transitional Economies.
Sources: "Russian Economic Monitor," *PlanEcon Report*, Vol. 11, nos. 30–31, Oct. 6, 1996, p. 9 (for Russia only); UN Secretariat of Economic Commission of Europe, *Economic Survey of Europe, 1994–1995*, New York, UN, p. 92.

drops were also registered in 1994 for Russia, Slovakia, and Bulgaria. As can be seen from Table 6.4, Russia's decreases were particularly severe in 1992 and again in 1994. According to various estimates, Russia's investment in 1995 amounted to less than 30 percent of the 1989 volume.

The breakup of the Soviet Union and the Council of Mutual Economic Assistance (CMEA) severely affected the direction and volume of foreign trade in each of the countries considered. In 1989 about a quarter of Soviet exports and imports went to or came from the CMEA countries (i.e., the Eastern European countries, then including Eastern Germany but excluding Albania and Yugoslavia). At the time, 40 percent of the Soviet Union's exports and about 50 percent of its imports were accounted for by trade with the developed countries. By 1994, the Russian Federation's trade with Eastern Europe had fallen to 12 and 8 percent of its exports and imports, respectively, while its trade with the developed countries had risen in both directions to

70 percent. As for volume, at current prices, Soviet trade in 1989 amounted to close to $110 billion for exports and $115 billion for imports, while the Russian Federation's trade in 1994 accounted for $48 billion for exports and $28 billion for imports. Each member of the CETE and SETE in turn had to adjust to these enormous shifts; yet the trade volumes of the two groups evolved differently. In the case of the CETE, trade (at current prices) accounted for $36 billion in exports and $33 billion in imports in 1989; they rose to $44 and $53 billion, respectively, in 1994. In the case of the SETE the shifts were downward: from $20 billion and $18 billion for exports and imports in 1989 (even including only truncated Yugoslavia), they fell to $14 and $13 billion, respectively, in 1994.[23] Most of these countries are heavily indebted. Russia's long-term foreign debt is estimated to have reached over $92 billion in 1994: the country is in substantial arrears on debt payments and will face large-scale repayment obligations for the next several years. The most heavily indebted among the countries of Eastern Europe – whose total debt was estimated at $104 billion – are Hungary, whose external debt was over $27 billion in 1994, and Poland, whose debt amounted to close to $44 billion.[24]

One of the crucial direct consequences of the economic reforms has been the fall in employment. Unemployment, which did not exist under central planning, surged forward as restructuring reforms gained momentum. Now, high unemployment causes not only loss of income and the expansion of poverty, but also increased social tension, which may seriously hinder both the pace and extent of the reforms. Unemployment certainly cannot be solved without high increases in output and the creation of new jobs in new activities. The prospects from these points of view, however, are as yet unfavorable; rather, there is a strong likelihood of massive long-term unemployment in most of these countries, if not all of them. The transition process will have to continue to adapt to increasing shifts toward more labor- and skill-intensive industries where most rapid growth may be registered (namely, in industries such as textiles and garments, foodstuffs, and service-based products). At the same time, these countries will have to find the unemployment compensation system that best fits their present and prospective development. (I turn to this issue in detail in the next section.)

For now let me add that as the patterns of demand have changed considerably, so too have the other dimensions of macroeconomic activity. Regular data on changes in the producer price index, which is a leading indicator for the direction of change in the consumer price index, are not available for most of these countries. The data on retail/consumer prices presented in Table 6.5 show clearly that the most severe inflation has plagued the Russian Federation and continues at very high rates. (The average monthly inflation rates

Table 6.5. *Russia and Eastern Europe: Evolution of Inflation in Retail and Consumer Prices (End of Year, Percent Changes), 1991–1995*

Country or Area	1991	1992	1993	1994 Est.	1995 Proj.
Russian Federation	144	2,318	841	203	145
CETE[a]					
Czech Republic	42	13	18	10	10
Slovak Republic	58	9	25	12	10
Hungary	32	22	21	21	28
Poland	60	44	38	30	23
SETE[b]					
Albania	104	237	31	16	5
Bulgaria	339	79	64	122	50
Romania	223	199	296	62	30

Note: Rounded figures.
[a]Central European Transitional Economies.
[b]South European Transitional Economies.
Source: Economics of Transition, Oxford University Press for the European Bank for Reconstruction and Development, Vol. 3, no. 4, 1995, p. 525.

there increased from 15 percent in 1991 to 33 percent in 1992. In 1993 the monthly rate fell to 20 percent and in 1994, to 10.3 percent.) In the CETE, the Czech and Slovak Republics seem closest to macroeconomic stabilization in the sense that they expect their yearly inflation rates to fall to single digits. The highest inflation rates in the CETE are those of Hungary and Poland. The persistence of great inflationary concerns in these countries despite the strong emphasis on macroeconomic stabilization – so much advertised early in the case of Poland by its Western economic advisers – suggests that there are limits to what can be achieved with purely macroeconomic measures in periods of basic reform and vast economic transformations. The Polish government cut its budget deficit in 1993 and 1994 and has pursued a stringent monetary policy; yet all this was not sufficient to cut down inflation. Many agree that taming inflation may require attention to microeconomic and structural issues, such as "market imperfections, competition, enterprise behavior, structure of public spending, and expectations of economic agents and the general public."[25] In the SETE, the high-inflation countries continue to be Bulgaria and Romania.

6.4. Readjusting Social Protection

After the collapse of their command-and-control regimes, Russia and the East European countries have increasingly been confronted by two types of critical problems concerning their social support systems. The first involves the emergence of new risks unknown in the past, namely massive unemployment and the attendant expanding poverty. The second concerns the need to readjust social protection with regard to the concepts of support needed, the mix of benefits in cash and kind, financing sources, and methods of organization and management.

These countries' early confidence in the possibility of handling unemployment by means of insurance and relatively high benefit levels soon vanished. As economic reforms got under way with the consequences we have been examining concerning the structure and levels of output and the pace of inflation, the early generosity declined rapidly. The duration and levels of all kinds of social benefits were reduced, and, in addition, eligibility criteria were tightened. Unemployment benefits were brought down throughout the region to between 27 and 38 percent of the average wage, and in the Russian Federation to as low as 13 percent. The redefinition of eligibility criteria drastically reduced the number of benefit recipients, to between 25 and 50 percent of the unemployed (see Table 6.6). The overall changes in the economy and in the labor markets strongly affected the spread of poverty. Millions of workers in the state sectors fell into the ranks of the unemployed and joined the new poor through direct wage losses, incapacity to reenter the workforce, or shortened work time and unpaid leaves. In every country for which data are available, the population living below some version of the poverty line sharply increased between 1989 and the mid-1990s. According to UNICEF data, the percentage of households (H) or the population (P) living in poverty increased between 1989 and 1992 as follows in the CETE: in the Czech Republic, from 5.7 to 18.2 percent (H); in Slovakia, from 7.1 to 18.3 percent (P); in Poland, from 20.5 to 42.5 percent (P). In the SETE, the datum for Bulgaria for 1992 was 53.6 percent (H), while for Romania the change over the period was from 27.3 to 51.1 percent (H). The UNICEF datum for Russia hit the highest level, indicating a shift from 16.0 to 66.8 percent (P) – a figure fitting the trends I indicated in Section 4.4 for that country.[26]

The readjustment of the social protection system raises a host of problems concerning, first of all, the restructuring of pensions, the dominant factor of the whole insurance system; the scrutiny of all kind of allowances and, in particular, family allowances; subsistence-level aid in cases of need (poverty relief); the development of health care; and the financing and administration of all the system's programs.

The transformation of the regionwide inherited structure involving five

Table 6.6. *Russia and Eastern Europe: Unemployment Levels and Benefits, 1994*

Country or Area	Percentage of Labor Force Unemployed (1)	Percentage of Unemployed Receiving Benefits (2)	Unemployment Benefits as Percentage of Average Wage (3)
Russian Federation	7.1[a]	NA	13
CETE[b]			
Czech Republic	3.2	47	27
Slovak Republic	14.6	23	31
Hungary	10.9	37	26
Poland	16.0	50	36
SETE[c]			
Albania	18.0	NA	NA
Bulgaria	12.8	37	35
Romania	10.9	41	28

Note: NA denotes "not available."
[a]Estimate.
[b]Central European Transitional Economies.
[c]South European Transitional Economies.
Sources: Column 1: UN Dept. of Economic and Social Information and Policy Analysis, *World Economic and Social Survey, 1995*, New York, UN, p. 18; Columns 2 and 3: UN Secretariat of Economic Commission of Europe, *Economic Survey of Europe, 1994–1995*, New York, UN, pp. 111, 118.

types of pensions (for old age, disability, loss of the breadwinner, early retirement, and services to the state – with many benefits distributed in kind) is certainly one of the most important and difficult tasks facing the region's governments. A combination of factors – the new configuration of income, output, and employment structures; demographic evolutions; changing concepts of social justice; and the new procedures replacing old insurance provisions – all tend to affect the preceding system of pensions. The latter are now assumed to have provided disincentives to work and save, to have been costly, to have offered inadequate protection in an inflationary environment, and to have been riddled with all kinds of other deficiencies. In the majority of the countries considered, independent insurance funds have been created, ending complete dependence on the state budget. The indexation of pensions has started or is projected, with linkages to either prices or wages. Funding is ensured mostly by contributions paid by employers, often with state budget guarantees. To better adjust pensions to contributions, the number of working years used to calculate pensions has been increased, while early retirement privileges (e.g., for dangerous jobs or those causing poor health) have tended to be eliminated. In general, the idea of separate risk and on ad hoc pension or other compensation for damage arising from a given occupation tends now to be discouraged. The search for effective risk management in the workplace, coupled with rehabilitation offered on an equal basis whatever the cause of the work disability, now attracts increasing attention in many of the countries we have been studying.[27]

Also under close scrutiny are family allowances. These used to be relatively high, employment-related, increasing with each new baby up to the third child, and differentiated on social grounds (single parent, handicapped children). The ratio of family allowances to wages was higher than in the market economies: they constituted, in fact, a wage subsidy. Reforms in process aim at cost containment via taxation of benefits, shortening of their duration (e.g., no benefits after the child leaves school), and keener differentiation by the age of the child, size of the family, and means testing to determine the "truly needy." Yet various studies initiated by the World Bank point out that in fact market wages do not take family obligations into account, that the size of the family is an important predictor of child poverty, and that there are practical difficulties in taxing family allowances. In any case, given their shrinking resources, the real value of family allowances has decreased in all these countries.[28]

The inherited health care system, though overcentralized, highly inefficient, and providing low-quality service, nonetheless was easily accessible, combined curative and preventive functions, and could be afforded by the general public. Its overall reform has similar objectives as those for pensions or family allowances, namely cost containment, increased accountability for doctors and hospitals, and better management. Deep changes have already occurred spontaneously (particularly in Russia) or have been carried out systematically, notably through privatizing the pharmaceutical industry and certain hospitals, clinics, and ambulance services. Cost containment in public health services entails, however, a lowering of standards, further deterioration of preventive services, and significant increases in copayments, along with stricter rules for access to hospital services. Unfortunately, as in the state enterprise sector, public health care delivery and financing suffers from the lack of appropriate cost accounting. Neither the health care providers (administrators, physicians, nurses, technicians) nor the consumers have proper knowledge of the cost of medical services and the risks associated with inefficiency in providing them. With the deterioration of public services, the ending of the state's monopoly, and increased free choice, one can expect a rapid development of standards of care – but only for those who can afford to pay.[29]

As a report of the International Labour Office has pointed out, long-term unemployment and widespread poverty will continue to remain major problems in the entire region. Since large changes in the structure of employment are bound to continue, given the necessary shifts in production and the reallocation of resources, the resultant reductions in the economically active population will also have deep social repercussions. As we have seen, privatization, restructuring, and trade liberalization have proceeded at different paces and in different forms in the countries considered; often the initial liberalization measures have been reversed and then reinstated, at times with diminished scope and forcefulness. Yet certainly these measures must be carried to their logical end. Proponents of rapid change argue that all this must necessarily continue at a rapid pace, since anything else would thwart the process of transition to market economies. The "gradualists" point out, I believe correctly, that another massive unemployment surge, in a wave leading to falling wages and increased income inequality and poverty, would have unwelcome and possibly unmanageable social repercussions. Moreover, the creation of effective institutions, along with the viable restructuring of product and labor markets – still ensuring that change occurs in the right direction – will require a number of years, well beyond the turbulent ones of the "first phase."[30]

6.5. Concluding Comments

Paul Starr rightly noted in 1990 that governments "sold assets, contracted out services, disengaged themselves from certain functions, and reduced barriers to entry into public monopolies" years before the post-1970s privatization drives in the West and the East. What is new in the recent drives is the adoption of privatization programs, that is, "packages of policies pursued by governments with the explicit objective of significantly recasting the role and relations of state, market, and civil society."[31] But, of course, vast differences exist with respect to this "recasting." In the West, notably in the United Kingdom and France, privatization drives have been directed at more than the stated goals of increasing efficiency and securing additional government revenues. They have also aimed at discarding certain well-entrenched ideas concerning the state's agenda and at demolishing certain political structures erected by left-wing parties on the basis of nationalizations and/or the extension of the powers of the municipalities. In the former command-and-control economies, the complexity, scale, and range of the programs of privatization have exceeded the scope of the West's intended changes. In the East, privatization was seen as part and parcel of the process transforming the socioeconomic and political foundations of the society. The privatization processes were in fact launched – especially in a country like Russia, menaced by a potential civil war – with the purpose of rapidly demolishing the party's command-and-control system; of dismantling its institutions, first and foremost the state's ownership of the entire country's unified system of production; and of discarding the party's "strategy of development" predicated on the systematic increase of heavy industry and manufacturing in general at the expense of all the other sectors of the economy.

In the West, privatization itself consisted of selling the private sector a number of large state-owned companies that were already, to a great extent, subject to market forces. On the other hand, in Russia and its former satellites, privatization involved not only transferring the ownership of certain state-owned enterprises to the public, but also creating a new range of institutions, imposing market discipline, and severing most of the connections that privatized firms had had with the state banks and the state's subsidies and preferential loans. Whatever the previous reforms carried out under the old regimes in Hungary, Poland, and Yugoslavia, which had replaced state control with supervision by other regional or local public agencies, these reforms never absolved the state from keeping these firms operating with preferential credit arrangements, subsidies, and tax privileges – that is, operating without market discipline. Put differently, Western privatization was carried out within a well-established framework of institutions and involved the recasting of certain relations between "the state, the market, and civil society." Privatization in the collapsing communist framework imposed, as part of the remodeling of the state, the remodeling of its foundations, structures, and functions in a new, changing economic environment.

The differences with regard to scale between the two types of privatization – Western and Eastern – can best be understood by recalling not only the differences between the two regions (and underlying systems) with regard to the structure of both assets and employment, but also the dissimilarities relating to technological change and obsolescence. The G7 countries have continually led in virtually all fields of modern technology. Yet, of course, in certain cases, they have also had to face the obsolescence of certain types of products and industries, which is unavoidable in any era of technological progress. When obsolescence starts to critically affect certain large, traditional, national or nationalized industries, like coal mining, for instance, the difficulties entailed in shutting them down or liquidating them appear at times insuperable. This has been the case with many British and French coal mines, with the depressed and degraded Borinage coal-mining region of Belgium, and with other mining areas. But in the case of Russia and Eastern Europe, technological obsolescence involves not only mining or a particular industry, but the great majority of the industries created there under the shelter of the autarkic communist strategy of economic development. In a tragic sense, and with deep implications concerning unemployment, poverty, and the dangers of civil war, a large part of the mining and manufacturing establishments in truncated Russia and Eastern Europe constitute a gigantic Borinage – a situation that raises well-nigh insurmountable problems concerning their conversion, retooling, partial restructuring, partial privatization, or closing. In addition, one should not overlook the fact that in the West both domestic and foreign capital owners can certainly muster the funds needed for acquiring establishments offered for privatization whatever their size, provided they can be usefully reconditioned and modernized. In the East domestic capital owners have been able to bid mostly for small state-owned enterprises, warehouses, and means of transport. Only occasionally have they managed to acquire (not necessarily legitimately) medium-sized and large establishments, while foreign capital has remained reluctant to assume large ownership positions in most of these countries.

Certainly all privatization projects included in any Western program, when concluded, have likely affected the distribution of income to a greater or lesser degree through shifts in the acquisition of supplies, the sale of outputs, and the setting of new wage, price, and workforce levels. In the East, the mass privatization programs have a fortiori affected the entire society with respect to not only income and wealth, but also the totality of relations between owners, managers, workers, and the state. Yet privatization has not been carried out there to what one might have assumed would be its natural conclusion. On the one hand, these states are still burdened, as we have seen, by many large and inefficient enterprises that cannot be either sold or properly restructured. On the other hand, some of the privatizations that have already been carried out are incessantly denounced as "giveaways" or as "tools" of the foreign capital suppliers and may still be overturned. The question of the scope of privatization in Russia and in most Central and Southern European countries is not yet fully answered, but certainly a total reversal is not even thinkable. Yet one should note that it may take decades for the state – itself not yet well settled and defined – to withdraw effectively from key ownership positions and from extensive controls over even the privatized enterprises, help develop widely interconnected market relations based on viable economic structures, encourage and support the acquisition of skills needed in a market economy, forge an adequate system of social protection, and overcome the basic problems of the transition to a workable market economy. In this sense nothing is yet definitely settled.[32]

In the West, as some authors have noted, privatization has been in many cases the last-tried solution in seeking to improve the performance of certain public enterprises – that is, after the use of such measures as reorganization, decentralization, commercialization, performance budgeting, management by objectives, productivity councils, and so on have failed.[33] In the East, where there are no discernible constituencies supporting it, large-scale privatization is still not seen as the first and last solution for improving the economy and society, since the cost of the transition – falling income and outputs, rising unemployment, and poverty – still weigh heavily on large strata of the population. Postcommunist Russia's economic options are in various respects even more limited than those of some of its former satellites and more restricted and uncertain than they seemed in 1992, at the time of Yegor Gaidar's premiership and the illusions of the "big bang." The Russian Federation, after a critical first phase of transition (1991–1995), is muddling through a period in which such targets as reaching the 1989 output level, achieving fiscal balance, reducing the rate of inflation to a single digit, and curbing mass unemployment are still far out of sight. I return to these issues in the next chapter.

Part IV

Outlook for the Twenty-first Century

Focusing in historical perspective on the role of the state with regard to public ownership and to welfare in the Western industrialized countries, on the one hand, and in Russia, on the other, I have tried to underline the correspondences that have arisen over time within and between these markedly dissimilar systems. Let me recall briefly the crucial moments and forms of these correspondences and their implications.

With regard to the industrial West, I pointed out that from the very emergence of the national states and the continuous expansion of market relations, the states began to exercise vast control over the types of production, openly protected and subsidized various industrial enterprises, and consolidated their own ownership and direct management over their countries' key industries. Eventually, within the mixed liberal–mercantilist and rapidly industrializing framework of the nineteenth century, the role of government decreased in some respects, but continued in certain Western countries with regard to the promotion of national industries, the subsidization of exports, and the limitation of imports. This direct role of the state expanded further during World War I and the interwar years, as well as during and after World War II. As we noted, the role of welfare also became increasingly significant from the end of the nineteenth century onward and gained in scope and importance during the interwar years and then again particularly after World War II.

As for Russia, from the time of Peter the Great and the reign of some of the following emperors, efforts were made to implant within that country's feudal surroundings various industries (particularly of a military nature) under state ownership or under the state's guidance and control. Western influences had various other important effects on Russia's policies, including the crucial 1861 attempt to demolish (at least in part) the state's serfdom foundations. As I pointed out, even the Bolshevik revolution of 1917 reconstructed the country's economy in many respects along a foreign model, namely along the lines of the German World War I–type economy (*Kriegswirtschaft*). After World War II, the Soviet system's own planning strategy, as well as its concentrated attention on the development of certain heavy industry branches, in turn influenced attempts in both Western countries and most of the less developed countries at centralized planning, broader industrialization, and expanded welfare.

Impressed by the alleged great Soviet successes in planning, industrialization, and economic growth and by the then expanding influence of the Soviet model, a number of well-known economists – the late Jan Timbergen, John K. Galbraith, and Walter W. Rostow, along with some less well known writers – suggested, from the 1950s to the 1970s, that both the capitalists and the communist systems were converging toward a "mixed order" exhibiting a similar mix of goals, controlling devices, processes, and information use. According to Tinbergen (*Lessons from the Past* [1963], *Convergence of Economic Systems East and West* [1967]) the West was moving from traditional factory optimization and management to the complex planning and coordination of entire industries, sectors, and finally, the economy as a whole. And the East was moving through growth and experience from the narrow concepts of the *Kriegswirtschaft* and from extreme scarcity to different patterns of organization and accelerated growth. For Galbraith (*The New Industrial State* [1967]) the economic nucleus of the mature industrial state is formed by the complex of large corporations, the locus of key decisions, long-term planning, and expansion of the economy as a whole. To implement its decisions, the "brain" of this complex, its "technostructure," requires a great measure of autonomy, which it eventually secures – whatever the political system. Convergence between the capitalist and the communist systems begins with modern large-scale production, heavy requirements of capital, sophisticated technology, and, as a prime consequence, "elaborate organization." For Walter W. Rostow (*The Stages of Economic Growth* [1960]), all societies are supposed to be, in their "economic dimensions," within one (or a number) of "stages of growth," defined in terms of real per capita income growth patterns on income distribution between consumption, investment, and leading sectoral complexes of production. Allegedly, the Soviet Union was "technically ready for the age of high mass-consumption" and would have entered into that phase if it could have been convinced that on the world scene there were better alternatives than the arms race or unconditional surrender.

The efforts of redefining the role of the state in the West and then the collapse of the Soviet Union and its former satellites have laid to rest most of the convergence theories, though in slightly revised forms they do reemerge sometimes cautiously, but now with reference to China. What I try to point out in the final chapter is that there is no single, fully predictable pattern of change concerning the role of the state with regard both to the highly developed countries and to Russia and the former party-state communist system. It is erroneous to speak of the historical end of the so-called epoch of the rise and fall of public ownership. I believe that attempts at "redefining" the state will continue, leading to changes not only in the scope and nature of public ownership and of welfare, but also in a variety of other directions. In many respects both public ownership and welfare are still "alive and well." Public control may even expand further in the West in areas in which the private sector cannot provide the services considered of "public interest" and may take new forms with regard to public–private mixed projects and investments or with regard to ways of circumventing budgetary pressures and limitations. Compelling situations concerning the patterns of employment, wages, and foreign competition may also involve various forms of subsidization and income transfers.

On the other hand, as I also indicate in the concluding chapter, it would be erroneous to imagine that the pattern of transition from the communist party-state system to primarily a market-based system would (or could) follow a single, easily traceable road. Russia and the USSR's former Eastern European satellites are far from tending toward a single, identical, structural model independent of their historical traditions and customs, their levels of development and social pressures. Russia's reemergence from the ruins of the Soviet economy and from the struggles and disastrous phases that followed it may tend toward a highly dirigiste kind of economy, if it can eventually curb the powers if its nomenklatura fiefdoms. Other former satellites may move closer to a truly market-determined type of economy. In most of these countries, economic restructuring, vast reallocation of the human capital, and effective privatization may prove more difficult and require much more time than was generally assumed after the collapse of the Soviet empire.

7 Contraction versus Expansion of the Scope of the State

7.1. The Underlying Issues

From the viewpoint of the twenty-first century, what are the prospects concerning the scope of the state – both in the developed industrialized countries of the West, the G7, and in the transitional economies from command-and-control to markets on which I have chosen to focus, namely the Russian Federation and the USSR's former East European satellites? Will the economic developments in the West lead to a further decline in the role of the state, not only with regard to public ownership and welfare but also in other respects, or will they rather tend to push toward combinations of various reductions with new extensions of the functions of the state? And as far as the indicated East European countries are concerned, will further reshaping and institutional adaptations of the state machines bring them closer to a free market economy like that of the United States, or rather to dirigiste economies in which the state always plays a decisive role as owner, regulator, and manipulator of firms that are mostly weak, though market oriented?

In order to tackle these crucial, all-encompassing questions, one must first identify the underlying issues concerning not only the actual but also the potential impact of a range of transformations that have taken place at an accelerating pace – in the West particularly since the late 1970s, and in the East since the middle to late 1980s. These questions concern in particular the nature and scope of changes in the structures of production in the economies considered; the interconnections between the changes in their industries and the growth of certain classes of services; the expansion of their cross-border activities in investment, trade, and the creation of an international production system; and, finally, the concomitant transformations that have taken place in the patterns of employment, unemployment, and earnings, as well as their impact on the behavior and efforts of the populations of each of the countries considered to adjust to them.

Specifically, in regard to the West, one must attempt to identify the scope, range, and general direction of changes in the sectoral structures of employment; the types of changes that have occurred, especially in manufacturing, production and employment, and the links created with certain new services; the influence of inward and outward flows of foreign direct investments (FDI) on gross fixed capital formation, trade, and the creation and/or destruction of jobs; the evolution of the size and composition of full- and part-time employment, as well as the shifts in the employment shares of blue- and white-collar workers, the rates of unemployment, and the impact of all the changes with respect to wage levels and income differentials.

With regard to the indicated Eastern countries, one will have to identify first the most likely prospects arising after the end of what I defined as the "first initial phase" of transformation (1989/1990–1995) that followed the collapse of the old system. The specific elements of concern are output growth, inflation, unemployment, and fiscal balance (i.e., stability), as well as the newly developing relations involving access to new technologies, foreign investment, and the global market. At the same time, one must sketch further possible changes involving privatization, welfare, and other state activities.

Incongruously, the most advanced industrialized countries of the West and the ruined economies of the East seem to suffer from the same kind of affliction, namely a widespread insecurity in the labor force due to these rapid, underlying, and vast structural changes. Certainly as far as the East European countries are concerned, few still nourish optimistic illusions about the possible avoidance of prolonged insecurity and uncertainty as these countries disentangle from their disastrous communist heritage. But as far as the Western economies are concerned, clear-cut differences of opinion persist about the strength and soundness of these feelings of insecurity, particularly in the United States. Thus, the distinguished economist Herbert Stein noted in the *New York Times* in a March 1996 article entitled "Good Times, Bad Vibes," that the country was indeed "swamped with reports that American workers feel terribly insecure, especially about their jobs." Stein added that while he didn't "doubt that the feeling of insecurity exists," he felt it necessary to point out that "what is less clear is that the feeling is very serious." Stein then remarked that in the United States in 1995, the rate of unemployment was on the average so low (5.6 percent) that in the previous twenty years the rate had been lower for only three years. Moreover, the proportion of the total population working was higher "than in any year in history," and highly publicized layoffs by large corporations involved only "a small number of people who enter or leave employment each year."[1] Stein was certainly right on the basis of the data that he used. But, I believe, this is only part of the story. What matters in addition, despite some immediate positive signs, are the long-term structural challenges and their impacts on the future patterns of employment and rewards. I turn to these issues in some detail in Section 7.2, with regard not only to the United States but also to the other industrialized countries. Afterward, I examine the likely prospects of development, under the impact of similar challenges in Eastern Europe in Section 7.3. I then focus on the comparative West–East prospects of change in the scope of the state in Section 7.4. Finally, in Section 7.5, I sketch in broad outline the successive redefinitions of the role of the state encountered throughout the present work.

7.2. Sources of Insecurity in the G7

The range and pace of long-term structural economic changes are reflected in the scope of shifts in the respective weights of the basic sectors – agriculture, industries, and services; in the amplitude of modifications in the respective importance of the manufacturing branches; and in the scale of transformations in the gamut of services. All these changes can be illustrated by the alterations in the way the workforce is used, that is, in the range and scope of its employment and/or unemployment, its required skills, and its rewards.

To start with, I tabulate the sectoral shifts in the structure of economic employment in the G7 over three recent decades, namely for the subperiods 1960–1973, 1974–1979, 1980–1989, and 1990–1993. As Table 7.1 shows, the period was marked by accelerated decreases in the weight of agriculture – most particularly in Japan, France, and Italy, which have caught up with the deep changes that had taken place in this sector long before in the United Kingdom and the United States. (Further recent decreases have also been registered in these countries, as well as in Canada and Germany.) The table further illustrates the decrease in the employment weight of industry, which between 1960–1973 and 1990–1993 declined at the rate of over 18 percent for the United Kingdom, 10 percent for France, 9 percent for the United States and Canada, 6 to 7 percent for Germany, and 5 percent for Italy – while growing less than 1 percent for Japan. To these joint drops in agriculture and industry correspond massive increases in employment in services – excluding government – remarkable particularly in the cases of the United Kingdom and the United States, where they reach, respectively, close to 18 percent and over 14 percent.

The changes in agriculture, as I noted above, follow traditional evolutions in the highly industrialized countries. The changes in manufacturing are brought about by a gamut of technological advances and by newly developing relations in the global market. We can perceive the structural changes in manufacturing in the G7 by observing in Table 7.2 first the relative weight of different branches in 1992 (the odd-numbered columns) and then changes in relative weights between 1984 and 1992 (the even-numbered columns). Clearly, the basic characteristic in the industrialized countries, as shown in

Table 7.1. *Group of Seven: Sectoral Shifts in the Structure of Employment, 1960–1993 (Percent Averages by Subperiods)*

Group of Seven	Sector	Average 1960–1973	Average 1974–1979	Average 1980–1989	Average 1990–1993
United States	Agriculture	5.9	3.9	3.2	2.8
	Industry	34.7	31.2	28.2	25.0
	Services	43.2	48.8	53.6	57.4
	Government	16.2	16.1	15.0	14.7
	Total	100.0	100.0	100.0	100.0
Japan	Agriculture	21.7	12.1	8.9	6.6
	Industry	33.4	35.7	34.7	34.3
	Services	} 44.9	45.7	49.9	53.2
	Government		6.5	6.5	5.9
	Total	100.0	100.0	100.0	100.0
Germany	Agriculture	10.4	6.2	4.6	} 85.1
	Industry	47.8	45.0	41.3	
	Services	31.5	34.8	38.8	
	Government	10.3	14.0	15.3	14.9
	Total	100.0	100.0	100.0	100.0
France	Agriculture	16.7	9.8	7.6	5.3
	Industry	38.9	37.8	32.7	29.0
	Services	} 44.4	33.7	37.6	42.2
	Government		18.7	22.1	23.5
	Total	100.0	100.0	100.0	100.0
Italy	Agriculture	24.6	16.1	11.6	8.2
	Industry	37.6	38.5	34.7	32.5
	Services	} 37.8	31.3	38.6	43.6
	Government		14.1	15.1	15.7
	Total	100.0	100.0	100.0	100.0
United Kingdom	Agriculture	3.8	2.8	2.5	2.2
	Industry	45.5	39.9	32.6	27.2
	Services	33.7	36.4	43.6	51.9
	Government	17.0	20.9	21.3	18.7
	Total	100.0	100.0	100.0	100.0
Canada	Agriculture	9.6	5.9	5.1	4.4
	Industry	32.0	29.3	26.2	23.2
	Services	} 58.4	44.9	49.1	51.8
	Government		19.9	19.6	20.6
	Total	100.0	100.0	100.0	100.0

Source: Based on OECD, *Historical Statistics, 1960–1993*, Paris, OECD, 1995, pp. 40, 42, 44.

Table 7.2. Group of Seven: Structure of Employment in Manufacturing, 1992 (Percentages) and 1992 Employment as Percentage of 1984

Industrial Structure	United States		Japan		Germany		France		Italy[a]		United Kingdom		Canada	
	1992	1992 as % of 1984	1992	1992 as % of 1984	1992	1992 as % of 1984	1992	1992 as % of 1984	1992	1992 as % of 1984	1992	1992 as % of 1984	1992	1992 as % of 1984
	(1)	(2)	(3)	(4)	(5)	(6)	(7)	(8)	(9)	(10)	(11)	(12)	(13)	(14)
Food, beverages, and tobacco	9.1	100	11.1	101	7.2	101	13.0	94	7.4	89	12.9	91	13.6	100
Textiles, apparel, and leather	10.0	84	10.3	93	5.4	77	9.0	69	17.7	88	9.9	74	9.0	75
Wood products and furniture	5.2	100	3.9	88	3.6	101	4.5	87	3.8	87	3.9	91	8.5	98
Paper, paper products, and printing	12.4	101	7.6	101	5.1	101	8.0	101	5.3	93	10.0	93	13.9	102
Chemical products	11.3	101	9.6	101	14.3	114	12.3	99	10.7	77	12.4	99	11.8	109
Nonmetallic mineral products	3.0	94	4.1	100	3.6	98	3.3	87	5.3	75	4.1	85	2.7	92
Basic metal industries	3.8	81	4.1	85	4.8	85	5.1	77	6.3	71	4.0	71	5.2	80
Fabricated metal products	43.2	91	47.3	101	55.3	114	42.4	89	42.1	95	41.2	82	33.0	101
Other manufacturing	2.0	101	2.0	100	0.7	105	2.4	92	1.4	217	1.6	90	2.3	97
Total manufacturing	100.0	95	100.0	103	100.0	108	100.0	89	100.0	88	100.0	85	100.0	97

[a]Data for Italy are for 1991.

Source: Computed from OECD, Industrial Structure Statistics, 1993, Paris, OECD, 1995, pp. 29, 57, 86, 94, 188, 199, 245.

columns 1–7, is the critical importance of heavy industry products. The figure for fabricated metal products ranges from 55 percent of the total employment in manufacturing in Germany to between 41 and 47 percent for all the others (except Canada, where it reaches 33 percent). A distant second in importance is the chemical products group, reaching in all the countries considered between about 10 and 14 percent. Yet the crucial structural changes over the relatively short but important period 1984–1992 (observable in the even-numbered columns) include the fall in employment in fabricated metal products (in the United States, France, and the United Kingdom) and the G7-wide decreases in basic metal industries (mainly iron and steel), the other heavy industry branch. In line with these changes, sharp drops in employment are registered in the light industry group, that is, in textiles, apparel, and leather goods (again, throughout the G7). Finally, there were overall falls in total manufacturing employment (in all G7 countries except Japan and Germany).

The causes of changes in the basic sectors are very different. Manufacturing, the core of industrialized countries, has been reshaped by a variety of continuous pressures – for concentration and/or for mergers; for downsizing or for expanding the scope of production; and for changing processes, shifting the relations between inputs and outputs, absorbing new technologies, improving the scale of factory operation and engineering design, rearranging information flows and transportation, and searching for growth opportunities in global markets. Incessant technological advances in the developed countries lead to decreases in certain types of light industries, easily inherited at certain stages by developing countries, as has been traditionally the case for textiles, apparel, and leather goods and continues to be the case now. Other factors leading to shrinkages in basic industries may be critical technological changes in production – as has been the case since the 1950s for iron and steel, and which has continued through the period considered with the development of new, efficient "minimills" – as well as the growth of new interconnections between manufacturing at the highest levels of development and diversified new business services involving engineering, information processing, accounting, legal, and other services.

One must remember, with regard to services, that while the latter make available to business and consumers the products of the goods-producing industries, in so doing they also channel a variety of inputs used themselves in the production of certain goods, and in this sense they may be viewed as producer services. Thus, the expansion of services illustrated in Table 7.1 is not the perverse result of deindustrialization, but rather the consequence of increasing new interconnections between industries in general and business services in particular. OECD data available for the 1980s show that massive increases in employment in services have generally been concentrated in business and finance. In fact, increases in the latter services ranged from 3 to 5 percent (for 1979–1990), compared with overall increases of 0.8 to 2.2 percent for total nongovernmental services. On the other hand, the rapid advances in telecommunications and information technologies have also expanded the boundaries of tradeability of many services. These advances have created new opportunities for long-distance service exports from the industrialized countries, whose estimated potential could possibly double these exports (now running at about $180 billion). As computer and telecommunication technologies transform the structure and quality of certain services, awareness of the importance of efficient producer services increases, and their development is seen as indispensable to sustained growth. As the convergence of computer and communication technologies promotes the growth of electronic networks, large corporations are continually expanding their relations through the Internet system. And, as in the case of trade, services are also becoming a crucial component of the flows of foreign direct investments (FDI).

A remarkable feature of recent decades has been the rapid growth of FDI and the acquisition of colossal real estate holdings by nonresidents, in developed and developing countries alike. In today's globalizing world economy, FDI flows enable its participants to contribute to and gain from the growth in specialization and in the size and scope of world markets. This de facto creation and expansion of an international production system is an important means for transnational corporations (TNCs – sometimes called multinational corporations [MNCs]) to secure and expand markets for their products, as well as to internalize cross-border transactions based on intrafirm divisions. The international production system also constitutes an "internal" market to which its individual members have privileged access. It has been estimated that in 1993 this simultaneously internal and international market accounted for one-third of world trade. Furthermore, access to larger markets strengthens the competitiveness of TNCs, through specialization and economies of scale in both host and home countries. The overall investment activities of the TNCs are best assessed by an examination of the size and structure of FDI. As can be seen from Table 7.3, the interior stock of the G7 reached $1.1 trillion in 1994, about three times its 1985 size, while its much larger exterior stock ($1.7 trillion) also more than tripled in relation to 1985. Characteristically, more than 40 percent of the interior stock was located in the United States, and about 35 percent of the G7 outward stock belonged to U.S. companies. The world outward stock, attributable to more than 250,000 affiliates controlled by at least 38,000 firms, stood at an estimated $2.4 trillion at the end of 1994 (the G7 share of this was on the order of 73 percent).[2]

The relations within the G7 of the yearly inflows and outflow of FDI to each country's gross fixed capital formation for the periods 1981–1985, 1986–1990, and 1993 are presented in Table 7.4. These relations furnish an

Table 7.3. *Group of Seven: FDI Inward and Outward Stock, 1985, 1990, and 1994 (Millions of Dollars)*

Group of Seven	Inward Stock				Outward Stock			
	1985	1990	1994		1985	1990	1994
United States	184,615	394,911	504,401		251,034	435,219	610,061
Japan	4,740	9,850	17,772		43,970	201,440	277,733
Germany	36,926	111,231	132,409		59,909	151,581	205,608
France	33,392	86,514	142,089		37,077	110,126	183,406
Italy	18,976	57,985	60,349		16,301	56,102	83,462
United Kingdom	64,028	218,213	214,231		100,313	230,825	281,170
Canada	64,657	113,054	105,606		40,947	78,853	105,606
Total	407,334	991,758	1,176,857		549,551	1,264,146	1,747,046

Source: UN, *World Investment Report, 1995: Transnational Corporations and Competitiveness*, New York, UN, pp. 406, 407.

Table 7.4. *Group of Seven: Ratios of Foreign Direct Investment Inflows and Outflows to Gross Fixed Capital Formation, and Ratios of Gross Fixed Capital Formation to GDP, 1981–1993*

Group of Seven	Inflows			Outflows		
	Annual Average			Annual Average		
	1981–1985	1986–1990	1993	1981–1985	1986–1990	1993
United States	2.9	6.9	4.7	1.7	2.8	7.8
	18.2	15.7	13.9	18.2	15.7	13.9
Japan	0.1	0.1	—	1.5	4.1	1.1
	29.0	30.0	30.1	29.0	30.0	30.1
Germany	1.2	2.0	0.5	3.4	6.8	5.1
	20.3	20.0	20.0	20.3	20.0	20.0
France	2.0	4.1	8.7	2.5	8.5	8.6
	20.4	20.7	19.1	20.4	20.7	19.1
Italy	1.1	2.2	1.6	1.8	2.3	3.2
	23.1	21.1	23.4	23.1	21.1	23.4
United Kingdom	5.7	14.6	10.3	12.0	18.7	18.4
	16.4	19.1	14.9	16.4	19.1	14.9
Canada	1.0	5.8	5.1	4.9	4.9	5.9
	20.7	21.7	18.3	20.7	21.7	18.3

Source: UN, *World Investment Report, 1995: Transnational Corporation and Competitiveness*, New York, UN, pp. 411–412, 421–422.

important measure of the critical levels that these flows are reaching. As shown in the table, in 1993, for instance, the ratios of the FDI inflows were close to 5 percent for the United States, slightly more than 5 percent for Canada, close to 9 percent for France, and over 10 percent for the United Kingdom. In that same year, the ratios of the outflow to capital formation were as high as 5 percent for Germany, close to 6 percent for Canada, close to 8 percent for the United States, close to 9 percent for France, and over 18 percent for the United Kingdom. Certainly, such inflows and outflows have an impact on the patterns of capital formation and employment inside and outside the G7, at levels not yet fully ascertained. According to a study by the International Labour Organization (ILO), the relocation of production by TNCs in the less developed countries has led to job losses and falling wages in the industrialized countries. Moreover, concludes the ILO study, "a continuation of current trends and investment will depress industrialized countries' living standards to the levels obtaining in cheaper labor countries.''[3] One must not, it is true, overlook the fact that a large share of the stock and flows of FDI are located or directed also in or toward the most developed countries. On the other hand, as various sources remind us, the international production system created by the TNCs involves an enormous mass of jobs. By the late 1980s and early 1990s, worldwide direct employment in the TNCs – that is, employment both at home and abroad – involved in the United States alone 25 million people and, in decreasing order of importance, close to 5.5 million for the United Kingdom, 4.5 million for Germany, over 4 million for Japan, over 3.6 million for France, 1.7 million for Canada, and 1.1 million for Italy.[4]

How did all the indicated changes – the enormous intersectoral shifts, the portentous transformation in manufacturing, the wide-ranging modifications in services, and the striking expansion of the international production system – affect, in combination with various other factors, the level and the patterns of employment, as well as the level of wages, in the developed countries on which we have been focusing? In a number of the G7 countries, the level of total employment tended to decrease in 1990–1993, in relation to 1963–1973, by significant percentages. This has been the case in France, Germany, Italy, and the United Kingdom. Contrariwise, total employment has increased in 1990–1993, in comparison with 1963–1973, in Japan, Canada, and, particularly, the United States (where, as a percentage of the population aged fifteen to sixty-four, employment rose from 63.1 percent in 1963–1973 to 71.9 percent in 1990–1993). To which factors may this important difference be attributed? In this relation it is not surprising to note that the G7 countries in which the level of total employment fell were also the countries that registered the highest levels of unemployment among the G7. On the other hand, the G7 countries that registered increases in their levels of total employment were, with the exception of Canada, those with the lowest levels of unemployment. As can be seen from Table 7.5, these levels were 3.1 percent for Japan and 5.6 percent for the United States in 1995, compared with over 11 percent for France and 12 percent for Italy – trends continuously happening for these countries from the 1960s on. Incidentally, in the case of Germany, while total unemployment for the country as a whole is indicated as having been in 1994 on the order of 9.6 percent, other OECD sources specify that unemployment in the former West Germany reached 9.2 percent that year, while in the former East Germany it was 16.0 percent.

In focusing on employment, one must also attempt to inquire which particular groups of the labor force were especially affected by unemployment. Was the rate of layoffs much the same for all workers, youth, and women? Did workers' displacement affect blue- and white-collar workers to different degrees? How did the composition of employment and unemployment evolve

Table 7.5. *Group of Seven: Unemployment as a Percentage of Total Labor Force, 1960–1995*

Group of Seven	Average					1995 Est.
	1960–1973	1974–1979	1980–1989	1990–1993	1994	
United States	4.8	6.7	7.2	6.5	6.1	5.6
Japan	1.3	1.9	2.5	2.2	2.9	3.1
Germany	0.8	3.4	6.8	7.3	9.6	9.3
France	2.0	4.5	9.0	10.0	12.2	11.5
Italy	5.3	6.6	9.9	11.0	11.3	11.9
United Kingdom	1.9	4.2	9.5	8.3	9.2	8.4
Canada	5.0	7.2	9.3	10.2	10.4	9.4
Total	3.1	4.9	6.9	6.7	NA	NA

Note: NA denotes "not available."

Sources: OECD, *Historical Statistics, 1960–1993*, Paris, OECD, pp. 2, 15; *OECD Economic Outlook*, no. 58, Dec. 1995, p. A24.

with respect to the shares of long-term unemployment and part-time employment? Is there a tendency toward the expansion of temporary work in relation to stable work?

The data available for (a) all persons, (b) youth, and (c) women clearly show that the highest unemployment rates in all the G7 countries have usually affected youth and, often but not always, women. The extreme cases, in 1993, for instance, were in France, where the rates for (a) were 11.6, for (b) 24.6, and for (c) 13.7 percent, and in Italy, where the rates for (a) were 10.2, for (b) 30.6, and for (c) 14.6 percent. In the other countries the rates for women equaled or were even below those for all persons. In the United States the rates were for (a) 6.7, for (b) 13.3, and for (c) 6.5 percent. Clearly in most of these countries the most deeply affected group continues to be the young. In the extreme case of France, in 1994, "more than half of all young people were not at work, while only a quarter were in jobs that paid market rates."[5]

Given the present pace of technological transformation, the data for the early 1980s and 1990s indicate that the percentage of blue-collar workers in total employment has generally tended to fall, while the percentage of white-collar workers has tended to rise in all the developed countries. For the OECD as a whole, the portion of white-collar workers employed in all occupations rose from 54 percent in 1981 to 60 percent in 1991. In the case of the United

States, the workforce percentages for blue- and white-collar employees shifted from 28–68 to 26–71. It would, however, be erroneous to conclude that in all cases, such changes were due to layoffs consistently affecting only blue-collar workers. As a report of the United States Council of Economic Advisers pointed out in April 1996, displacement rates for older, white-collar workers have risen, although they have remained low relative to those for younger, blue-collar, and less educated workers. These changes in the pattern of job displacement, adds the report, "may be a reason for the reports of heightened anxiety regarding job loss."[6] The anxiety has been increased further by a new so-called step-by-step layoff method. In the process of downsizing, certain big companies – like AT&T, for instance (which set out to cut tens of thousands of jobs) – devised an ad hoc method for massively trimming their white-collar workforce. In order to better link employment to pay and effort, each member of AT&T was asked to complete a resumé specifying his or her job experience and accomplishments. On the basis of the evaluation of each resumé, the executives of each department were called upon to determine which employee would be "assigned" to a job, and which one would be "unassigned" (i.e., would be dismissed). In sum, as an employee of AT&T put it, "everybody has been asked to step out into a parking lot" in this new system of "layoffs step by step."[7]

The data available suggest that, by and large, most of the jobs available in the G7 were full time. Yet there is clearly a tendency in many of these countries toward a significant increase in the proportion of jobs held by part-time or temporary workers ("temps"). Thus, from 1973 to 1983 and then to 1992–1993 the number of temps rose continually in Japan, from 13.9 to 16.2 and then to 21.1 percent of the total workforce. For Germany the corresponding figures were 10.7, 12.6, and 14.1 percent; for France, 5.9, 9.7, and 12.7 percent; for the United Kingdom, 16.0, 19.4, and 23.5 percent; for Canada, 9.7, 15.4, and 17.3 percent. In the United States the trend has not been continuously upward, namely 15.6, 18.4, and 17.5 percent.[8] While part-time work reflects in certain cases the preference of certain workers for "job flexibility" (which may explain at least up to a point why the share of women who are temps is very high), it is also evident that temp arrangements reflect a deep preference of certain companies for indefinite-term contracts allowing them to avoid the charges and obligations connected with stable work. In France, for instance, official exemptions from employer social insurance obligations have been granted (since 1992) both for "hiring a part-time worker on an indefinite contract, and for switching an employee to part-time work in order to avoid 'redundancy.'"[9]

Parallel to the growth in the share of part-time employment (and often in the share of workers holding multiple jobs), sharp increases have been registered in the shares in unemployment of the long-term unemployed, that is, persons continually unemployed for more than one year. In the depressed year 1992, the latter shares were on the order of 11.2 percent for the United States and Canada, 15.4 for Japan, 33.5 percent for Germany, 35.4 percent for the United Kingdom, 36.1 percent for France, and 58.2 percent for Italy. Incidentally, the previously cited April 1996 report of the Council of Economic Advisers points out that U.S. data from 1981 to 1993 indicate that "job losers were more likely to be permanently dismissed rather than temporarily laid-off." The parallel growth of part-time employment and long-term unemployment (so-called structural unemployment) in Europe constitutes gnawing sources of uneasiness in the workforce of the industrialized countries.

The impact of heavy unemployment and/or the greater risk of job displacement have led to significant and persistent losses in average real wages and to increases in income inequality. Typically, in countries of relative high unemployment, like Germany and France, OECD documents assert that "real product wages started to moderate significantly" (from 1993 on) and that "wage moderation has been instrumental in maintaining low inflation and in pricing labor back to work." On the other hand, in countries of low unemployment, "the share of wages in value added has fallen sharply since 1982."[10] In the specific case of the United States, where the rates of unemployment were low, the indicated structural shifts in the patterns of both employment and unemployment between 1970 and 1990 led to a situation characterized by the Council of Economic Advisers as one in which "average real wage growth slowed and income inequality widened." Recent net increases in employment have occurred in occupations that typically pay above-median wages; but these additions to the workforce have had "only a marginal effect on aggregate wage data" because net employment growth represents only a small percentage of total employment.[11] According to computations from other sources, the median family income in the U.S. was in 1993 at virtually the same level as in 1973 ($36,959 in 1993 vs. $36,893, at 1993 prices), with the average real hourly and weekly earnings falling systematically during the period considered.[12]

In sum, throughout the industrially advanced countries, the overall impacts of structural changes in production employment and unemployment and the concomitant spread of transnational production and of downsizing at big companies, combined with the indicated effects on wages and income inequality, have increased feelings of anxiety about jobs. Job apprehensions have fragmented communities, splintered families, and diluted self-confidence. In many cases the uneasiness has been particularly traumatic because of the deep contrast experienced in the developed countries between the post-1973 period and the preceding post–World War II period, when continuous improvement for all seemed absolutely certain.[13]

7.3. Sources of Uncertainty in Russia and Eastern Europe

The full analysis of the complex tendencies at work in the countries transiting from command-and-control to broad market relations, as well as the projection of their economic development in the years ahead, are rendered difficult by the instability of the sociopolitical conditions prevailing in some of them, by their still evolving efforts to build up their legal and institutional frameworks, and, last but not least, by their different policies with respect to goods, factors of production, money markets, and the internal and external flow of commodities. According to the estimates available for the period following the first critical phase of transition (1989/1990 or 1991 to 1995), the main issues for all these countries were still the slow rates of growth of the GDP, the high short- and long-term unemployment rates, inflation rates ranging from 10 to 60 percent, and, with few and temporary exceptions, their troublesome financial imbalances (see Figure 7.1).

As I indicated in the preceding chapter, as far as GDP was concerned, by 1995, none of these countries had reached their 1989 level (see Figure 6.1). According to World Bank estimates, in 1993 the per capita income levels of the countries of the area placed them in the ranks of "developing economies," somewhere between Nigeria and Mexico. Albania fitted into the category of "low-income" economies. The bulk of the other countries belonged to the "lower-middle-income" economies. Only Hungary had acceded to the "upper-middle-income" economies, in the company of Malaysia and Chile.[14] Even assuming comfortable rates of growth in per capita income for the bulk of the countries considered, these per capita incomes would at best range between $1,500 and $3,600, stretching from the "lower-middle-income" to the "upper-middle-income" groups. The projections of GDP growth available (as illustrated in Figure 7.1) are far from implying that most of these countries could reach their pretransition per capita income levels before the turn of the century.

The actual levels of unemployment (see Table 6.6 and Figure 7.1) continue to jeopardize the growth of output, hamper the processes of transition, and foster social tensions. The reallocation of human capital remains a key issue in the overall attempts at reform and struggle for restructuring. Officially, the levels of unemployment are relatively low, as already indicated, because of a wide variety of manipulations involving "hidden" unemployment and reductions – through voluntary departures or imposed early retirement – in the activity rates among the population. Accordingly, even with a strong recovery, actual unemployment is not likely to decrease; in the absence of such a recovery, the prospects are for further increases in unemployment. And, since the decreases in employment have been small relative to the falls in output – particularly so in the case of the Russian Federation – the falls in produc-

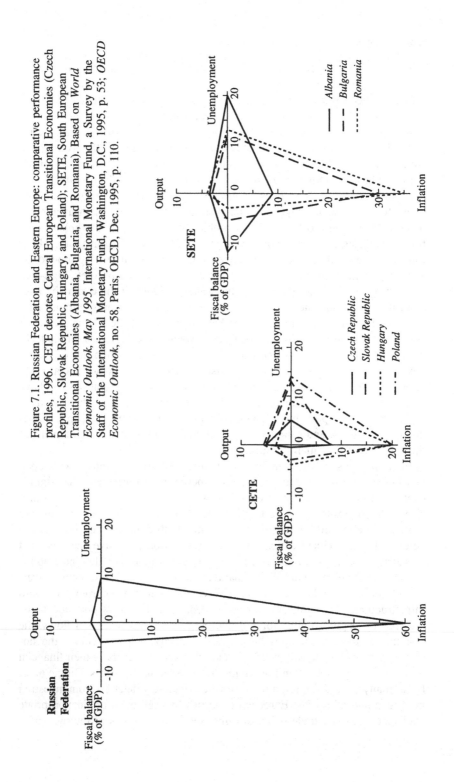

Figure 7.1. Russian Federation and Eastern Europe: comparative performance profiles, 1996. CETE denotes Central European Transitional Economies (Czech Republic, Slovak Republic, Hungary, and Poland); SETE, South European Transitional Economies (Albania, Bulgaria, and Romania). Based on *World Economic Outlook, May 1995*, International Monetary Fund, Washington, D.C., 1995, p. 53; *OECD Economic Outlook*, no. 58, Paris, OECD, Dec. 1995, p. 110.

tivity rates have appeared especially heavy at a time when, more than ever, restructuring would have required their growth. According to the International Labour Office productivity has started to increase only in Hungary and Poland, where employment has declined concomitantly with the recovery in output. Critical factors in all these countries are the growth of long-term unemployment, the heavy incidence of the latter among the young and women, and the widening regional disparities. As was the case also during the first phase of transition, many people who have been cut from the formal economy, in towns as well as in the countryside, have also lost access to many forms of social payments and welfare. Clearly, long-term unemployment will continue to be a critical problem in the area as a whole, where further changes in the structure of employment must necessarily take place. Indeed, the transition process will have to be relentless in shifting production and employment out of uncompetitive capital-goods and obsolete high-tech industries. The bulk of these were the proud creations of the command-and-control system, and they were able to survive even then only through subsidies and insulation from world market forces. The dismantlement of such complexes as the Russian "city of steel," Magnitogorsk, grown on the technology of the 1930s, or of the calamitous Chernobyls, which dot the entire area, encounter deep resistance, and raise difficult economic and social problems. Yet the shift toward more labor- and skill-intensive operations will have to continue throughout this area, as business trends indicate that the most rapid growth in exports has been in industries such as textiles, apparel, leather goods, foodstuffs, and resource-based products; and, in domestic markets, in the services of the small privatized firms.[15]

Economic instability combined with reluctant support and/or with open resistance to reform prevent substantial increases in investment and significant cuts in certain areas of production, while long-term growth dictates precisely the opposite. It is certainly imperative to increase investment and reorient its allocation; but large investments, both domestic and foreign, are deterred by the evident danger of instability. Serious, massive changes must be carried out in the production processes, the structure of the value-added chains, the scale and scope of the markets, the diffusion of new technologies, the retraining of the labor force, and the development of the current backward infrastructures. In many of these countries, capital inflows continue to be dwarfed by capital flight. Notwithstanding restrictions on capital flows, the opening of these economies have enabled newly rich residents – the nomenklatura capitalists and the black-market lords – to diversify their financial portfolios away from often low-yield, high-risk domestic assets. On the other hand, many potential foreign investors are effectively deterred from investing in Russia and other East European countries by high inflation, inappropriate exchange rates and trade policies, limits set on dollar rates of returns, and a lack of reliable information on business conditions. Foreign banks are kept out by barriers to entry and (as far as loans are concerned), by the risks of lending to domestic intermediaries (given the lack of reliable balance sheet information), weaknesses of most banks' asset portfolios, and limited reliable supervision. Yet, although economic growth primarily requires sustained efforts to mobilize domestic financial resources, these economies could reap considerable benefits from larger foreign direct investments than is still the case.[16]

Throughout the region, fiscal imbalances – particularly strong, for diverse reasons, not only in the Russian Federation, but also in Hungary and Bulgaria – are likely to continue for a number of years, except in the Czech Republic. In the latter nation, a number of favorable factors are at play, including prudent fiscal policies, wage moderation coupled with a certain increase in productivity, and the availability of employment opportunities in nearby Germany. The polar opposite case is the Russian Federation, where strong pressures favoring high inflation and fiscal imbalance have been continuously at work since 1991. A flood of presidential decrees has consistently favored these special interests and has increased the erosion of fiscal discipline. A variety of factors – the bloody war in Chechnya, crucial elections, the contractions of Russia's traditional tax base (state industrial production, retail trade turnover, wages), the newly acquired powers of the regions over tax revenue sources, and other revenue-shrinking reforms – have all contributed to financial imbalance and high inflation. The limited scope for nonmilitary finance of the budget deficit suggests that the inflation rate in the 50 to 60 percent per year range may continue well beyond the end of the century. It is estimated that the Russian state's revenue declined from some 46 percent of the GDP in 1991 to 36 percent of the much-diminished GDP of 1995, and this declining trend may well continue in the years ahead.[17]

In the CETE the picture is somewhat less grim. As far as Poland is concerned, the prospects for balancing the budget remain limited without reforms – in particular with regard to social protection – and investments in human capital and infrastructure continue to be low and in pressing need of expansion. On the other hand, the scope of fiscal choices facing the policy makers may broaden, as output increases and surpasses the 1989 level. In Hungary also many difficult adjustments are at work, given in particular the presence there of unsustainable deficits in the budget and in the current account of the balance of payments. The measures envisaged involve massive devaluation, sharp cuts in government employment, and the overhaul of the social protection programs. In the high-inflation SETE, financial instability continues to be far greater than in the CETE, and the prospects for single-digit inflation by the turn of the century seem far less certain for this group than for the CETE.[18]

The key factor underpinning growth in all these countries is, besides the beginnings of the revival of trade among them, their integration into world trade, especially Western European trade. In order to further expand this integration, trade liberalization, along with privatization and the restructuring of trade, must regain much ground lost in the entire region under a variety of pressures. Not only in the Russian Federation or in the SETE, but also in Poland and Hungary, initial import liberalizations have been temporarily reversed by reintroductions of quantitative restrictions and selective tariff increases. In addition, export controls, including surrender of foreign exchange earnings, are still in place. The overall ability of the countries of the region to attract sizeable investment flows is still small (as indicated in Chapter 6), though, as I have noted, marked differences exist in this respect between them in function, level of development, and scope.

While still small, foreign direct investment (FDI) flows have had a significant impact in some cases, fostering the transfer of advanced technologies and modern management practices. In some countries FDI has been at the core of market-oriented legislation around which subsequent basic laws have been formulated. The main investors – Germany, Italy, and the United Kingdom – have been particularly active in Hungary, Poland, and Romania; countries of the European Free Trade Area have invested in Slovakia. The productivity and sales of companies with foreign participation have increased more than those of domestic firms and continue to be among the best performers in the region, thanks to their direct access to modern technology, capital, marketing, and management skills. Such companies have displayed a remarkable patience in the handling of the often changing situations in the area, and only a few have failed. Most of the foreign affiliates in the region have contributed appreciably to the growth of manufacturing. As the UN *World Investment Reports* have pointed out, in Hungary, for instance, 40 percent of FDI has gone into manufacturing, contributing greatly to the growth in industrial output. Significant output increases have been registered there, notably in telecommunications equipment, electronic-based equipment, and computer-based machinery, in which foreign investors have played a prominent role. Foreign affiliates in the area, totaling 55,000 by the mid-1990s, have grown in importance in various fields, including financial banking and insurance services. The foreign ownership of shares has grown remarkably not only in Hungary but also in the Czech Republic and Poland. As for the development of the infrastructure, foreign investors have played crucial roles, notably in the upgrading of telecommunications. Deutsche Telekom has been active in the Russian Federation and Hungary, and Ameritech (in association with Matad) has also been active in the latter country; Cable & Wireless has invested in Bulgaria and, jointly with other companies, in the Czech Republic. In the primary sector, most of the actual and committed FDI has been geared toward the development and exploitation of the vast energy and mineral reserves of some countries of the region.[19]

Certainly growth in the area will depend primarily on the scope and effectiveness of privatization and restructuring; fiscal and financial discipline; increases in output, employment, and productivity; and integration into world trade. To support and expand this growth, FDI can play a much larger role, but many negative reactions to FDI, rooted in deep-seated feelings against the "penetration of foreign capital," are evident throughout the region. In addition, FDI projects generally require special authorizations concerning foreign exchange, licenses, or registrations, sometimes made conditional on export performance or profitability tests. Moreover, obtaining the appropriate permissions often involves lengthy and discouraging procedures. In sum, these countries need to take account of the considerable benefits that can be obtained from FDI in the form of joint ventures, acquisitions, and new businesses. There are still strong incentives for foreign firms to invest in the region: these countries have significant economic potential that cannot and should not be neglected.

The advocates of simultaneous rapid changes with respect to price and trade liberalization, financial balance, privatization, and restructuring assert that any and all kinds of slowing down thwart the processes of transformation. But, as I have already remarked, these advisers overlook the social costs that broad, relentless changes involved a fortiori after the end of the unsettling first critical phase (1989/1991–1995). As a report of the International Labour Office points out – at least with regard to the Russian Federation and some other countries of the area – another massive wave of unemployment would lead to a further fall in real wages that would deepen income inequality and poverty, threatening the social stability needed for the transition process. It is increasingly evident that the buildup of effective new institutions, as well as the efficient restructuring of production, finances, as well as the labor market, will have to continue, even in the most favorable circumstances, well into the twenty-first century.[20]

7.4. Comparative Perspectives on the Role of the State

The processes began by the governments of Margaret Thatcher at the end of the 1970s in the United Kingdom and by Ronald Reagan at the beginning of the 1980s in the United States concerning the downsizing of the state – particularly with respect to public ownership and welfare – continue in all the Western countries on which we have focused our attention. It may seem paradoxical, though, that these conservative policies triumphant in the Anglo-Saxon world in the late twentieth century should be akin in many respects to the European liberal antistate philosophy of the late nineteenth century –

a body of thought directed at the time against powerful authoritarian states and the influences of socialism. It is certain that the liberal ideas of such eminent economists as Ludwig von Mises and Friedrich A. Hayek have had a great impact on modern Anglo-Saxon conservative thought. Hayek, who consistently asserted that the growth of state interventionism had not been a reflex reaction on the part of various states to the need to solve social problems but rather the consequence of the "erosion of liberalism," simply dismissed the whole of the welfare state as "that hodgepodge of ill-assembled and often inconsistent ideals."[21] With regard to public ownership, as von Mises put it in a nutshell, the big problem is indeed that "as soon as an undertaking is no longer operated under the profit motive" – that is, as soon as it becomes a public property – "other principles must be adopted for the conduct of its affairs." But then the crux of the matter is who decides where a criterion can be found for adjudging the usefulness of such services and how one can ascertain whether these services "are not too heavily paid for."[22]

Be that as it may, privatization, along with policies aiming to shrink taxes and especially government spending with special emphasis on welfare, remains the order of the day at the end of the twentieth century. The United Kingdom, the pacesetter for privatization in the West with the sale of some fifty major public businesses since 1979, now plans to pass on the nuclear power industry to the private sector and to press ahead with programs to expand private investment in the provision of both capital assets and services in areas previously restricted to the public sector.[23] In Germany, where privatization has been carried out successfully in the former communist East Germany, but where such policies have not been making much headway in the West, attention is shifting to bringing down the public expenditure share in GDP to its "preunification level" (i.e., from 50 to 46 percent of GDP) by the year 2000, with hopes of reducing public spending particularly with respect to public health, labor programs, public pensions, and similar obligations. As OECD reports on Germany put it, "The welfare state is endangered" not only by the demographic problem and by the rise of unemployment, but also by other difficulties that force the government to target "benefit entitlements, tax loopholes, and concessions more efficiently."[24] In France, officially, the focus of industrial policy remains privatization, but, as I already indicated, certain obstacles delay its scheduled implementation. It is with respect to social protection in general that the whole gamut of long-term programs is under close consideration, aiming in particular to modify the system of unemployment benefits, reform the social security system, and make broad changes with respect to public health and the "generosity" of the pension systems.[25] Finally, in the United States, the pacesetter for welfare reform in the West, projected cuts, embodied in the mid-1990s in bills of the

House of Representatives, would drastically reform the myriad federal programs loosely grouped under the heading of welfare – AFDC cash benefits, food stamps, school meal subsidies – as well as making reductions in cost-of-living adjustments. These and similar measures would eventually combine with the restructuring of Social Security and of social assistance projects, health care programs, and income transfers in general.

Thus, in all these countries, the processes of limiting the scope of the state continue to unfold with the target of dismantling chunks of the welfare state, while asserting as main objectives (1) liquidating or reducing the state budget's deficit in order to promote private savings and investment; (2) taking into account growing demographic problems or the rise of long-term unemployment (or both); and (3) introducing new orientations in social policy, notably for handling any income transfers more efficiently, while better assessing their potentially negative impact on incentives to work.

Does that mean that the critical processes of contracting the role of the state, started in many respects legitimately in the late 1970s and early 1980s, will prevent the further expansion of the scope of the state in new directions? I don't think so. The complex issues relating to the indicated shifts in the structure of production in the West, the implications of the growth of the transnational production system, and the uncertainties and uneasiness with regard to job stability, skill utilization, and long-term unemployment are already calling forth demands for all kinds of state intervention and may increase such demands in the future.

With respect to the United Kingdom, for instance, recall that even when privatization and deregulation were in full swing, it was wrong to assume that pushing back the frontiers of the state was the whole story. Indeed, downgrading the powers of the municipalities led to increases in the central role of the state. Furthermore, even as the necessity of new orientations in social policy is proclaimed, the presence of "structural" problems concerning persistent unemployment has given rise to a broad consensus that "U.K. skill outputs have been inadequate and remedial public action has become necessary." In short, since the UK government does not see the "enhancement of market forces in education and training as in itself sufficient to realize its education and training goals," reforms are to target "active labor market policies" concerning the long-term unemployed, including better basic education, training, and counseling.[26] In Germany, slower growth and higher unemployment have called forth substantial increases in state subsidization – in the eastern German economy focusing on railways, agriculture, housing, and general development; in the west, on maintaining existing industrial structures.[27] In France, as usual, the whole gamut of state interventions and subsidizations is already at work, helping out key banks and supporting initiatives in favor of job creation, training, and labor contracts, as well as renovations of public housing – all without either changing the scope of the measures already aimed at modifying social security or hampering attentive examination of long-term scenarios involving further reforms of social policy.[28] In the United States itself, the apparent consensus on the end of "big government" may be at risk. As a Report of the Council of Economic Advisers on job creation and employment puts it, although many more jobs have been created here than have been destroyed, "a dynamic economy inevitably imposes costs on some workers." In the specific conditions of the United States, during the past decade some of other costs are that job losers have been likely to be permanently rather than temporarily laid off, that older workers have been subject to greater risks of job displacement, and that average real wage loss due to displacement has been profound and persistent.[29] As long as the structural shifts indicated in the preceding section do not increase the social weight of these "long-term challenges," movements to limit the safety-net programs (particularly welfare dependency) and shrink state interventionism in general will likely gain ground. On the other hand, if the scope of the indicated challenges grows and particularly if the uneasiness about jobs and unemployment increases, it is not at all excluded that state intervention under many forms – from subsidizing ailing industries, to direct investment in all kinds of infrastructure, and even to various kinds of public works – would again be the order of the day.

Infinitely more complex doubts, dilemmas, and policy combinations have occurred in the East, where efforts to circumscribe the role of the state – by demolishing and discarding the main command-and-control structures – have combined with a tendency to maintain and/or expand state interventionism in old or new directions. Conflicting amalgamations will continue to be tried, not only in the Russian Federation but also in most of the other economies turning toward effective market relations. The obsolescence of much of their industrial installations, the deepening structural shifts, the wide and inescapable intersectoral changes, and the growth of long-term mass unemployment are bound to call forth conflicting and reluctant approaches to liberalization, restructuring, privatization, and labor market policies. Great emphasis will have to be put on training and retraining labor to increase its mobility, along with efforts to reintegrate disadvantaged groups, reduce unemployment, and raise productivity. Among other measures considered or in the process of implementation are state assistance for the development of new businesses, subsidies and credits for small-scale enterprises, and wage subsidies to slow down the pace of employment dislocations. As in the West during restructuring crises, attention is also being paid to the ways in which labor supply could be cut, through diverse schemes such as increased youth enrollments in educational institutions, extended maternity leaves, and early retirement.[30]

From an economic point of view, what type of state is likely to emerge in the East from the mixing and balancing of the conflicting and often chaotic tendencies generated by the processes of transition to the market? Will the basic characteristics of such states be similar to those of the developed Western countries? Will they approach the structural-institutional setup of the developing economies? In order to answer these questions, one must recall that the size and scope of a state at any point in time result from the interaction of a set of factors, including notably the historical evolution of the country considered in a number of fields and its ensuing traditions and frameworks of activity; the size, structure, operations, and evolving strength of its business community; the extent to which the state has been substituting for business in providing certain goods and services (which business might or might not have provided); the interrelations between the business community's methods of governance and the economic policies of the state; the socioeconomic conditions prevailing at critical economic junctures (e.g., recessions, massive unemployment); and the impact of politicians' and the "intellectual elite's" philosophies on ad hoc state policies.

The marked differences in economic management existing even between developed countries is best illustrated by contrasting the organization and functioning of Germany's business with those prevailing in the Anglo-Saxon world. In the German system, the key feature is the importance of cross-shareholdings (a feature also developed in France) in the allocation and control of capital assets, both among nonfinancial enterprises and between banks and nonfinancial enterprises – a system supporting long-term contracts between firms. In the Anglo-Saxon system, market-based processes command the efficient allocation of capital and shape the relations between shareholders/owners, managers, employees, suppliers, and customers. The shareholders have little direct influence on management and, when dissatisfied, sell their equity holdings and thus put pressure on managers for course correction in order to avoid a fall in share prices and the possibility of hostile takeovers. In this system, the central element is the stock market; in the German system the crux of the matter is the direct and continuous participation of banks, business partners, and employees in running companies. The Anglo-Saxon system may be more innovative and adaptable to technological change; the German system may perform more methodically and securely in areas of large-term comparative advantage (but may at times be more prone to bureaucratic inertia and/or excessive regulation).[31]

For evident reasons, including of course the absence of appropriate meaningful institutions and of developed markets, the German system of business governance, with all kinds of adaptations, has proved congenial to less developed countries. In these countries, not private banks, but rather commanding state banks have been called upon to exercise continuous surveillance and control, extending subsidies and other forms of support to

the relatively small and slow-growing business enterprises. In such economies, a core public sector may continue to be quite large and inefficient,
remaining a drag on economic growth. State interventions may remain ubiq-
uitous and not necessarily always clearly defined. It is within this kind of
framework that business may be called upon to develop in Eastern Europe
for years to come. The type of state that emerges in the area, through the
halting processes of transition to developed markets, may be by and large,
from the economic point of view, similar to the precommunist regimes or in
many respects comparable to the setups in neighboring Greece or Turkey
(with closely similar problems concerning privatization, restructuring, and
deregulation; raising the efficiency of the public sector core; imposing hard
budget cuts; improving the tax system; and reforming the safety net). Assuming that social upheavals are avoided in a country like the Russian Federation,
its state will very likely continue to develop along similar lines. As the indicated reforms are put in place, these countries should in time, on the basis
of private ownership, free trade, and other appropriate measures, narrow the
gap in living standards that separates them from their more advanced neighboring countries. As a senior economist of the IMF reminds us, deep institutional changes creating an environment more conducive to the success of
orthodox policies are likely to take place in the area as a whole only after
several years of experience with market economics.[32]

7.5. Concluding Comments

In his famous work *The Road to Serfdom*, written in 1944, Friedrich A.
Hayek warned the Western world against the dangers of losing individual
freedom because of the continuous expansion of the scope of the state. Hayek
asserted that for over 200 years, the "rule of freedom" that had been
achieved in England seemed destined to spread over the rest of the world.
But from 1870 on, the reign of these ideas started to retreat and a different
set of ideas began to advance from the East – that is, from Germany –
stressing "organization," "planning," and "socialism." This challenged
what up to then had been meant by the term *Western civilization*, that is,
"liberalism and democracy, capitalism and individualism, free trade, and any
form of internationalism and love of peace." Unfortunately, added Hayek,
the people of the West imported the ill-fated German ideas and started to
believe that their own former ideals and convictions were "hopelessly out-
moded."[33]

Following Hayek, Robert Skidelsky asserts in his 1996 book, *The Road
from Serfdom*, that the "great ideological struggle of the twentieth century"
has been between "collectivism" (Skidelsky's analogue of Hayek's serfdom)
and liberalism (in its nineteenth-century sense of limited government and

"release of the individual from social fetters"). Fortunately, adds Skidelsky, a fundamental rethinking of the role of the state and markets occurred around 1980: "In essence, the state's role was redefined as that of providing public goods – goods which the market cannot supply – rather than that of supplanting the market in pursuit of the state's objectives." It was the rise of Thatcherism and Reaganism, as well as the fall of communism, that tilted the "global ideological balance" from a stress on "collectivism" to an emphasis on "economic freedom."[34]

Reviewing Skidelsky's work (and implicitly also Hayek's book), Herbert Stein rejected the idea that the world was moving "in one direction." Now, as in the past, as he puts it, "we cannot escape the difficult task of trying to judge whether particular state activities are legitimate in a free society, whether they are conducted on too large or too small a scale and whether they are effectively managed."[35] Indeed, when we get beyond the simplifying Hayek (or Skidelsky) alternative, we have to specify what has actually happened and for what particular reasons the state's characteristics with respect to size and scope have been modified.

These are the central issues on which this book has focused. What I have tried to show is that a fuller light can be thrown on these matters only if one takes into account the correspondences and divergences existing between the evolutions in the West and the East concerning the role of the state. Accordingly, I have followed, in historical perspective, two basic lines of exposition and analysis. The first has concerned developments in the great Western countries (which I limited herein to the United Kingdom, France, Germany, and, from the nineteenth century on also, the United States); the second, developments that took place in Russia, particularly after 1917, and in the USSR's former satellites in Europe. I have attempted to show how and why the actions of these nations' political leaders have, within differently evolving historical frameworks, aimed to expand the role of the state and then to reverse some of these policies.

To start with, let me recall in broad outline how I perceived the chain of events and their rationale in the West. In pursuing the vigorous expansion of the role of the state and of all kind of enterprises under its ownership and control through the seventeenth and eighteenth centuries, during the epoch of so-called merchant capitalism, the modern European states in the making aimed not only at pulling their economies out of their feudal shells and unifying, organizing, and transforming them, but also at securing for their countries a dominant position among all the nations. Vesting enormous economic powers in the hands of the state was viewed, as I pointed out, as indispensable for both security and conquest. The mercantilist ideas about the state's right, for these purposes, to own, control, initiate, or support any industry and trade were treated as axiomatic. Then, as the newly emerging frameworks of industrialization and urbanization began to take shape from the end of the eighteenth century on, developing through the nineteenth century until World War I, the competition (or combat) for dominance among the indicated Western nations required the achievement of the highest levels of industrialization and military power. The increasing liberal critiques against state interventionism and in favor of liberty for the growing private industries and trade did not prevent these Western states from maintaining certain previously established state ownership positions and even promoting various new state industries. Nor could they prevent the expansion of the states' regulatory, supervisory, and controlling powers over "free" private industry and commerce. The further search for a dominant position centered now not only on imitating, copying, competing with, and surpassing the industrial achievements in the leading countries, but also in launching colonial expeditions for the acquisition of sheltered new markets – a direction that only the United States could in a sense avoid through its own consolidation and integration from the Atlantic to the Pacific, particularly after the Civil War. The economists of the time accepted more or less readily the mixing of mercantilist emphases with liberal approaches in the practices of their respective states. Be that as it may, the quest to surpass any and all of their peers finally led Germany, and then the other advanced nations, after numerous miscalculations, to the disasters of World War I. The following postwar period again brought to the fore serious social tensions, nourished by recessions, unemployment, expanding income inequality, and poverty – as had also been the case in the last quarter of the nineteenth century, when the beginnings of state-run welfare programs started to take shape. These deepening tensions, however, also brought forth the unfortunate creation and rapid consolidation of the state-run Nazi economy. Its expansion, and the brutal assaults opening World War II, constituted yet another attempt to grasp the dominant position in Europe and the world, finally bringing Germany to its defeat and total collapse. In the post–World War II era, various socialist influences that had gained ground for decades, especially with regard to industrial planning, expansion of the public sector, and increased welfare and income transfers, ultimately ran into an impasse. From the 1970s on, as we have seen, this impasse brought about successful attempts to limit and then reverse these policies, particularly with regard to public ownership and to welfare. These tendencies toward shrinking the scope of the state in these respects may, however, combine in the future with possible new expansions of the role of the state in some other directions.

Let me now recall also briefly the broad lines that I sketched concerning the rise and fall of the backward and despotic party-state system implanted in Russia and the USSR's former satellites. After various structural changes, including first of all the elimination of private property from all the economy's sectors, the giant but economically retarded Soviet Union attempted to overcome its backwardness by launching a replica of the intercapitalist drives of the nineteenth and twentieth centuries for industrial, military, and technological supremacy. To achieve this goal, Stalin, who matched in many respects Ivan the Terrible, pursued his drive to "catch up with and to surpass the highest indices of capitalism" with cruel and unflinching resolution. For that purpose, he adopted an inflexible strategy of development (constant emphasis on heavy industry and on machine tools) and attempted to unify the entire economy as a "single factory" guided as an engineering servomechanism by Moscow party-state bureaucrats on the basis of rigid economic plans. After limited successes, heavily paid for – including the buildup of a military-industrial complex endowed with nuclear capabilities – the war-type economy of the USSR began running into increasing difficulties. Its challenge to the West started to decrease from the early 1980s on. Finally, the USSR and its satellites "imploded" between 1989 and 1991. Russia – a replica of the German war economy of World War I (but excluding private property), a replica of the intercapitalist drives for dominance (but excluding the capacity for rapid innovations and assimilation of advancing technology), and finally, the would-be replica of advanced economies (but in fact incapable of surmounting its own backwardness) – is now emerging from the collapse of the command-and-control system, is transiting to a market economy and does not present in any way an immediate challenge to the great powers.

This does not mean, however, that party-state analogues to the Nazi or even to the Soviet party-state cannot either endure (as is the case with communist China) or reemerge under new disguises in the future. But in pondering this latter eventuality, it would be good to remember in the West, on the basis of experience, that an ounce of prevention is worth a pound of cure.

Notes

1. Public Ownership and Welfare

1. Pierre Deyon, *Le mercantilisme*, Paris, Questions d'Histoire, Flammarion, 1969, pp. 15–16.
2. Adam Smith, *An Inquiry into the Nature and Causes of the Wealth of Nations* (1776), ed. by Edwin Cannan, New York, The Modern Library, 1937, pp. 418–419; W. Cunningham, *The Growth of English Industry and Commerce*, Cambridge, At the University Press, 1882, p. 368; W. Cunningham, *The Growth of English Industry and Commerce in Modern Times*, Cambridge, At the University Press, 1892, pp. 16–17; D. C. Coleman, "Editor's Introduction," and "Eli Heckscher and the Idea of Mercantilism," in D. C. Coleman, *Revisions in Mercantilism*, London, Methuen, 1969, pp. 1–19, 93; and Jacob Viner, "Power Versus Plenty as Objectives of Foreign Policy in the Seventeenth and Eighteenth Century," in ibid., p. 71.
3. John U. Nef, *Industry and Government in France and England, 1540–1640*, Ithaca, Cornell University Press, 1940, pp. 89, 103–105, 107, 115.
4. Deyon, *Le mercantilisme*, p. 31; Cunningham, *The Growth of English Industry and Commerce in Modern Times*, pp. 110–111.
5. Sydney Checkland, *British Public Policy, 1776–1939: An Economic, Social and Political Perspective*, Cambridge University Press, 1983, p. 15.
6. Deyon, *Le mercantilisme*, pp. 26–27; Nef, *Industry and Government*, pp. 58–61, 85, 88; Shepard B. Clough, *France: A History of National Economics, 1789–1939*, New York, Scribner's 1939, pp. 19–22; Robert Catherine and Pierre Gousset, *L'état et l'essor industriel; du dirigisme colbertien à l'économie concertée* (The state and industrial development; from Colbert's dirigisme to the coordinated economy), Paris, Berger-Levrault, 1965, pp. 72–73; and M. Félix Joubleau, *Etudes sur Colbert, ou exposition du système d'economie politique suivi en France de 1661 à 1683* (1856) (Studies on Colbert, or Exposition of the system of political economy followed in France from 1661 to 1683) (1856), New York, Franklin, 1971, esp. vol. 1, pp. 329–332.
7. Clough, *France: A History of National Economics*, pp. 24–25; Deyon, *Le mercantilism*, pp. 28–29; see Henry E. Sée, *Economic and Social Conditions in France During the Eighteenth Century*, trans. by Edwin H. Zeydel, New York, Knopf, 1927, pp. 158–159; and L. H. Haney, *History of Economic Thought*, New York, Macmillan, 1936, pp. 172–175.

8. Haney, *History of Economic Thought*, pp. 146–165; Albion W. Small, *The Cameralists – the Pioneers of German Social Polity* (1909), New York, Franklin, 1969, pp. viii, 2–6, 20, 588–589; Autorenkollektiv, *Frundlinien des Ökonomischen Denkens in Deutschland, von den Anfängen bis zur Mitte des 19. Jahrhunderts* (Collective of authors: Outlines of economic thought in Germany from the beginning to the middle of the nineteenth century), Berlin, Akademie, 1977, pp. 162–163; on the critics of the cameralists, pp. 186–189.

9. Clive Trebilcock, *The Industrialization of the Continental Powers, 1780–1914*, London, Longman, 1981, pp. 26–27; Ulrich P. Ritter, *Die Rolle des Staates in den Frühstadien der Industrialisierung: Die preusische Industrieförderung in der ersten Hälfte des 19. Jahrhunderts* (The role of the state in the early stages of industrialization: The Prussian promotion of industry in the first half of the nineteenth century), Berlin, Duncker and Humblot, 1961, pp. 77–78; Haney, *History of Economic Thought*, p. 147.

10. Small, *The Cameralists*, pp. 588–589.

11. Eli F. Heckscher, *Mercantilism*, trans. by M. Shapiro, London, Allen and Unwin, 1962, pp. 24–25. Schumpeter points out that the Physiocrat position was in fact contradictory: laissez-faire and free trade could not be "abolished without a good deal of government 'interference' "; put differently, "Quesnay urged upon government what really was an activist policy." Cf. Joseph A. Schumpeter, *History of Economic Analysis*, ed. by Elizabeth B. Schumpeter, New York, Oxford University Press, 1954, p. 230. I believe, however, that this does not invalidate either Heckscher's definition of physiocracy (presented in the text above) or the thrust of the Physiocratic policy, namely the eventual confinement of the state only to the protection of life, liberty, and property.

12. Smith, *An Inquiry*, p. 627. The critique of mercantilism appears in Book 4, pp. 397–627.

13. S. F. Mason, *Main Currents of Science Thought*, New York, Schuman, 1953, pp. 408–409.

14. Checkland, *British Public Policy*, pp. 16–18; Sydney Checkland, *The Rise of Industrial Society in England, 1815–1885*, London, Longmans, 1964, pp. 358–359; and Cunningham, *The Growth of English Industry and Commerce in Modern Times*, pp. 16–17, 256–259.

15. See Alfred Marshall, *Industry and Trade*, London, Macmillan, 1920, pp. 93–94; and W. H. B. Court, *A Concise Economic History of Britain from 1750 to Recent Times*, Cambridge University Press, 1954, pp. 216–217, 218–219, 319.

16. Checkland, *British Public Policy*, pp. 121, 196–203.

17. Merle Fainsod, Lincoln Gordon, and Joseph C. Palamountain Jr., *Government and the American Economy*, 3rd ed. New York, Norton, 1959, p. 734.

18. Thomas K. McCraw, "Mercantilism and the Market: Antecedents of the American Industrial Policy," in Claude E. Barfield, and William A. Schambra, eds., *The Politics of Industrial Policy*, Washington, D.C., American Enterprise Institute for Public Policy Research, 1986, pp. 35–41.

19. F. W. Taussig, *The Tariff History of the United States*, New York, Capricorn Books, 8th rev. ed., 1964: on 1830–1860, pp. 109–154, on 1861–1913, pp. 155–

447. Harold F. Williamson, ed., *The Growth of the American Economy*, New York, Prentice-Hall, 1951, pp. 535–537; and Robert R. Russell, *A History of American Economic System*, New York, Appleton-Century-Crofts, 1964, pp. 192–194, 399–400.

20. Fainsod, Gordon, and Palamountain, *Government and the American Economy*, pp. 114–116, 737–739; Russel, *A History*, pp. 157–158, 242–272; and Irwin Unger, *These United States: The Questions of Our Past*, Vol. 1 (to 1877), Englewood Cliffs, N.J., Prentice-Hall, 1986, pp. 416–418.

21. Jean Clinquart, "L'administration des douanes et le contrôle du commerce extérieur" (Customs administration and the control of foreign trade), in Michel Bruguière et al., *Administration et contrôle de l'économie, 1800–1914* (Administration and control of the economy, 1800–1914), Geneva, Droz, 1985, pp. 146–151; Charles Asselain, *Histoire économique de la France du XVIII; se siècle à nos jours, 1 De l'Ancien Régime à la première guerre mondiale* (Economic history of France from the seventeenth century to the present: From the "Old Regime" to the First World War), Paris, Editions du Seuil, 1984, pp. 136–137; and Clough, *France: A History of National Economics*, pp. 109, 130–139, 180–183, 230–234.

22. Alain Plesis, "Les rapports entre l'Etat et la Banque de France jusqu'en 1914" (Relations between the state and the Bank of France up to 1914), in Bruguière, *Administration et contrôle*, pp. 49, 60–62; Asselain, *Histoire économique de la France*, pp. 81–82; Robert, Delorme and Christine André, *L'etat et l'économie: Un essai d'explication de l'évolution des dépenses publiques en France, 1870–1980* (The state and the economy: An explanatory essay on the evolution of public outlays in France, 1870–1980), Paris, Editions du Seuil, 1983, pp. 220–223; Catherine and Gousset, *L'état et l'essor industriel*, pp. 127–129; and Warren C. Baum, *The French Economy and the State*, Princeton, N.J., Princeton University Press, 1958, pp. 171–172.

23. See Schumpeter, *History of Economic Analysis*, pp. 412–413, 504–505; and Theodore S. Hamerow, *Restoration, Revolution, Reaction: Economics and Politics in Germany, 1815–1871*, Princeton, N.J., Princeton University Press, 1958, pp. 12–16. See also Haney, *History of Economic Thought*, pp. 405, 410–418.

24. Rolf Engelsing, *Sozial und Wirtschaftsgeschichte Deutschlands* (Social and economic history of Germany), Göttingen, Vandenhoeck and Ruprecht, 1973, pp. 161–163; Hans-Ulrich Wehler, *Deutsche Gesellschaftsgeschichte* (German social history), Munich, C. H. Beck, 1987, pp. 499–507; Helmut Böhne, *An Introduction to the Social and Economic History of Germany: Politics and Economic Change in the Nineteenth and Twentieth Centuries*, trans. by W. R. Lee, New York, St. Martin's, 1978, pp. 88–91; and Jean-Pierre Rioux, *La révolution industrielle, 1780–1880* (The industrial revolution, 1780–1880), Paris, Editions du Seuil, 1971, pp. 110–111.

25. See Gustav Stolper, *German Economy, 1870–1940: Issues and Trends*, New York, Reynal and Hitchcock, 1940; W. O. Henderson, *The State and the Industrial Revolution in Prussia, 1740–1870*, Liverpool, Liverpool University Press, 1967, p. xxiii, and New York, Reynal and Hitchcock, 1940, pp. 70–77; and W. O.

Henderson, *The Rise of German Industrial Power, 1834–1914*, Berkeley, University of California Press, 1975, pp. 173–179.

26. Arthur C. Pigou, *The Political Economy of War*, new and rev. ed., London, Macmillan, 1940, pp. 30, 67, 70.

27. See Maurice J. Clark, Walton H. Hamilton, and Harold G. Moulton, eds., *Readings in the Economics of War*, Chicago, University of Chicago Press, 1918, pp. 272–284, 345–346; and Howard L. Gray, *War Time Control of Industry: The Experience of England*, New York, Macmillan, 1918, pp. vii–xv, 1–60. Kathleen Burk, *War and the State: The Transformation of British Government, 1914–1919*, London, Allen and Unwin, 1982, pp. 7–12, 20–28, 151–152; and David French, *British Economic and Strategic Planning, 1905–1915*, London, Allen and Unwin, 1982, pp. 51, 74, 98, 127.

28. Clough, *France: A History of National Economics*, pp. 234–239, 260–261; C.-J. Gignoux, *L'industrie française: Vocation de la France* (French industry: Vocation of France), Paris, Boivin, 1952, pp. 124–127; and Jean Bouvier, Fernand Braudel, and Ernest Labrousse, *Histoire economique et sociale de la France: L'ére industrielle et la société d'aujourdi'hui (siècle 1880–1980): Le temps des guerres mondiales et de la grande crise (1914 vers 1950)* (Economic and social history of France: The industrial era and today's society [century, 1880–1980] – The time of the world wars and about the great crisis [1914 – toward 1950]). Paris, Presses Universitaires de France, tome 4, vol. 2, 1980, pp. 633–639.

29. Friedrich A. Hayek, *The Road to Serfdom*, Chicago, University of Chicago Press, 1944, p. 9; Ernst Schulin, *Walther Rathenau, Repräsentant, Kritiker und Opfer Seiner Zeit* (Walther Rathenau: Representative, critic, and victim of his time), Göttingen, Musterschmidt, 1979, pp. 62–70; Gerhard Hecker, *Walther Rathenau und Sein Verhältnis zu Militär und Kriege* (Walther Rathenau and his relationship to the military and to war), Boppard, Harold Boldt, 1983, pp. 202–237; Theodor Schieder, *Staatensystem als Vormacht der Welt, 1848–1918* (States system as the world's highest power, 1848–1918), Berlin, Propyläen, 1977, pp. 390–393; and Clark, Hamilton, and Moulton, eds., *Readings in the Economics of War*, pp. 197–201.

30. Clark, Hamilton, and Moulton, eds., *Readings in the Economics of War*, pp. 245–256, 286–304, 330–343, 347–355, 371–399; Bernard M. Baruch, chairman, *American Industry in the War: A Report of the War Industries Board (March 21)*, ed. by Richard H. Hippelheuser, New York, Prentice-Hall, 1941, pp. 3–9, 305–308; and Robert D. Cuff, *The War Industries Board: Business–Government Relations During World War I*, Baltimore, Johns Hopkins University Press, 1973, pp. 1–12, 68–75, 148–149, 241–242.

31. W. A. Robson, "The Public Service Board: General Conclusions," in W. A. Robson, ed., *Public Enterprise: Developments in Social Ownership and Control in Great Britain*, London, Allen and Unwin, 1937, pp. 359–361, 365; H. A. Clegg and T. E. Chester, *The Future of Nationalization*, Oxford, Basil Blackwell, 1953, pp. 3–9, 18–19; W. Thornhill, *The Nationalized Industries: An Introduction*, London, Nelson, 1968, pp. 2–7, 19–24, and the appendix by major public corporations; and Frank Welsh, *The Profit of the State: Nationalized Industries and Public Enterprises*, London, Maurice Temple Smith, 1982, p. 75.

32. K. B. Smellie, *A Hundred Years of English Government*, New York, Macmillan, 1937, pp. 328–329.
33. Leonard Tivey, *Nationalization in British Industry*, rev. ed., London, Jonathan Cape, 1973, pp. 39–70; Jean-Jacques Santini, ed., *Les privatisations à l'étranger: Royaume Uni, RFA, Italie, Espagne, Japan* (Privatizations abroad: United Kingdom, GFR, Italy, Spain, Japan), Paris, La Documentation Française, 1986; Trevor May, *An Economic and Social History of Britain, 1760–1970*, New York, Longman, 1987, pp. 383–384, 390–401; Dennis Swann, *The Retreat of the State: Deregulation and Privatization in the U.K. and U.S.*, Ann Arbor, University of Michigan Press, 1988, pp. 189–212 and appendix 320–322; John Wickers and George Yarrow, *Privatization: An Economic Analysis*, Cambridge, Mass., MIT Press, 1988, pp. 139–141.
34. See notably Hubert Bonin, *Histoire économique de la France depuis 1880* (Economic history of France since 1880), Paris, Masson, 1988, pp. 50–55, 74–79, 98–102; Baum, *The French Economy and the State*, pp. 173–174; Bouvier, Braudel and Labrousse, *Histoire économique et sociale de la France*, pp. 697–700; and Delorme and André, *L'état et l'économie*, pp. 237–245.
35. Pierre Rosanvallon, *L'état en France de 1789 à nos jours* (The state in France from 1789 to our time), Paris, Editions du Seuil, 1990, pp. 244–247.
36. Ibid., pp. 247–250; see also Lionel Zinsou, *Le fer de lance: Essai sur les nationalisations industrielles* (The spearhead: Essay on industrial nationalizations), Paris, Olivier Orban, 1985, pp. 47–48; and Stephens Cohen, Serge Halimi, and John Zysman, "Institutions, Politics, and Industrial Policy in France," in Barfield and Schambra, eds., *The Politics of Industrial Policy*, p. 115.
37. Jean-Maxime Lévêque, *Dénationalisations: Mode d'emploi* (Denationalizations: Directions for use), Paris, Albin Michel, 1985, pp. 139–145.
38. Jacques Bourdon, Jean-Marie Pontier, and Jean-Claude Ricci, "Les privatisations en France" (Privatization in France), in Centre de Recherches Administratives d'Aix-Marseille, *Les privatisations en Europe* (Privatization in Europe), Paris, Editions CNRS, 1989, pp. 120, 128–130.
39. Fritz Blaich, ed., *Die Rolle des Staats für die wirtschaftliche Entwicklung* (The role of the state in economic development), Berlin, Duncker and Humblot, 1982, pp. 16–19; and Gustav Stolper, Karl Häuser, and Knut Borchardt, *The German Economy, 1870 to the Present*, New York, Harcourt, Brace and World, 1967, pp. 101–104.
40. Stolper, Häuser, and Borchardt, *The German Economy, 1870 to the Present*, pp. 129–137; Ludwig von Mises, *Nation, State, and Economy: Contributions to the Politics and History of Our Time*, trans. from the German by L. B. Yeager, New York, New York University Press, 1983, pp. 179–173; and Ludolf Herbst, *Der Totale Krieg und die Ordnung der Wirtschaft: Die Kriegswirtschaft im Spannungsfeld von Politik, Ideologie und Propaganda 1939–1945* (Total war and the coordination of the economy: The war economy in the domain of politics, ideology and propaganda, 1939–1945), Stuttgardt, Deutsche, 1982, p. 66.
41. Josef Esser, " 'Symbolic Privatization': The Politics of Privatization in West Germany," in John Wickers and Vincent Wright, *The Politics of Privatization in Western Europe*, London, Frank Cass, 1989, pp. 61–65; Michel Fromont and

Heinrich Siedentopf, "Les privatisations en République Fédérale d'Allemagne" (Privatization in the German Federal Republic), in Centre de Recherche Administratives d'Aix-Marseille, *Les privatisations en Europe*, p. 161; and Blaich, ed., *Die Rolle des Staats*, p. 18.

42. See Annmarie Hauck Walsh, *The Public Business: The Politics and Practices of Government Corporations*, Cambridge, Mass., MIT Press, 1978, pp. 3, 354–355, 370, 373; and U.S. General Accounting Office, *Profiles of Existing Government Corporations: A Study Prepared for the Committee on Government Operations*, House of Representatives, 100th Congress, Second Session, Dec. 1988, Washington, D.C., U.S. GPO, 1989, pp. 4–5.

43. Albert S. Abel, "The Public Corporation in the United States," in W. G. Friedman and J. F. Garner, eds., *Government Enterprise: A Comparative Study*, New York, Columbia University Press, 1970, pp. 183–184; Fainsod, Gordon, and Palamountain, *Government and the American Economy*, pp. 742–747; and Howard R. Smith, *Government and Business: A Study in Economic Evolution*, New York, Ronald, 1958, pp. 402–412.

44. Friedmann and Garner, eds., *Government Enterprise*, p. 186; Harold Hoontz and Richard W. Gable, *Public Control of Economic Enterprise*, New York, McGraw-Hill, 1956, p. 709; U.S. General Accounting Office, *Profiles*, pp. 17–19; and Paul W. MacAvoy and George S. McIsaac, "The Performance and Management of United States Federal Government Corporations," in Paul W. McAvoy, W. T. Stanbury, George Yarrow, and Richard J. Zeckhauser, eds., *Privatization in State-Owned Enterprises: Lessons from the United States, Great Britain and Canada*, Boston, Kluwer, 1989, pp. 77–78.

45. Steve H. Hanke and Barney Douwdle, "Privatizing the Public Domain," in Steve H. Hanke, ed., *Prospects for Privatization*, Proceedings of the Academy of Political Science, vol. 36, no. 3, 1987, p. 114.

46. Walsh, *The Public Business*, p. 6; and Friedmann and Garner, eds., *Government Enterprises*, pp. 189–192.

47. Computed from U.S. Department of Commerce, Bureau of Economic Analysis, *Fixed Reproducible Tangible Wealth in the United States, 1925–89*, Washington, D.C., U.S. GPO, 1993, tables A13 and A14, pp. 294, 332–343.

48. For details, see Pat Thane, *Foundations of the Welfare State*, London, Longmans, 1982, pp. 32–38.

49. Sir William Beveridge, *Social Insurance and Allied Services Report* (photocopy of the English edition), New York, Macmillan, 1942, p. 5; Charles E. Clarke, *Social Insurance in Britain*, Cambridge, At the University Press, 1950, pp. 1–7, 11; and Thane, *Foundations*, pp. 44–45, 79, 95–96.

50. Ernest L. Bogart, *Economic History of Europe, 1760–1939*, London, Longmans, 1942, pp. 478–479, 666–667; George Dorion, and André Buionnet, *La sécurité sociale* (Social security), Paris, Presses Universitaires de France, 1983, pp. 6–10.

51. Hajo Holborn, *A History of Modern Germany, 1840–1945*, New York, Knopf, 1969, pp. 291–293; Federal Minister for Labor and Social Affairs, *Survey of Social Security in the Federal Republic of Germany*, Bonn, At the Ministry, 1972, p. 21; Thane, *Foundations*, pp. 102–103, 108–110; Gerhard A. Ritter, *Socialver-*

sicherung in Deutschland und England (Social security in Germany and England), Munich, C. H. Beck, 1983, pp. 28–31; and Jeans Alber, *Der Sozialstaat in der Bundesrepublik, 1950–1983* (The Welfare State in the Federal Republic of Germany, 1950–1983), Frankfurt, Campus, 1989, pp. 45–49.

52. Beveridge, *Social Insurance*, 9–11; Clarke, *Social Insurance*, pp. 20–26; OECD, *The Reform of Health Care: A Comparative Analysis of Seven OECD Countries*, Paris, OECD, 1992, pp. 113–115; and Eric Midwinter, *The Development of Social Welfare in Britain*, Buckingham, Open University Press, 1994, pp. 90–103.

53. Dorion and Buionnet, *La sécurité sociale*, pp. 10–14; Christian Charpy and Hugues de Jouvenel, *Protection sociale: Trois scénarios contrastés à l'horizon 2000* (Social protection: Three contrasting scenarios at the approach of the year 2000), Paris, Association Internationale des Futuribles, 1986, pp. 6–9, 12–14; and OECD, *The Reform of Health Care*, p. 45.

54. Federal Minister for Labor and Social Affairs, *Survey of Social Security*, pp. 21–24; and Michael Wilson, "The German Welfare State: A Conservative Regime in Crisis," in Allan Cochrane and John Clarke, *Comparing Welfare States: Britain in International Context*, London, Sage with the Open University, 1993, pp. 141, 148–152.

55. Fainsod, Gordon, and Palamountain, *Government and the American Economy*, pp. 766–797; Joseph A. Pechman, Henry J. Aaron, and Michael K. Taussig, *Social Security: Perspectives for Reforms*, Washington, D.C., Brookings Institution, 1968, pp. 28–38; David G. Davies, *United States Taxes and Tax Policy*, Cambridge University Press, 1986, p. 168; OECD, *The Reform of Health Care Systems: A Review of Seventeen OECD Countries*, Paris, OECD, 1994, pp. 317–321; and OECD, *Economic Surveys, 1993–1994: United States*, Paris, OECD, 1994, pp. 76–78.

2. An All-Encompassing Party-State

1. Jean-Pierre Machelon, "L'idée de nationalisation en France de 1840 à 1914" (The idea of nationalization in France from 1840 to 1914), in Bruguière, et al., *Administration et contrôle*, pp. 1–2.

2. Karl Marx and Friedrich Engels, "The Communist Manifesto," in C. Robert Tucker, ed., *The Marx–Engels Reader*, New York, Norton, 1972, pp. 346–347, 352.

3. See Hans Kelsen, *Sozialismus und Staat: Eine Untersuchung der politischen Theorie des Marxismus* (Socialism and the state: An analysis of the political theory of Marxism), Vienna, der Wiener Volksbuchhandlung, 1965, pp. 95–105; also Karl Kautsky, *The Road to Power*, Chicago, Bloch, 1909, pp. 26–30, 55.

4. Cf. V. I. Lenin, "The State and Revolution," in V. I. Lenin, *Marx, Engels, Marxism*, 3rd English ed., Moscow, Foreign Language Publishing House, 1947, pp. 356–357.

5. Karl Marx, "The Holy Family," "Capital I," and "The German Ideology," excerpted in Z. A. Jordan, ed., *Karl Marx: Economy, Class and Social Revolution*, London, Michael Joseph, 1971, pp. 143, 238–239, 273.

6. Jacques Blanc and Chantal Brulé, *Les nationalisations françaises en 1982* (French nationalizations in 1982), Paris, La Documentation Française, 1983, pp. 9–11.

7. See notably ibid., p. 12; and Zinsou, *Le fer de lance*, pp. 53–54.

8. James Mavor, *An Economic History of Russia: The Rise and Fall of Bondage Right*, New York, Hutton, 1914, vol. 1, pp. 80–81.

9. See notably Bertrand Gille, *Histoire économique et sociale de la Russie du Moyen Age au XXe siècle* (Economic and social history of Russia from the middle ages to the twentieth century), Paris, Payot, 1949, pp. 98–100; Stanislav G. Strumilin, *Ocherki ekonomicheskoi istorii Rossii i SSSR* (Essays on the economic history of Russia and the USSR), Moscow, Nauka, 1966, pp. 302–333, 507–508; and M. E. Falkus, *The Industrialization of Russia, 1700–1914*, London, Macmillan, 1972, pp. 21–25. On the peasant workforce, see esp. Jerome Blum, *Lord and Peasant in Russia from the Ninth to the Nineteenth Century*, Princeton, N.J., Princeton University Press, 1961, pp. 308–316.

10. R. D. Charques, *A Short History of Russia*, New York, Dutton, 1956, pp. 106, 107, 115, 116, 133–134; and George Vernadsky, *A History of Russia*, New York, Bantam, 1961, pp. 177–178; also George Vernadsky, "Serfdom in Russia," in Sydney Harcave, ed., *The Scope and Nature of Russian History from Ancient Times to the Abolition of Serfdom*, New York, Crowell, 1962, pp. 226–228; and Blum, *Lord and Peasant*, pp. 552–560.

11. Cf. notably Sergei Pushkarev, *The Emergence of Modern Russia, 1801–1917*, trans. by Robert McNeal and Tora Yedlin, Edmonton, Alberta, Pica Pica, 1985, pp. 28, 36, 43, 146, 208.

12. W. O. Henderson, *Germany, France, Russia, 1800–1914*, London, Frank Cass, 1961, pp. 202–203; Theodore von Laue, *Sergei Witte and the Industrialization of Russia*, New York, Atheneum, 1969, pp. 19, 33–35, 60–63, 72–77; Falkus, *The Industrialization of Russia*, pp. 62–63; and Peter Gatrell, *Government, Industry and Rearmament in Russia, 1900–1914*, Cambridge University Press, 1994, pp. 169, 206–209, 277–281.

13. Pushkarev, *The Emergence of Modern Russia*, p. 282.

14. See Gille, *Histoire économique et sociale de la Russie*, pp. 221–224; Clark, Hamilton, and Moulton, eds., *Readings in the Economics of War*, pp. 202–205; and Lewis H. Siegelbaum, *The Politics of Industrial Mobilization in Russia, 1914–17: A Study of the War-Industries Committees*, New York, St. Martin's, 1983, pp. 31, 85–88, 156–158.

15. See William E. Butler Peter B. Maggs and John B. Quigley Jr., *Law After Revolution*, New York, Oceana, 1988, pp. 8–9.

16. William Henry Chamberlain, *The Russian Revolution, 1917–1921*, New York, Macmillan, 1960, vol. I, pp. 320–327; Walter Pietsch, *Revolution und Staat: Institutionen als Träger der Machten Sowjetrussland, 1917–1922* (Revolution and state: Institutions as the carriers of power in Soviet Russia, 1917–1922), Köln, Verlagwissenschaft und Politik, 1969, pp. 140–145; Sharlet Robert et al., eds. *P. I. Stuchka: Selected Writings on Soviet Law and Marxism*, Armonk, N.Y., Sharpe, 1988, pp. 12–13; Karen Dawisha, "State and Politics in Developed So-

cialism," in John A. Hall, ed., *States in History*, Oxford, Blackwell, 1986, pp. 222–223; and *Konstitutsiia [Osnovnoi Zakon] Soiuza Sovetskikh Sotsialisticheskikh Respublic* (Constitution [Fundamental Law] of the Union of Soviet Socialist Republics), adopted October 7, 1977, *Russian Studies Series*, no. 82, 1977.

17. See notably Chamberlain, *The Russian Revolution*, pp. 325–326; Vladimir Gsovski, *Soviet Civil Law: Private Rights and Their Background Under the Soviet Regime*, Ann Arbor, University of Michigan Law School, 1948, pp. 10–15; René David and John N. Hazard, *Le droit Sovietique* (Soviet law), vol. 2, ed. by John N. Hazard, *Le Droit et l'Evolution de la Societé dans L'U.R.S.S.* (Law and the evolution of society in the U.S.S.R.), Paris, Librarie Générale de Droit et de Jurisprudence, 1954, p. 8; and Konstantin Katzarov, *The Theory of Nationalization*, The Hague, Martinus Nijhoff, 1964, p. 34.

18. Nikolai, I. Bukharin, *Economics of the Transformation Period, with Lenin's Critical Remarks* (1920), New York, Bergman, 1971, pp. 15, 36. It is interesting to note that the belief that the socialist state required a centralized administration was common to both wings of the Russian Social Democratic Labor Party, as indeed it was to European Marxists. See Richard Pipes, *The Formation of the Soviet Union: Communism and Nationalism, 1917–1923*, Cambridge, Mass., Harvard University Press, 1954, p. 241.

19. Gsovski, *Soviet Civil Law*, pp. 13–14; and Butler, Maggs, and Quigley, *Law After Revolution*, pp. 18–19.

20. Bukharin, *Economics of the Transformation*, pp. 114–116. See also N. I. Bukharin, and E. A. Preobrazhenski, *The ABC of Communism*, trans. by Eden Paul, London, Unwin, 1922, pp. 334–335.

21. Bukharin, *Economics of the Transformation*, pp. 145–146, 219.

22. As quoted by Laszlo Szamuely in *First Models of the Socialist Economic Systems: Principles and Theories*, Budapest, Akadémiai Kaidó, 1974, p. 7.

23. Gsovski, *Soviet Civil Law*, p. 18.

24. Nicolas, Spulber, *Soviet Strategy for Economic Growth*, Bloomington, Indiana University Press, 1964, pp. 30–31.

25. Gsovski, *Soviet Civil Law*, pp. 21–23, 292–296, 314–316; and David and Hazard, *Le droit Sovietique*, vol. 1, pp. 126–129, 131–132; vol. 2, pp. 12–14.

26. N. Ia. Petrakov et al., *Nep i khozraschet* (NEP and economic accounting), Moscow, Ekonomika, 1991, pp. 1–67; Rossiiskaia Akademiia Nauk, Institut Nauchnoi Informatsia po obschestvennym naukam (Russian Academy of Science, Institute of Scientific Information on the Social Sciences), *Organizatsionny formy i metody gosudarstvennogo regulirovaniia ekonomiki v period novoi ekonomicheskoi politiki* (Organizational forms and methods of the state's regulation of the economy in the NEP period), Moscow, 1992, pp. 7–43.

27. See Nicolas Spulber, ed., *Foundations of Soviet Strategy for Economic Growth: Selected Soviet Essays, 1924–1930*, Bloomington, Indiana University Press, 1964, pp. 359–360, 393–400.

28. Gsovski, *Soviet Civil Law*, pp. 558–562, 569, 707–710, 768–769.

29. Nicolas Spulber, *The Soviet Economy: Structure, Principles, Problems*, rev. ed.,

New York, Norton, 1969, pp. 8–9, 39–46. The Soviet camps are estimated to have contained around 2.5 million inmates after World War II.

30. S. Ioffe Olimpiad and Peter B. Maggs, *The Soviet Economic System: A Legal Analysis*, Boulder, Colo., Westview, 1987, p. 14.

31. Spulber, *The Soviet Economy*, p. 7; Goskomstat, *Promyshlenost' SSSR: Statisticheskii sbornik* (Soviet industry: Statistical collection), Moscow, Finansy i Statistika, 1988, p. 42; and Nicolas Spulber, *Restructuring the Soviet Economy: In Search of the Market*, Ann Arbor, University of Michigan Press, 1991, p. 186.

32. See Nicolas Spulber, *Organizational Alternatives in Soviet-type Economies*, Cambridge University Press, 1979, pp. 20, 22–24.

33. Ibid., pp. 51, 56, 84.

34. M. S. Gorbachev, "Strengthening the Key Element of the Economy," *Pravda and Izvesta*, Dec. 10, 1990, trans. in *Current Digest of the Soviet Press*, vol. 42, no. 49 (1990), pp. 8–9.

35. Russian Goskomstat, *Statisticheskoe Obozrenie* (Statistical review), Oct. 1994, pp. 64, 66.

36. See, e.g., M. S. Lantsev, *The Economic Aspects of Social Security in the USSR*, Moscow, Progress Publishers, 1976, pp. 10–13.

37. Gaston V. Rimlinger, *Welfare Policy and Industrialization in Europe, America, and Russia*, New York, Wiley, 1971, pp. 249–252.

38. Pavel Stiller, *Sozialpolitik in der USSR, 1950–80: Eine Analyse der quantitative und qualitativen Zusammenhänge* (Social policy in the USSR, 1950–80; An analysis of quantitative and qualitative interrelations), Baden-Baden, Nomos, 1983, pp. 91–99.

39. See notably Stiller, *Sozialpolitik*, pp. 108–110, 300–302; and M. L. Zakharov and E. G. Tuchkova, *Azbuka sotsial'nogo obespecheniia* (ABCs of social insurance), Moscow, Znanie, 1987, esp. on pensions, pp. 102–148; V. S. Chekhutova and T. V. Mit'kina, *Finansovye resursy sotsial'nogo obespecheniia* (Financial Resources of social insurance), Moscow, Finansy i Statistika, 1986, pp. 14–27; M. L. Zakharov and R. Tsivilyov, *Social Security in the USSR*, Moscow, Progress Publishers, 1978, pp. 21, 27, 32, 97–111; and Lantsev, *The Economic Aspects*, pp. 24, 52, 67–80.

40. For a detailed study, see Christopher Mark Davis, "Developments in the Health Sector of the Soviet Economy, 1970–1990," in *Gorbachev's Economic Plans, Study Papers*, submitted to the Joint Economic Committee, Congress of the United States, 100th Congress, First Session, Joint Committee Print, Washington, D.C., U.S. GPO, 1987, vol. 2, pp. 312–335.

41. See Michael V. Alexeev, "Soviet Residential Housing: Will the 'Acute Problem' be Solved?" in *Gorbachev's Economic Plans*, vol. 2, pp. 282–296.

42. Anthony B. Atkinson, and John Micklewright, *Economic Transformation in Eastern Europe and the Distribution of Income*, Cambridge University Press, 1992, esp. pp. 220, 237–241.

43. For a rare contrary opinion, see Joseph S. Berliner, "Socialism in the Twenty-First Century," in Michael Keren and Gur Ofer, eds., *Trials of Transition: Economic Reform in the Former Communist Bloc*, Boulder, Colo., Westview, 1992, p. 2.

3. *Limiting the State's Size and Scope*

1. Peter Jenkins, *Mrs. Thatcher's Revolution: The Ending of the Socialist Era*, London, Jonathan Cape, 1987, p. 5.
2. Margaret Thatcher, *The Downing Street Years*, New York, HarperCollins, 1993, pp. 6–7.
3. *Economic Report of the President*, transmitted to Congress Feb. 1982 together with the *Annual Report of the Council of Economic Advisers*, Washington, D.C., U.S. GPO, 1982, pp. 3–10. The idea of a "long overdue redirection" of the role of the federal government has found many defenders. Among them, Robert Higgs, in an otherwise interesting and well-documented study on the growth of state power, asserts that Democrat and Republican politicians alike have failed to stem "the decline of the commitment to limited government and extensive private property," a decline allegedly started from 1900 on. According to Higgs, even Reagan's partisans, though genuinely in favor of "a return to a free market" failed to achieve their goals because they focused "not on institutional change" but rather on budget numbers. Or, concludes Higgs, "number juggling is not the stuff of evolution." See Robert Higgs, *Crisis in Leviathan: Critical Episodes in the Growth of American Government*, New York, Oxford University Press, 1987, pp. 2, 256.
4. Herbert Stein, *Governing the $5 Trillion Economy*, New York, Oxford University Press, 1989.
5. Jenkins, *Mrs. Thatcher's Revolution*, pp. 168–169, 174, 178–180; and Thatcher, *The Downing Street Years*, pp. 339, 676–677.
6. Transcript of Second Inaugural Address by Reagan, *New York Times*, Jan. 22, 1985, p. 7.
7. *America's New Beginning: A Program for Economic Recovery*, Washington, D.C., The White House, Office of Press Secretary, Feb. 18, 1981, pp. 10–11; Robert Pear, "The Reagan Revolution: The Plans, the Progress," *New York Times*, Jan. 31, 1983, pp. 8–9; and AFL-CIO, *Reaganomics: The Second Dose*, Washington, D.C., American Federationist, 1982, pp. 12–13, 23.
8. *Contract with America: The Bold Plan by Rep. Newt Gingrich, Rep. Dick Arney and the House Republicans to Change the Nation*, ed. by Gillespie Ed and Bob Schellhas, New York, Random House, 1994.
9. See notably Lester M. Salamon, "The Changing Tools of Government Action: An Overview," and Lloyd D. Musolf, "The Government-Corporation Tool: Permutations and Possibilities," in Lester M. Salamon, assisted by Michael S. Lund, eds., *Beyond Privatization: The Tools of Government Action*, Washington, D.C., Urban Institute Press, 1989, pp. 20, 231–239; see also Dennis Swann, *The Retreat of the State: Deregulation and Privatization in the U.K. and U.S.*, Ann Arbor, University of Michigan Press, 1988, pp. 76–85; Richard J. Zeckhauser, and Murray Horn, "The Control and Performance of State-Owned Enterprises," in MacAvoy, Stanbury, Yarrow, and Zeckhauser, eds., *Privatization and State-Owned Enterprises*, pp. 12–15; Walsh, *The Public Business*, pp. 40–47; W. Friedman, "Government Enterprise: A Comparative Analysis," in Friedman and Garner, eds., *Government Enterprise*, pp. 303–307; Murray, L. Weidenbaum, *The*

Modern Public Sector: New Ways of Doing the Government's Business, New York, Basic, 1969, pp. vii, 4–6, 198–199; Claude Berthomieu, *La gestion des enterprises nationalisées: Critique de l'analyse marginaliste* (Management of nationalized enterprises: Critique of the marginalist analysis), Paris, Presses Universitaires de France, 1970, pp. 11–12; and Koontz, *Public Control of Economic Enterprise*, pp. 680–681.

10. Armand Bizaguet, *Le secteur public et les privatisations* (The public sector and privatization), Paris, Presses Universitaire de France, 1988, pp. 6–12.
11. R. Drago, "Public Enterprises in France," in Friedman and Garner, eds., *Government Enterprise*, p. 107.
12. Musolf, "The Government Corporation Tool," pp. 232–233.
13. Weidenbaum, *The Modern Public Sector*, pp. 189–190.
14. Peter Saunders and Friedrich Klau, *The Role of the Public Sector: Causes and Consequences of the Growth of Government*, Paris, OECD, 1985, p. 75.
15. W. Friedman, "Government Enterprise," p. 325.
16. W. A. Robson, "Ministerial Control of the Nationalized Industries," in Friedman and Garner, eds., *Government Enterprise*, pp. 61–65.
17. Drago, "Public Enterprises in France," pp. 120–121.
18. Albert S. Abel, "The Public Corporation in the United States," in Friedman and Garner, *Government Enterprise*, pp. 194–195.
19. Walsh, *The Public Business*, p. 332.
20. As quoted by R. Mathew Bishop and John Kay, in "Privatization in Western Economies," in Horst Siebert, ed., *Privatization: Symposium in Honor of Herbert Giersch*, Tübingen, J. C. B. Mohr, 1992, p. 194. Emphasis added.
21. Ludwig von Mises, *Bureaucracy* (1944), Cedar Falls, Iowa, Center for Futures Education, 1983, p. 59.
22. See Vito Tanzi, "Introduction," and Robert H. Floyd, "Some Topical Issues Concerning Public Enterprises," in *Public Enterprises in Mixed Economies*, Robert H. Floyd, Clive S. Gray, and R. P. Short, eds., Washington, D.C., International Monetary Fund, 1984, pp. xiv–xv, 4–5.
23. Warren C. Baum, *The French Economy and the State*, Princeton, N.J., Princeton University Press, 1958, p. 189.
24. William C. Shepherd, et al., *Public Enterprise: Economic Analysis of Theory and Practice*, Lexington, Mass., Lexington, 1976, p. 41.
25. See in particular Paul W. McAvoy and George S. McIsaac, "The Performance and Management of United States Federal Government Corporations," in McAvoy, Stanbury, Yarrow, and Zeckhauser, eds., *Privatization and State-Owned Enterprises*, pp. 107–120, 128. See also William S. Vickery, "Actual and Potential Pricing Practices Under Public and Private Operation," in William J. Baumol, ed., *Public and Private Enterprise in a Mixed Economy: Proceedings of a Conference Held by the International Economic Association*, New York, St. Martin's, 1980, pp. 286–287; and Maurice, R. Gardner, "Has Public Enterprise Failed?" in V. V. Ramanadham, *Privatization in the U.K.*, London, Routledge, 1988, pp. 30–31.
26. Floyd, "Some Topical Issues," pp. 12–15; and Ramanadham, *Privatization*, p. 31.

27. David E. Sappington and Joseph E. Stiglitz, "Privatization, Information, and Incentives," Working Paper No. 2196, Cambridge, Mass., National Bureau of Economic Research, Mar. 1987, p. 1.
28. Carl Shapiro and Robert D. Willig, "Economic Rationales for the Scope of Privatization," in N. Suleiman Ezra and John Waterbury, eds., *The Political Economy of Public Sector Reform and Privatization*, Boulder, Colo., Westview, 1990, pp. 56–57.
29. Joseph E. Stiglitz, *Economics of the Public Sector*, New York, Norton, 1986, p. 165; Swann, *The Retreat of the State*, p. 82.
30. Nicolas Kaldor, "The Economic Consequences of Mrs. Thatcher," in N. Butler, ed., *Fabia Tract 486*, speeches 1979–1982, London, 1982, p. 11.
31. Sam Peltzman, "The Control and Performance of State-Owned Enterprises: Comment," in MacAvoy, Stanbury, Yarrow, and Zeckhauser, eds., *Privatization and State-Owned Enterprises*, pp. 69–71; and Dieter Bös, *Public Enterprise Economics: Theory and Application*, Amsterdam, North Holland, 1986, pp. 18–20.
32. Maurice Marchand, Pierre Pestilau, and Henry Tulkens, "The Performance of Public Enterprises: Normative, Positive, and Empirical Issues," in Marchand, Pestilau, and Tulkens eds., *The Performance of Public Enterprises: Concepts and Measurements*, Amsterdam, North Holland, 1984, p. 34; and Nicholas Kaldor, "Public or Private Enterprise – The Issues to Be Considered," in Baumol, ed., *Public and Private Enterprise . . .* , p. 37.
33. Joseph Stiglitz, "On the Economic Role of the State," in Arnold Heertje, ed., *The Economic Role of the State*, Oxford, Basil Blackwell, 1989, pp. 38–39.
34. Janet Rothenberg-Pack, "The Opportunities and Constraints of Privatization," in William T. Gormley Jr., ed., *Privatization and Its Alternatives*, Madison, University of Wisconsin Press, 1991, p. 282.
35. Stiglitz, "On the Economic Role," p. 56.
36. William T., Gormley Jr., "The Privatization Controversy," in Gormley, ed., *Privatization and Its Alternatives*, p. 3.
37. See *OECD Economic Surveys, 1994–1995: United Kingdom*, Paris, OECD, 1995, p. 91; John Vickers and Vincent Wright, *The Politics of Privatization in Western Europe*, London, Frank Cass, 1989, pp. 4–9; John Vickers, and George Yarrow, "Privatization in Britain," in MacAvoy, Stanbury, Yarrow, and Zeckhauser, eds., *Privatization and State-Owned Enterprises*, p. 243; John Vickers, and George Yarrow, *Privatization: An Economic Analysis*, Cambridge, Mass., MIT Press, 1988, pp. 155–157; and Yair Aharoni, *The Evolution and Management of State-Owned Enterprises*, Cambridge, Mass., Ballinger, 1986, p. 324.
38. Michel Bauer, "The Politics of State-Directed Privatization: The Case of France, 1986–88," in Vickers and Wright, *The Politics of Privatization*, pp. 49–60. Cosmo Graham and Tony Prosser, *Privatizing Public Enterprises: Constitutions, the State, and Regulation in Comparative Perspective*, Oxford, Clarendon Press, 1991, pp. 75–76; Thomas Crampton, "In Europe, the Market Is Overflowing with Privatization Issues," *International Herald Tribune*, June 18–19, 1994, p. 19; Jacques Neher, "After Sell-Off of Prime Properties, Slowdown Is Likely in Privatization Program," *International Herald Tribune*, June 7, 1994, p. 10; and Eric Leser, "Les investisseurs étrangers échaudés par les precedentes dénationalisa-

234 Notes to Pages 88–95

tions" (Foreign investors discouraged by preceding denationalizations), *Le monde*, June 8, 1945.

39. Josef Esser, " 'Symbolic Privatization': The Politics of Privatization in West Germany," in Vickers and Wright, *The Politics of Privatization*, pp. 61–73; Michel Fromont, and Heinrich Siedentopf, "Les Privatisations en République Fédérale d'Allemagne" (The privatizations in FRG), in Centre de Recherches Administratives d'Aix Marseille, *Les privatisations d'Europe* (The European privatizations), Paris, Centre National de la Rechershe Scientifique, 1989, pp. 159–167; for a list of the direct participation of the federal government and of autonomous institutions, see Jacques Ziller, "Les enterprises du secteur publique in RFA" (The enterprises of the public sector in FRG), in *Les enterprises du secteur publique dans les pays de la Communité Européenne* (The enterprises of the public sector in the countries of the European Community), Brussels, Estitut European d'Administration Publique, pp. 455–461.

40. Smith, *The Wealth of Nations*, p. 776.

41. *Statistical Abstract of the United States, 1994*, Washington, D.C., U.S. Department of Commerce, Bureau of the Census, 1994, p. 225.

42. Scott Lehman, *Privatizing Public Lands*, New York, Oxford University Press, 1995, pp. 3–16; Randall Fitzgerald, *When Government Goes Private: Successful Alternatives to Public Services*, New York, Universe Books, 1988, p. 200.

43. 104th Congress, 1st Session, S. 852, "To Provide for Uniform Management of Livestock Grazing on Federal Land and for Other Purposes," May 25 (legislative day, May 15), 1995; Timothy Egan, "Grazing Bill to Give Ranchers Vast Control of Public Lands," *New York Times*, July 21, 1995, pp. 1, C18; "Babbitt Offers Interest Groups More Input in Lands Policy," *Congressional Quarterly* (Feb. 19, 1994), p. 430; and "Grazing-Fee Plan Bites the Dust," *Congressional Quarterly* (Dec. 31, 1994), p. 3610.

44. Keith Schneider, "Bold Plan Seeks to Wrest Control of Federal Lands," *New York Times*, Apr. 8, 1995. Emphasis added.

45. Lehman, *Privatizing Public lands*, pp. 13, 14.

46. Steve H. Hanke and Barney Dowdle, "Privatizing the Public Domain," in Hanke, ed., *Prospects for Privatization*, p. 115; see also Karl Hess, Jr. and Jerry Holechek, "Beyond the Grazing Fee: An Agenda for Rangeland Reform," Cato Institute, *Policy Analysis*, no. 234, July 13, 1995; and, Fitzgerald, *When Government Goes Private*, p. 205.

47. Fitzgerald, *When Government Goes Private*, p. 221.

48. *The Human Cost of Contracting Out: A Survival Guide for Public Employees*, compiled by Krista Schneider, Washington, D.C., AFL-CIO Public Employee Department, 1993, pp. 10–17; and Keith Schneider, "U.S. Admits Waste in Its Contracts," *New York Times*, Dec. 3, 1992.

49. Weidenbaum, *The Modern Public Sector*, pp. 9, 12, 32–33, 190–191.

50. Jonathan Bradshaw, "Development in Social Security Policy," in Catherine Jones, ed., *New Perspectives on the Welfare State in Europe*, London, Routledge, 1993, pp. 44–47; Johnathan Bradshaw, "Social Security," and Gerald Wistow, "The National Health Service," both in David Marsh and R. A. W. Rhodes, eds.,

Implementing Thatcherite Policies: Audit of an Era, Buchingham, Open University Press, 1992, pp. 81–97, 100–116; Dennis Kavanaugh, *Thatcherism and British Politics: The End of Consensus?*, Oxford, Oxford University Press, 1987, pp. 212–217; and Joel Krieger, *Reagan, Thatcher and the Politics of Decline*, New York, Oxford University Press, 1986, pp. 96–101.

51. Dorion and Buionnet, *La sécurité sociale*, pp. 12–20, 124–125; Charpy and Jouvenel, *Protection sociale*, pp. 24–29; and *OECD Economic Surveys 1993–1994*, pp. 58–90.

52. Eberhard Wille and Volker Ulrich, "Bestimmungsfaktoren der Ausgabenentwicklung in der gesetzlichen Krankenversicherung (GKV)" (Determinant factors in the development of expenditures of statutory health insurance), in Karl-Heinrich Hansmeyer, ed., *Finanzierungsprobleme der sozialen Sicherung II* (Financing problems of social security II), Berlin, Duncker and Humblot, 1991, pp. 11–13, 74–75, 79; Cochrane and Clark, *Comparing Welfare States*, pp. 141–162; and Helmut Winterstein, *Das System der Sozialen Sicherung in der Bundesrepublik Deutschland* (The system of social security in the Federal Republic of Germany), Munich, Vahlen, 1980, pp. 32–40.

53. *Contract with America*, pp. 17, 65–69, 115–123.

54. See the entire issue of *AARP Bulletin Special Report Commemorating the 60th Anniversary of the Social Security System*, June 1995, and particularly within it: Julie Rovner, "Social Security Lauded for Its Achievements – But What of the Future?"; Robert M. Ball, "Five Easy Steps Making Sure the System Endures"; and "Social Security: Q & A." See also Horace B. Deets, "Just What Is an Entitlement?" and Senator Daniel Patrick Moynihan, "The Case Against Entitlement Cuts," in *Modern Maturity* (Nov.–Dec. 1994), pp. 5, 7, 13–14.

55. Aldona Robbins, "Salvaging Social Security," *Wall Street Journal*, July 3, 1995.

56. See the intervention of Senator Pete Domenici on Medicare, *Congressional Record*, July 28, 1995 (Senate), pp. S10869–S10871; Robin Toner and Robert Pear, "Medicare Turning 30, Won't Be What It Was," *New York Times*, July 23, 1995, pp. 1, 12; "Secret Attack on Have-Nots," *New York Times*, Oct. 20, 1996 (editorial); and *The Reform of Health Care Systems: A Review of Seventeen OECD Countries*, Paris, OECD, 1994, pp. 317–320.

57. *Reform of Health Care Systems*, pp. 320–321; Adam Clymer, "An Accidental Overhaul: Major Revamping of Health Care System Could Be Byproduct of Steep Budget Cuts," *New York Times*, June 26, 1995; Daniel Patrick Moynihan, "The Devolution Revolution," *New York Times*, Aug. 6, 1995, op-ed; Kevin Sack, "Public Hospitals Around Country Cut Basic Service," *New York Times*, Aug. 20, 1995; Robert Pear, "Republicans Draw Plan for Slowing Medicare Growth," *New York Times*, Sept. 10, 1995; Robert Pear, "Republicans Proposing End to Care Guarantee to Poor," *New York Times*, Sept. 20, 1995; and Robert Toner, "Senate Approves Welfare Plan That Would End Aid Guarantee: A Landmark Shift," *New York Times*, Sept. 20, 1995, pp. 1, 17.

58. Vickers and Wright, *The Politics of Privatization*, pp. 27–28; and Julian Le Grand and Ray Robinson, eds., *Privatization and the Welfare State*, London, Allen and Unwin, 1984, pp. 3–6, 15.

59. Lawrence, H. Thompson, "The Social Security Reform Debate," *Journal of Economic Literature*, vol. 21 (Dec. 1983), pp. 1443–1446.
60. Margaret S. Gordon, *Social Security Policies in Industrial Countries*, Cambridge University Press, 1988, pp. 82–83, 218–220.
61. Nicolas Spulber, *The American Economy: The Struggle for Supremacy in the 21st Century*, Cambridge University Press, 1995, pp. 30–33.
62. Richard A. Musgrave, "The Reagan Administration's Fiscal Policy: A Critique," in Wm. Craig Stubblebine and Thomas D. Willett, eds., *Reaganomics: A Midterm Report*, San Francisco, ICS Press, 1983, p. 130.

4. Restructuring the State's Foundations

1. N. Fiodorov, "According to Incomplete Data," *Izvestiia*, Jan. 4, 1990, p. 2, trans. in *Current Digest of the Soviet Press* (henceforth CDSP), vol. 42, no. 1 (1990), pp. 28–29.
2. A. Prokhanov, "The Tragedy of Centralism," *Literaturnaia Rossiiá*, Jan. 5, 1990, trans. in ibid., no. 4 (1990), p. 1.
3. "Economic Report of Premier Ryzhkov to the Supreme Soviet," press release FBIS-Sov-90-102, May 25, 1990.
4. "A Step Toward Freedom," interview conducted by M. Gurtovoi, *Pravda*, Apr. 26, 1990, trans. in CDSP, vol. 42, no. 17, pp. 1–2.
5. "Transition to a Market Economy," mimeo, JPRS-UEA-90-034, Sept. 28, 1990.
6. Bocharov, M., "500 Days of Hope and Risk," *Literaturnaia gazeta*, Aug. 15, 1990, trans. in CDSP, vol. 42, no. 33 (1990), p. 4.
7. I. Demechenko, "The First Day of the 500," *Izvestiia*, Nov. 1, 1990, trans. in ibid., no. 44 (1990), p. 27.
8. "Osnovnye napravleniia stabilizatsii narodnogo khoziaistva i perekhoda k rynochnoi ekonomike" (Basic guidelines for the stabilization of the national economy and the transition to a market economy), *Pravda*, Oct. 18, 1990, pp. 1–4.
9. B. N. Yeltsin, "I Have Made My Choice," *Komsomolskaia pravda*, Feb. 22, 1991, trans. in CDSP, vol. 43, no. 7 (1991), p. 1.
10. V. S. Pavlov, "Report at the USSR Supreme Soviet," *Pravda* and *Izvestia*, Apr. 23, 1991, trans. in ibid., no. 16 (1991), pp. 1–6.
11. "On Terminating the Activity of the Organizational Structures of Political Parties and Mass Public Movements in State Agencies, Institutions and Organizations of the RSFSR," *Sovetskaia Rossiia*, July 23, 1991, p. 1, trans. in ibid., no. 29 (1991), pp. 1–2.
12. B. N. Yeltsin, "I Pledge to My People That a Reform Cabinet Will Be Formed and I Am Counting on Understanding and Support from Deputies and Every Resident of the Russian Republic," *Izvestia*, Oct. 28, pp. 1–2, trans. in ibid., no. 43 (1991), pp. 1–6.
13. International Monetary Fund, the World Bank, Organization for Economic Cooperation and Development, European Bank for Reconstruction and Development, *The Economy of the USSR: Summary and Recommendations*, Washington, D.C., the World Bank, 1990, p. 18.

14. Jeffrey Sachs, "Poland and Eastern Europe: What Is to Be Done," in András Köves and Paul Marer, eds., *Foreign Economic Liberalizations: Transformations in Socialist and Market Economies*, Boulder, Colo., Westview, 1991, pp. 236–237. Emphasis added.

15. Olivier Blanchard et al., *Reform in Eastern Europe*, Cambridge, Mass., MIT Press, 1991, pp. xi, xii, 1.

16. Dornbusch Rudiger, "Strategies and Priorities for Reform," in *The Transition to a Market Economy*, Vol. 1: *The Broad Issues*, ed. by Paul Marer and S. Zecchini, eds., Paris, OECD, 1991, pp. 169–183.

17. "On Measures for Freeing Up Prices," *Rossüskaia gazeta*, Dec. 25, 1991, trans. in CDSP, vol. 43, no. 52 (1991), p. 6.

18. Yeltsin, "I Pledge to My People," p. 2.

19. "At First Glance, We Are Nearing the Abyss: The Government Is Convinced We Are Moving Away from It," *Rossiiskaia gazeta*, Jan. 11, p. 3, trans. in *The Current Digest of the Post-Soviet Press* (henceforth CDPSP), vol. 44, no. 1 (1992), pp. 1–4.

20. Yeltsin, "Speech by the President of Russia," *Rossüskaia gazeta*, Jan. 17, pp. 1–2, trans. in ibid., no. 2 (1992), pp. 1–3.

21. "The Reform in Russia, Spring '92," *Moskovskie novosti*, May 24, 1992, trans. in CDPSP, vol. 44, no. 25 (1992), pp. 17–18.

22. See notably Gaidar Yegor, "Russia and the Reform," *Izvestia*, Aug. 19, 1992, trans. in CDPSP, vol. 44, no. 33 (1992), p. 6; "The 'Industrial Union' Faction Presents an Ultimatum to the Government," *Izvestiia*, Aug. 12, 1992, trans. in CDPSP, vol. 44, no. 33 (1992), p. 7; and M. Berger, "Head of Russia's Central Bank Calls for Reexamination of Reform Plan," *Izvestiia*, Aug. 24, 1992, pp. 1–2, trans. in CDPSP, vol. 44, no. 34 (1992), p. 24.

23. See "In Place of a Poor Russia Without Rich People, Build a Rich Russia Without Poor People," *Rabochaia tribuna*, Nov. 17, pp. 1–2, trans. in CDPSP, vol. 44, no. 46 (1992), pp. 1–2; and "Borderline Situation," transcribed by G. Tsitriniak, *Literaturnaia gazeta*, Oct. 28, trans. in CDPSP, vol. 44, no. 46 (1992), pp. 11–12.

24. Yevgeni Yasin, "The Economy on a Seesaw," *Moskovskie novosti*, no. 33, Aug. 15, 1993, p. 47, trans. in CDPSP, vol. 45, no. 32 (1993), p. 4; and Y. Yasin, "Russia Cannot Pull Out of the Crisis with This Kind of Parliament," *Novoe vremia*, Aug., 1993, trans. in CDPSP, vol. 45, no. 32 (1993), p. 5.

25. "If I Were Chernomyrdin," *Komsomoiskaia pravda*, Sept. 15, 1993, p. 3, trans. in CDPSP, vol. 45, no. 37 (1993), p. 7; "The Reformer Has Turned to Rescue the Reform or the Country?" *Nezavisimaia gazeta*, Sept. 18, 1993, p. 1, trans. in CDPSP, vol. 45, no. 37 (1993), p. 6.

26. Y. Yasin, "Old Debates and New Problems," *Sevodnia*, Jan. 12, 1994, p. 9, trans. in CDPSP, vol. 46, no. 2 (1994), pp. 1–2.

27. Mikhail Berger, "The End of the Era of Market Romanticism," *Izvestiia*, Jan. 18, 1994, trans. in ibid., no. 3 (1994), pp. 1–2; and "Gaidar Gives Chernomyrdin a Chance to Be Russia's Chief Reformer," *Izvestiia*, Jan. 18, in ibid., pp. 1–2.

28. E. Rostova, "Fiodorov's Interview," *Novaia Ezhednevnaia gazeta*, Jan. 22, 1994,

p. 1, trans. in CDPSP, vol. 46, no. 4 (1994), pp. 5–6; and R. Arifdzhanov, "Gorbachev-Era Economic Advisers Propose an Old-Style New Life to Yeltsin and Chernomyrdin," *Izvestiia*, Jan. 29, 1994, pp. 1–2, trans. in ibid., pp. 2–3.

29. G. Yavlinski, "Another Transitional Period Strategy Is Possible," *Nezavisimaia gazeta*, Feb. 10, 1994, p. 4, trans. in ibid., no. 11 (1994), p. 15.

30. Jeffrey D. Sachs, "Russia's Struggle with Stabilization," and John Williamson, "Comments," in *Transition*, vol. 5, no. 5 (May–June 1994), pp. 9, 11.

31. "The Opposition Has One Last Chance After 1996," *Literaturnaia gazeta*, no. 21, May 1995, p. 1, trans. in CDPSP, vol. 47, no. 22 (1995), pp. 7–9.

32. A. Bekker, "Non-Payment Crisis Was Provoked by Self-Seeking Directors," *Sevodnia*, Feb. 4, 1995, trans. in CDPSP, vol. 47, no. 5 (1995), p. 20; and A. Bekker, "Bankruptcy: Life After Death," *Sevodnia*, Feb. 16, 1995, p. 2, trans. in ibid. no. 7 (1995), p. 19.

33. Olivier Blanchard et al., *Reform in Eastern Europe*, pp. xiv–xv.

34. Jeffrey Sachs, *Accelerating Privatization in Eastern Europe: The Case of Poland*, Helsinki, World Institute for Development of Economic Research of the UN (UNU/WIDER), Apr. 1991 (mimeo), pp. 1–40.

35. "Russia's National Interest [Should] Be Taken into Account in the Future," *Sevodnia*, Apr. 12, 1995, p. 2, trans. in CDPSP, vol. 47, no. 15 (1995), p. 17.

36. See Rustam Narzikulov, The Cost of a Balanced Budget," *Sevodnia*, Apr. 1, 1995, p. 1, trans. in ibid., no. 13 (1995), p. 5; Vladislav Borodulin, "Banks Offer Credit to the Government," *Kommersant*, Mar. 31, 1995, p. 1, in ibid, p. 5; "Banks Find Their Biggest Borrower," *Kommersant*, Apr. 1, 1995, p. 6, in ibid., p. 5; "Deal of the Century? The Elusive Russian Bank Proposal," *Transition*, vol. 6, no. 4 (Apr. 1995), p. 17; and Alessandra Stanley, "Russian Scandal Threatens Future of Privatization," *New York Times*, Jan. 28, 1995.

37. See Tsentr Ekonomicheskoi Kon'iunktury (Center of Economic Trends), *Rossiia, 1995* (Russia, 1995), Moscow, 1995, p. 152; Lev Makarevich, "Banks Unable to Help Peasants Until Land Reform Is Carried Out," *Finansovye Izvestiia*, no. 60, Aug. 29, 1995, trans. in CDPSP, vol. 47, no. 37 (1995), pp. 10–11; and Boris Boiko, "Land Legislation," *Komersant*, Sept. 2, 1995, trans. in ibid., pp. 12–14.

38. Sergei Chagaiev, "Y. Gaidar Presents the Government's Program to the Deputies," *Izvestiia*, Oct. 6, 1992, p. 1, trans. in ibid., vol. 44, no. 40 (1992), p. 5.

39. Y. Gaidar, "Trial by Elections," *Izvestiia*, June 28, 1995, trans. in ibid., vol. 47, no. 26 (1995), p. 6; Andrei Bagrov, "Cold and Inevitable Vengence," Boris Fiodorov's press conference, *Kommersant*, Oct. 15, 1996, trans. in ibid., vol. 48, no. 41 (1996), p. 11.

40. Steven, Emanger, "A Corrupt Tide in Russia from State-Business Ties," *New York Times*, July 3, 1995.

41. See notably Vasili Knonenko, "Russian Authorities Prepare an Attack on Organized Crime," *Izvestiia*, May 26, 1994, p. 1, trans. in CDPSP, vol. 46, no. 21 (1994), pp. 1–3; "The President Takes Extraordinary Measures to Combat the Rampage of Crime," *Izvestiia*, June 15, 1994, p. 1, trans. in ibid., no. 24 (1994), pp. 1–3; V. Saltaganov, "Crime in the Sphere of Economics Is a Threat to Russia's National Security," *Ekonomika i zhizn*, no. 37, Sept. 1994, trans. in

ibid., no. 37 (1994), pp. 1–3; "The 'Nationality' Column on a Survey About Gangs," *Izvestiia*, Oct. 21, 1994, p. 5, trans. in ibid., no. 45 (1994), pp. 14–15; Alexei Makharin, "Both Democrats and Communists Support the New Criminal Code," *Sevodnia*, Aug. 2, 1995, p. 5, trans. in ibid., vol. 47, no. 31 (1995), pp. 1–4; and Olga Krishtanovskaia, "Russia's Mafia Landscape," *Izvestiia*, Sept. 21, 1995, p. 5, trans. in ibid., no. 38 (1995), pp. 1–5.

42. Jeffrey Sachs, "Why Corruption Rules Russia," *New York Times*, Nov. 29, 1995.

43. Andrei Neschadin, "Russia's Gray Economy," *Izvestiia*, Sept. 29, 1994, p. 9, trans. in CDPSP, vol. 46, no. 38 (1994), pp. 5–6; also Krishtanovskaia, "Russia's Mafia," pp. 1–2.

44. Michael Gray, "Russia Fights Crime and Corruption," *Transition*, vol. 6, no. 11–12 (Nov.–Dec. 1995), pp. 7–8.

45. Based on *Rossiia 1995*, Tsentr Ekonomicheskoi Koniunktury (*Russia, 1995*, Center of Economic Business Fluctuations), Moscow, Mar. 1995, pp. 64–68.

46. Olga Krishtanovskaia, "Russia's New Millionaires," *Izvestiia*, Sept. 7, 1994, p. 9, trans. in CDPSP, vol. 46, no. 36 (1994), pp. 1–3.

47. *Trends in Developing Economies*, Washington, D.C., World Bank, July 1995, p. 448.

48. *Rossiia, 1995*, p. 64; Igor Karpenko, "Government Approves Stage-by-Stage Options for Adjusting Pensions," *Izvestiia*, Aug. 11, 1994, pp. 1–2, and "Official Statistics Show Average Russian Can Easily Feed Himself," *Sevodnia*, Aug. 11, 1994, both trans. in CDPSP, vol. 46, no. 32 (1994), p. 13, and J. Klugman, "Poverty in Russia – An Assessment," *Transition*, vol. 6, no. 9–10 (Sept.–Oct. 1995), p. 1. See also: Nicholas Barr, *Income Transfers and the Social Safety Net in Russia*, Washington, D.C., World Bank, 1992.

49. Alexander Bekker, "Government Approves Reform Concept," *Sevodnia*, May 20, 1995, p. 2, trans. in CDPSP, vol. 47, no. 20 (1995), p. 15.

50. Zbigniew Hockuba, *Between Plan and Market: Economy of Chaos*, Warsaw, Polish Policy Research Group, Warsaw University, no. 23, 1993, p. 21.

51. Mikhail Berger, "The Government Has Prepared a Reform Program. What Will the Russian Parliament and the Group of Seven Say to This?" *Izvestiia*, June 30, 1992, trans. in CDPSP, vol. 44, no. 26 (1992), p. 7; and I. Savvateiva, "Produce 'Capitalism in the Main' in Three Years," *Komsomolskaia pravda*, July 1, 1992, p. 1, trans. in ibid., no. 30 (1992), p. 7.

52. Jeffrey Sachs and Wing Thye Woo, "Understanding the Reform Experiences of China, Eastern Europe, and Russia," in Chung H. Lee and Helmut Reisen, eds., *From Reform to Growth: Countries in Transition in Asia and Central and Eastern Europe*, Paris, OECD, 1994, pp. 23–48. See also the introduction and summary, p. 18.

53. See "Reform of China's State-Owned Enterprises: A Progress Report of Oxford Analytica," *Transition*, vol. 6, no. 11–12 (Nov.–Dec. 1995), pp. 16–19; and Subrata Ghatak, *Development Economics*, London, Longmans, 1978, pp. 40–43.

54. Joseph S. Berliner, "Perestroika and the Chinese Model," in Robert W. Campbell, ed., *The Post-Communist Economic Transformation*, Boulder, Colo., Westview, 1994, pp. 249, 253, 275–276.

55. Sergei Chagaiev, "Yegor Gaidar Presents the Government Programs to the Deputies," *Izvestiia*, Oct. 6, 1992, trans. in CDPSP, vol. 44, no. 40 (1992), p. 5.

56. Michael Richardson, "A Revised Look at China's Poverty: World Bank Says It Is Worse Than Previously Thought," *Herald International Tribune*, Sept. 26, 1996.

5. Options and Outcomes in the Industrial Economies

1. Herbert Stein, "We Can't Afford Voodoo 2," *New York Times*, Feb. 7, 1996, p. A15.

2. John Maynard Keynes, *The General Theory of Employment Interest and Money*, New York, Harcourt Brace, 1936, pp. 1–22, 379. Emphasis added.

3. Frank Hahn and Robert Solow, *A Critical Essay on Modern Macroeconomic Theory*, Cambridge, Mass., MIT Press, 1995, pp. 1–7, 135, 150–154. However, there is now a tendency to address the problem of market imperfection within the standard neoclassical framework of rational expectations and infinitely living representative households. See J. J. Rotemberg and M. Woodford, "Dynamic General Equilibrium Models with Imperfectly Competitive Product Markets," in Thomas F. Cooley, ed., *Frontiers of Business Cycle Research*, Princeton, N.J., Princeton University Press, 1995, pp. 243–293.

4. Adam Smith, *The Wealth of Nations*, pp. 767–768.

5. *Economic Report of the President*, transmitted to the Congress, Feb. 1996, together with the *Annual Report of the Council of Economic Advisers*, Washington, D.C., U.S. GPO, 1996, p. 291.

6. Bizaguet, *Le secteur public et les privatisations*, p. 61.

7. Paul Starr, "The Limits of Privatization," Economic Policy Institute, Washington, D.C., 1987, pp. 2–7.

8. Thatcher, *The Downing Street Years*, p. 8.

9. For an extensive examination of these issues, buttressed with worldwide examples, see the detailed report of Charles Vuylsteke, *Techniques of Privatization of State-Owned Enterprises, vol. 1: Methods and Implementation*, Washington, D.C., World Bank, 1988; also Madsen Pirie, *Privatization*, Aldershot, Wildwood House, 1988, esp. pp. 69–293; and Pierre Guislain, *Les privatisations: Un défi stratégique, juridique, et institutionel* (Privatization: Strategic, juridical, and institutional challenge), Brussels, DeBoeck-Wesmael, 1995.

10. Pirie, *Privatization*, p. 70.

11. Peter Young, *Privatization Around the Globe: NCPA Policy Report No. 120*, Dallas, Texas, National Center for Policy Analysis (mimeo), 1986, p. 4; and Andrew Pendleton and Jonathan Winterton, "Introduction: Public Enterprise Industrial Relations in Context," in Pendleton and Winterton, eds., *Public Enterprise in Transition: Industrial Relations in State and Privatized Corporations*, London, Routledge, 1983, p. 12.

12. Pirie, *Privatization*, pp. 142–143; and Schneider, *The Human Cost of Contracting Out*, pp. 12, 16.

13. The foreign investors complained that "France sold us its old tin and wanted to

make us believe that it was silver." See *Le Monde*, June 8, 1995; see also *International Herald Tribune*, June 18–19, 1994.

14. Judith Rehak, "Profiting from Privatization: Choose Well, Choose Wisely," *Herald International Tribune*, June 18–19, 1994, p. 15.

15. *OECD Economic Surveys, United Kingdom, 1995*, Paris, OECD, 1995, pp. 30–31, 91.

16. Governor Jean-Claude Trichet, Banque de France, 1993, *Annual Report*, given to the president of the republic and Parliament, Paris, Banque de France, 1993, pp. 30–31; idem, 1994, *Annual Report*, pp. 38–39; and *OECD Economic Surveys, France, 1995*, Paris, OECD, 1995, pp. 50–51.

17. Guislain, *Les privatisations*, p. 17; and *OECD Economic Surveys Germany, 1995*, Paris, OECD, 1995, pp. 23–25, 75–76.

18. European Commission, *Panorama of EU Industry, 1994: An Extensive Review of the Situation and Outlook of the Manufacturing and Services Industries in the European Union*, Luxembourg, Office for Official Publications of the European Communities, 1994, pp. 114–115.

19. Jeff Gerth, "As Payroll Shrinks, Government's Costs for Contracts Rise," *New York Times*, Mar. 18, 1996, pp. A1, A12.

20. Ellen Nedde, *Welfare Reform in the United States*, International Monetary Fund Working Paper no. 95-124, Washington, D.C., Nov. 1995, pp. 2–3.

21. John Vickers and Vincent Wright, eds., *The Politics of Privatization in Western Europe*, London, Frank Cass, 1989, p. 23; Cento Veljanovski, *Selling the State: Privatisation in Britain*, London, Widenfeld and Nicolson, 1987, pp. 9–14, 17–19; Raymond Vernon, "A Technical Approach to Privatization Issues: Coupling Project Analysis with Rules of Thumb," in Ravi Ramamurf and Raymond Vernon, eds., *Privatization and Control of State-Owned Enterprises*, Washington, D.C., World Bank, 1991, pp. 68–69; and Ahmed Galal and Mary Shirley, eds., *Does Privatization Deliver? Highlights from a World Bank Conference*, Washington, D.C., World Bank, 1994, pp. 114–115.

22. For the French case see the listing in Michel Bauer, "The Politics of State-Directed Privatization: The Case of France, 1986–1988," in Vickers and Wright, *The Politics of Privatization*, p. 59; see also Cosmo Graham and Toni Prosser, *Privatizing Public Enterprises: Constitutions, The State, and Regulation in Comparative Perspective*, Oxford, Clarendon Press, 1991, pp. 156–159, 173; and Guislain, *Les privatisations*, pp. 146–147.

23. Vickers and Wright, *The Politics of Privatization*, p. 25.

24. Ibid., p. 27.

6. Options and Outcomes in the Transitional Economies

1. Steven L. Solnick, "Federal Bargaining in Russia," *East European Constitutional Review*, vol. 4, no. 4 (Fall 1995), pp. 52–58.

2. For a detailed analysis of Russia's evolving legal system, see the comprehensive study of William G. Frenkel, *Commercial Law of Russia: A Legal Treatise*, Irvington, New York, Transnational Juris Publications, 1995.

3. Ibid., pp. 1 A (25) and (29).
4. Ibid., pp. II B (1–3), II C (1), and II H (4 and 8).
5. See N. Spulber, *Organizational Alternatives in Soviet-Type Economies*, Cambridge University Press, 1979.
6. Gianmaria Ajani, "La circulation des modèles juridiques dans le droit post-socialiste" (The circulation of juridical models in post-socialist law), *Revue internationale de droit comparé*, no. 4 (Oct.–Dec. 1994), p. 1096.
7. Ibid., pp. 1101–1103.
8. Iván Major, *Privatization in Eastern Europe: A Critical Approach*, Aldershot, Elgar, 1993, pp. 2, 51–58.
9. See OECD, *Economic Surveys, 1994–1995: Germany*, Paris, OECD, 1995, pp. 71–73; Hans-Peter Brunner, "German Blitz-Privatization: Lessons for Other Reforming Economies?" *Transition*, vol. 6, no. 4 (Apr. 1995), pp. 13–14; Ferdinand Protzman, "East Nearly Privatized: Germans Argue the Cost," *New York Times*, Aug. 12, 1994; and "Restructuring of State-Owned Enterprises in Eastern Europe," UN, *Economic Survey of Europe in 1993–1994, U.N.*, New York, United Nations, 1994, pp. 174–184.
10. See, for its beginnings, Guillermo de la Dehesa, "Privatization in Eastern and Central Europe," Washington, D.C., Group of Thirty, Occasional Papers, no. 34, 1991, pp. 17–21; for a detailed study of privatization in Russia, the Czech Republic, and Hungary, see Katherina Pistor and Joel Turkewitz, "Coping with Hydra-State Ownership After Privatization," a paper in *Corporate Governance in Central Europe and Russia*, from the Joint Conference of the World Bank and the Central European University Privatization Project, Dec. 15–16, 1994, Washington, D.C. Transitional Economic Division, Policy Research Department, World Bank, 1994.
11. For all the countries considered, see Roman Frydman, Andrezej Rapaczynski, John S. Earle, et al., *The Privatization Process in Central Europe*, Budapest, Central European University Press, 1993; also, *Economic Survey of Europe in 1994–1995*, pp. 198–199.
12. OECD, *Short-Term Economic Indicators in Transitional Economies: Sources and Definitions*, Paris OECD, 1994, p. 9; UN, *Economic Survey of Europe in 1994–1995*, p. 72.
13. *Panorama privatizatsii*, vol. 4, no. 79 (Feb. 1996), p. 39.
14. *World Investment Report, 1995*, pp. 99–102.
15. See *Russian Federation: IMF Economic Review*, no. 16, 1944, p. 58. For the other experiences, see notably Daniel S. Fogel and Suzanne Etcheverry, "Reforming the Economies of Central and Eastern Europe," in Daniel S. Fogel, ed., *Managing Market Economies: Cases from the Czech and Slovak Republics*, Boulder, Colo., Westview, 1994, p. 27; on restructuring Hungary and Poland in, see the detailed and instructive accounts: "Restructuring of Large State-Owned Enterprises," in the respective two countries in *Economic Survey of Europe in 1993–1994*, pp. 185–198 and 199–211; also see "Hungary," in *Trends in Developing Economies, 1995*, Washington, D.C., World Bank, July 1995, p. 239; and "Bulgaria," in ibid., p. 63; for more on Bulgaria, also see Christo Dalkalachev, "Pri-

vatization in Bulgaria,'' in V. V. Ramanadham, ed., *Privatization: A Global Perspective*, London, Routledge, 1993, pp. 171–173.

16. ''Selected Aspects of Structural Reform in the Transitional Economies,'' *Economic Survey of Europe in 1994–1995*, pp. 205–211; see also Andy Mullineux, *Progress with Financial Sector Reform in Six Transforming Economies*, Birmingham, Birmingham Business School, International Finance Group Working Paper no. 95–04: on Poland, pp. 5–6; on the Czech Republic, pp. 9–10; and on Bulgaria, pp. 19–20.

17. Boris Pleskovic, ''Banking Reform in the Transitional Economies: A Hard Nut to Crack,'' *Transition*, vol. 5, no. 1 (1994), pp. 5–6.

18. *Economist* Intelligence Unit (EIU), *Country Profile Russia, 1994–95*, London, EIU, 1995, pp. 35–56.

19. *Economic Survey of Europe in 1993–1994*, p. 170; Stilpon Nestor and Scott Thomas, ''Privatization Through Liquidation,'' *OECD Observer*, no. 192 (Feb.–Mar. 1995), pp. 36–38.

20. Paul R. Williams and Paul E. Wade, ''Bankruptcy in Russia: The Evolution of a Comprehensive Russian Bankruptcy Law,'' *Review of Central and East European Law*, no. 5 (1995), pp. 511–532.

21. *U.N. Statistical Yearbook, 1993*, New York, UN, 1995, pp. 153–169.

22. *Trends in Developing Economies in 1995*, Washington, D.C., World Bank, 1995, pp. 4, 65, 241, 442, 446, 451, 481.

23. *Economic Survey of Europe in 1994–1995*, pp. 251–252.

24. World Bank, *Trends in Developing Economies in 1995*, p. 450; and *World Economic and Social Survey 1995*, pp. 335–336.

25. UN Department of Economic and Social Information and Policy Analysis, *World Economic and Social Survey, 1995*, New York, UN, 1995, p. 20.

26. *Restructuring Social Security in Central and Eastern Europe: A Guide to Recent Development, Policy Issues and Options*, Geneva, International Social Security Association, 1994, p. 57.

27. Ibid., pp. 9, 10, 18, 63; for detailed presentations, see *The Financing of Social Insurance in Central and Eastern Europe*, Social Security Documentation European Series, no. 20, Geneva, International Social Security Association, 1993, pp. 3–9.

28. *Restructuring Social Security*, pp. 20–21.

29. Ibid., pp. 19–20, 63–64.

30. *World Employment, 1995: An ILO Report*, Geneva, International Labour Office, 1995, p. 116.

31. Paul Starr, ''New Life of the Liberal State,'' in Ezra N. Suleiman and John Waterbury, eds., *The Political Economy of Public Sector Reform and Privatization*, Boulder, Colo., Westview, 1990, p. 30.

32. On the West–East privatization differences see notably Cheril Gray, ''Economic Transformation: Issues, Progress, and Prospects,'' in *Transition*, vol. 2, no. 5 (May 1991), p. 79; ''The Challenge of Legal Reform in Hungary: An Assessment and Some Proposals,'' *Transition*, vol. 3, no. 9 (Oct. 1992), pp. 6–8; Jan Winiecki, *Privatization in Poland: A Comparative Perspective*, Kieler Studien,

Bübingen, J. C. B. Mohr, 1992, pp. 40–46; Paul G. Hare, Anna Canning, and Timothy Ash, "The Role of Government Institutions in the Process of Privatization," in Hendrikus J. Blommestein, and Bernard Steunenberg, eds. *Government and Markets: Establishing a Democratic Constitutional Order and a Market Economy in Former Socialist Countries*, Dordrecht, Kluwer, 1994, pp. 142–157; Roman Frydman, and Andrezej Rapaczynski, *Privatization in Eastern Europe: Is the State Withering Away?* Budapest, Central University Press, 1994, pp. 141–167; and Saul Estrin, *Key Issues in the Realignment of Central and Eastern Europe: Privatizations in Central and Eastern Europe*, London, Longmans, 1994, pp. 127–317.

33. Winiecki, *Privatization*, p. 46.

7. Contraction versus Expansion of the Scope of the State

1. Herbert Stein, "Good Times, Bad Vibes," *New York Times*, Mar. 14, 1996. Emphasis added.

2. UN Conference on Trade and Development, Division of Transnational Corporations and Investment, *World Investment Report, 1995: Transnational Corporations and Competitiveness*, New York, United Nations, 1995, pp. 5–7, 192–193, 224.

3. *World Employment, 1995: An ILO Report*, p. 50.

4. Aurelio Parisotto, "Direct Employment in Multinational Enterprises in Industrialized and Developing Countries in the 1980s: Main Characteristics and Recent Trends," in Paul Bailey, Aurelioi Parisotto, and Geoffrey Renshow, eds., *Multinationals and Employment, The Global Economy of the 1990s*, Geneva, International Labour Office, 1993, p. 36.

5. *The OECD Job Study: Facts, Analysis, Strategies*, Paris, OECD, 1994, p. 14; and *OECD Economic Surveys: France, 1995*, Paris, OECD, 1995, p. 52.

6. *Job Creation and Employment Opportunities: The United States Labor Market, 1993–1996*, a report by the Council of Economic Advisers with the U.S. Department of Labor, Office of the Chief Economist, Washington, D.C., Council of Economic Advisers, Apr. 23, 1996, p. 9.

7. "Don't Go Away Mad, Just Go Away," *New York Times*, Feb. 13, 1996.

8. *The OECD Job Study*, p. 14; and *Job Creation and Employment Opportunities*, p. 6.

9. *OECD Economic Surveys: France, 1995*, Paris, OECD, 1995, pp. 64–65.

10. *OECD Economic Surveys: Germany, 1995*, p. 17; and *OECD Economic Surveys, France, 1995*, p. 58.

11. *Job Creation and Employment Opportunities* p. 8.

12. Lawrence Mishel and Jared Bernstein, *The State of Working America, 1994–95*, New York, Sharpe, 1994, pp. 28, 116.

13. Concerning the indicated contrast, see the *New York Times*, Mar. 10, 1996, and the series started by it on Mar. 3, 1996.

14. *World Bank, World Development Report, 1995: Workers in an Integrated World*, Oxford, Oxford University Press for the World Bank, 1995, pp. 162–163.

15. *World Employment 1995: An ILO Report*, pp. 105–114.
16. *World Economic Outlook, May 1995: A Survey of the Staff of the International Monetary Fund*, Washington, D.C., IMF, 1995, pp. 58, 60.
17. Adrienne Cheasty, "The Revenue Decline in the Countries of the Former Soviet Union," *Finance and Development*, vol. 33, no. 2 (June 1996), pp. 33–34.
18. See *OECD Economic Outlook*, no. 57, June 1995, pp. 113–114.
19. UN, *World Investment Report, 1994: Transnational Corporations, Employment and the Workplace*, New York, United Nations, 1994, pp. 103–105; and UN, *World Investment Report, 1995: Transnational Corporations and Competitiveness*, New York, United Nations, 1995, pp. 99–102, 108–115.
20. *World Employment 1995*, p. 116.
21. Hayek, *The Road to Serfdom*, pp. 2–4; see also Ronald Max Hartwell, "Capitalism and the Historians," in Fritz Machlup, ed., *Essays on Hayek*, New York, New York University Press, pp. 75, 81–82, 86.
22. Ludwig von Mises, *Bureaucracy*, Cedar Falls, Iowa, Center for Futures Education, 1969 (1983), pp. 60–63.
23. *OECD Economic Surveys: United Kingdom, 1995*, p. 91.
24. *OECD Economic Surveys: Germany, 1994*, p. 113; and *1995*, p. 65.
25. *OECD Economic Surveys: France, 1995*, pp. 38–41, 50.
26. *OECD Economic Surveys: United Kingdom, 1995*, pp. 47, 57, 69, 86. Emphasis added.
27. *OECD Economic Surveys: Germany, 1995*, pp. 79–80.
28. *OECD Economic Surveys: France, 1995*, pp. 19, 29, 34, 58.
29. *Job Creation and Employment Opportunities: The United States*, p. i.
30. *World Employment, 1995: An ILO Report*, pp. 118–125.
31. *OECD Economic Surveys: Germany, 1995*, pp. 84–85, 95, 97, 99, 124.
32. "Quotation of the Month: The IMF's Role in the Transition Has Come Under Increasing Scrutiny" (excerpted from Loza Kekic's study, "The IMF and Eastern Europe"), *Transition*, vol. 6, no. 9–10 (Sept.–Oct. 1995), p. 17.
33. Hayek, *The Road to Serfdom*, pp. 22–23.
34. Robert Skidelsky, *The Road from Serfdom: The Economic and Political Consequences of the End of Communism*, New York, Allen Lane and Penguin, 1996, pp. 16, 19, 27, 117.
35. Herbert Stein, "Out from Under: The Road from Serfdom," *New York Times Book Review*, Feb. 25, 1996, p. 8.

Index

246